TESTING THE NEW DEAL

The Working Class in American History

Editorial Advisors
David Brody
Alice Kessler-Harris
David Montgomery
Sean Wilentz

A list of books in the series appears at the end of this book.

TESTING THE NEW DEAL

The General Textile Strike of 1934 in the American South

JANET IRONS

University of Illinois Press

Urbana and Chicago

© 2000 by the Board of Trustees of the University of Illinois
All rights reserved
Manufactured in the United States of America
∞ This book is printed on acid-free paper.

Library of Congress Cataloging-in-Publication Data
Irons, Janet Christine.
Testing the New Deal : the general textile strike of 1934 in the
American South / Janet Irons.
    p.   cm. — (The working class in American history)
Includes bibliographical references and index.
ISBN 0-252-02527-X (acid-free paper)
ISBN 0-252-06840-8 (pbk. : acid-free paper)
1. Textile Workers' Strike, Southern States, 1934.
2. Textile workers—Southern States—History.
3. Trade-unions—Textile workers—Southern States—History.
4. United Textile Workers of America—History.
I. Title. II. Series.
HD5325.T421934I76   2000
331.892'877'00975—dc21   99-6498
CIP

1 2 3 4 5 C P 5 4 3 2 1

CONTENTS

Acknowledgments   vii

Introduction   3

1   Customary Rights   13

2   Homegrown Unions   29

3   Union-Management Cooperation   38

4   New Rules   49

5   Dirty Deal   63

6   A Battle of Righteousness   79

7   We Must Get Together in Our Organization   97

8   No Turning Back   110

9   Anatomy of a Strike   120

10   Which Side Are You On?   140

11   Aftermath   154

Conclusion   175

Appendix A: UTWA Southern Locals in 1934   183

Appendix B: Estimates of Southern Membership in the UTWA in 1934   188

Notes   191

Selected Bibliography   239

Index   255

ACKNOWLEDGMENTS

Many people and institutions made this book possible. Financial support for researching and writing this book came from the Andrew J. Mellon Foundation, the Appalachian Center at Berea College, the Rieve-Pollock Foundation, the American Council of Learned Societies, the Faculty Professional Development Committee of the Pennsylvania State System of Higher Education, and an Annual Campus Grant from Lock Haven University. Two semester-long leaves from Lock Haven University also gave me much needed time to research and write.

I owe large intellectual debts to many scholars whose works are cited throughout the text that follows, but I want to especially recognize Ed Akin, Mary Frederickson, James Gettys, Jacquelyn Hall, Sara Judson, Gretchen McLaughlin, and Tom Terrill for sharing their personal knowledge about southern textile workers and guiding me to sources. Kier Jorgensen, who at the time I completed my research was research director of the Amalgamated Clothing and Textile Workers' Union (ACTWU), provided me with valuable research materials over the course of several years. Eula McGill, a volunteer organizer in 1934 and a retired textile union official, introduced me to former union activists in northern Alabama. Eula's own recollections, offered over a month of stimulating car drives on Alabama's interstate highways and country roads, helped ground me in the reality of textile worker unionism in the 1930s. My grateful thanks to all.

I am also grateful for the help of the librarians who provided capable assistance locating sources: Jerry Hess, Bill Creech, and Tab Lewis at the National Archives, Les Hough and Bill Dinwiddie at the Southern Labor

Archives at Georgia State University, the staff at Perkins Library at Duke University, and Bernadette Heiney of Stevenson Library at Lock Haven University of Pennsylvania. William Chafe, Elizabeth Faue, Gary Fink, Michael Goldfield, Jacquelyn Hall, Kathy Lamb, Sidney Nathans, Bryant Simon, George Stoney, Allan Thurman, Jane Thurman, Peter Wood, and Robert Zieger read and generously commented on versions of the manuscript at various stages of its decade-long history. Their insights and suggestions have saved me from error and made this a much better book.

Over the last dozen years I have been privileged to be part of a number of supportive communities of scholars, beginning with the wonderful collection of faculty and graduate students who studied at Duke University while I was there. Larry Goodwyn was a true mentor; while setting an example through his own work, he encouraged me to follow my instincts, and at crucial stages brought needed direction and focus to this project. In Pennsylvania I found intellectual stimulation, valuable criticism, and the support necessary to finish this book from the Lock Haven University Summer Writing Workshop, the Penn State Labor History Workshop, and Irwin Marcus and Elizabeth Ricketts at Indiana University of Pennsylvania. Janet Gross offered me a place to write when I had none. Elizabeth Faue put me in touch with scholars who broadened my thinking beyond a southern focus. Staughton Lynd has been a source of vital intellectual stimulation and encouragement. I am especially grateful to George Stoney, Judith Helfand, and the staff of "The Uprising of '34" for encouraging me to finish the book, and for sharing with me their research and creative efforts.

Mark Wherley at the Deasy Geographics Lab at the Pennsylvania State University exercised great patience and skill constructing the map of the South that graces page 2 of this book. Thanks also go to Richard Wentworth, Emily Rogers, and the editorial staff at the University of Illinois Press for their competent, professional work bringing this book into print.

During the time I was working on this book, family and friends eased my burden in many ways. Though it is impossible to thank everyone by name, special mention goes to Jennifer Gunn, Bob Arnold, Karen and Frank Guzek, and Allison Porter and Michael Zucker, all of whom offered me a home away from home during my field research. Throughout, Allan Thurman has been a patient and steadfast supporter. And heartfelt appreciation goes to Rebecca and Elizabeth, whose cheerful tolerance of the presence of this project in our home made my job much easier.

I owe a large debt to the retired textile workers who took the time to talk with me about their memories of the 1930s. The list of former textile workers interviewed represents no social scientific study. Rather, I sought people whose names appeared in newspaper articles, documents, or letters in the National Archives. I especially sought people who lived in mill towns where labor unrest had a specific importance for an understanding of the 1934 strike. The recent deaths of two veteran southern textile union leaders, Joseph Jacobs and Lucille Thornburgh, are a reminder of how few participants in the 1934 strike are still alive. This book is written for them and in memory of others who tried and failed.

TESTING THE NEW DEAL

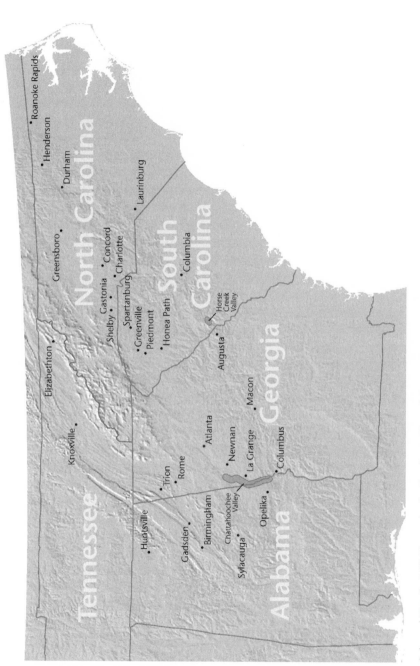

Selected Textile Mill Towns in the Southern United States, 1934

INTRODUCTION

It was Wednesday, September 5, 1934, and the southern backcountry of the United States was in an uproar. Car- and truckloads of young men and women, workers in the South's cotton textile factories, caravaned from mill town to mill town across the rural hilly terrain stretching northeast to southwest, from western North Carolina to northwest Georgia. Encircling textile mills still in operation, these "flying squadrons" demanded that the machinery be turned off and workers be let off their jobs. Their collective power was intimidating. The two hundred or so people, for example, who arrived at the Long Shoals Cotton Mills in Lincoln County, North Carolina, on September 5 were "yelling so loud," recalled the mill's owner, that "I could scarcely hear my voice." When he asked who was the group's leader, "they yelled back they had no leaders." The mill owner quickly shut down his plant.[1]

Actions like these constituted the opening salvos of the General Textile Strike of 1934 in the American South. Altogether some 170,000 workers—two-thirds of the southern textile labor force—left their jobs, making this strike the largest labor protest in the South's history.[2] The walkout's dimensions continue to awe veteran labor leaders. One southern observer called the event "the closest thing to a revolution I've seen in this country. It was an outpouring of hundreds and hundreds and thousands of people."[3]

Of course, no single incident can capture the strike's variegated nature; the southern textile industry comprised hundreds of locally owned mills scattered across five states (North and South Carolina, Georgia, Tennessee, and Alabama). Many mills were closed down by their own workers; others struggled to operate with skeletal staffs. A full one-third of southern mill workers stayed at their jobs. Some, geographically isolated from the currents sweeping the southern mills, chose to work; others, perhaps given little choice, were escorted to work by armed guards. The holiday mood turned somber as southern mill owners and state governors deployed approximately twenty-three thousand soldiers, deputies, and private guards to contain the walkout. When union organizers attempted to get mill workers in Russellville, Alabama, to participate, for example, they "were met, threatened, and repelled by a gang of armed hoodlums, who followed them far out of town and shot up their autos."[4] In some instances armed conflict led to death. At the strike's most famous battle site, Honea Path, South Carolina, armed guards stationed inside the Chiquola Mill fired into a crowd of over a hundred people gathered in the mill yard, killing seven union members and injuring over seventy-five others.

Yet the closing down of southern mills by the so-called flying squadrons remains the strike's most vivid emblem. The workers' sheer audacity symbolized that this was no narrow economic contest between employee and employer. No longer hidden in their rural mill villages, crisscrossing the South's newly paved highways in cars bought on the installment plan, cotton mill workers dramatically challenged southern elite control not only of the region's economy but also of its public space. Indeed, so threatening were such actions to the southern social order that one mill owner called the general strike "perhaps the gravest emergency which has confronted our people since Reconstruction days."[5]

The apparent power of the general textile strike stands in stark contrast to the speed and finality of its defeat. After three weeks, the AFL-affiliated United Textile Workers Union (UTW) called off the walkout in return for government assurances that abuses in the mills would be addressed. President Franklin Roosevelt himself urged workers to return to their jobs. But when former strikers showed up at the mill gates for work, seventy-five thousand of them were turned away, blacklisted throughout the industry. Those who were allowed to return to work were forced, as one worker remembered it, to "humble down" to their employer. Few government recommendations were implemented. To the contrary, conditions in the southern mills deteriorated rapidly after the strike. So painful was the defeat that in many communities the strike was never spoken of again. Sixty years later, in interviews by scholars and filmmakers, survivors of the strike spoke of it only reluctantly. What good, they wondered, would it do to reopen old and painful wounds?

The pain and tragedy of the strike's defeat has profoundly influenced historical renderings of the event. In particular, the silence of strike participants created a vacuum in the historical record that in subsequent years was filled by incomplete explanations or outright distortions from a number of sources. Most often, the strike has simply been overlooked in the history books. Until recently, those who wished to make the strike part of the South's history found that there was no framework within which it could be understood. It was hard to square the militant outspokenness conveyed by striking southern textile workers not only with their subsequent silence, but also with mill workers' own history: isolated in company-owned mill villages, politically disfranchised, and held in contempt by their social betters in southern towns. It hardly seemed possible that a group of relatively powerless and geographically far-flung workers could build an organization capable of coordination on a regional, even national scale. Stereotypes persisted of southern textile workers as inappropriate material for union organization because of their "passive" nature, or their "agrarian individualism." Until recently, if the 1934 strike was acknowledged, its occurrence was attributed to the manipulations of the workers by "outside" unions. Such an explanation was favored especially by southern manufacturers, who contended that the 1934 strike was organized and inspired by the northern-based United Textile Workers Union. This notion of an outside union fit more comfortably with the notion that southern textile workers were incapable of organizing themselves into unions.

Inside the circles of American labor, a completely different myth about 1934 emerged. For labor leaders, the problem was how to come to terms with the walkout's tragic defeat, particularly in light of the success of the U.S. labor movement in many other industries in the late thirties. Leaders of organized labor concluded that the 1934 strike was "premature," an unfortunate result of the impatience of southern workers, who failed to wait before they struck until they were more prepared, and until the landmark 1935 federal labor legislation protecting the right of workers to unionize had been passed.[6] Such an explanation made it possible for historians of labor to marginalize the meaning of the 1934 strike. So disconnected did the strike become from the currents of American labor history that the eminent historian Irving Bernstein concluded that it left behind "no heritage beyond bitter memories."[7]

Recent developments have created an opportunity to reassess these conclusions. Most important among these developments has been the decline in the fortunes of organized labor in the United States in the 1970s and 1980s.[8] This sea change in labor's fortunes has prompted historians to seek explanations not only for organized labor's successes, but also for labor's long-term weaknesses. Congratulatory histories of the New Deal and the rise of labor in the 1930s have now been supplemented by more nuanced accounts that acknowledge the constraints as well as the opportunities for workers and their leaders created by New Deal policies. The pivotal developments of the decade—the passage of the Wagner Act and the rise of a new industrial union, the CIO—form not the starting point for an understanding of labor insurgency in the 1930s, but are understood as themselves the products of labor struggles going back at least a generation.[9] In this context, the 1934 textile strike constitutes a powerful case study, revealing the relationship between worker insurgency, labor leaders, and government in the crucial first years of the New Deal, when federal labor policy and the relationship between organized labor and the federal government were still in flux.[10]

The setbacks for organized labor in the 1970s and 1980s have also tempered somewhat the historical arrogance of many in the labor movement who previously had been frustrated by the failure of unions in the South to thrive as successfully as they had in the rest of the country. The new humility has made possible fresh interpretations of southern labor history that de-emphasize the character failings of southern millhands. Beginning in the late 1980s, a new generation of researchers successfully challenged long-held stereotypes of southern cotton mill workers as passive and individualistic. They revealed that within the walls of the mill villages, hidden from public view, southern textile workers demonstrated a capacity for mutual aid and militant protest. Family, community, and religious traditions had nourished a sense of collective purpose and solidarity. These reinterpretations of textile workers' culture made sense out of millhands' periodic strikes despite the absence of formal union organization.[11]

Historians have also begun to rethink the idea that southern textile workers were so isolated in their mill villages that they were unconnected to the larger political world.[12] The thousands of letters that southern textile workers wrote to President Roosevelt during the 1930s amply testify to their active involvement in New Deal issues. To be sure, southern industrial workers never became the political force in Roosevelt's Democratic party that northern industrial workers did.[13] Thanks to an absence of local government in the rural South and to barriers such as the poll tax and literacy tests, only an estimated 35 percent of southern millhands voted.[14] With few exceptions, the southern congressional delegation represented the interests of the region's elites.[15]

Yet in a broader sense textile workers in the 1930s did become politically active. By means of the New Deal, the federal government extended its reach into the lives of the South's poor for the first time since Reconstruction. While in the case of Reconstruction a Republican government had reached over the heads of southern elites and extended aid to southern blacks, in 1933–34 a Democratic administration was sending a message of hope to white southern industrial workers, over the heads of their bosses, the South's powerful textile manufacturers. How southern textile workers mobilized in response to the New Deal is a key to explaining the passion of the '34 strike.

———

New Deal programs inspired southern textile workers because they held out the promise that the catastrophic consequences of the Great Depression would be managed with a measure of justice. As a political response to an economic crisis, the New Deal represented the contention that the social order of America rested on more than the right to make money. Business activities, New Dealers said, must take place within a set of guidelines that ensured that the suffering that accompanied the Great Depression did not happen again.

Among the New Deal programs that most inspired textile workers was the National Industry Recovery Act (NIRA). The NIRA's provisions regulating production, wages, hours, and workloads were an admission that laissez-faire theories, so cherished by classical economists, did not work, at least not in highly competitive industries like the textile industry. Instead, the practices of textile manufacturers during the 1920s had created a crisis of overproduction, as each firm, in an attempt to capture a larger share of an already saturated market, had produced more.

The industry crisis and the New Deal response to it was a concern not only to industry, but to workers as well. Ordinary millhands had a vital stake in attempts to regulate production, since textile employers had passed the burdens of cutthroat competition onto the workers. Using new machinery and "efficiency experts" to streamline their operations, mill owners had replaced "customary workloads" with workloads determined by time and motion studies. Millhands had called the result the "stretch-out," since such restructuring invariably resulted in heavier loads for some workers while causing others to be laid off.

Even before the New Deal, southern millhands had begun to resist the stretch-out with explosive protests. Increased workloads had not only exhausted them, but also disrupted the balance of work, family, and community life that was the hallmark of the southern labor system. Cutthroat competition had also altered workers' relationships with each other as they were driven to the limits of their physical abilities to save their jobs. The names of the locations of these pre–New Deal battles are familiar to almost any student of labor history: Gastonia, Marion, Elizabethton.

What has been less understood is how southern textile workers redefined the meaning of these protests with the coming of the Depression and the New Deal. Now they battled their employers not only to defend their livelihoods and their communities, but also to advance to goals of the New Deal itself. When textile manufacturers increased workloads, they were not only exploiting workers, they were adding to the overproduction already hobbling the industry. When employers laid off those whose jobs were no longer necessary because of the stretch-out, they contributed to the other scourge of the Depression: unemployment. Textile workers thus believed that the restructuring of their workplace threatened not only their own customary work practices but the fundamental goals of ending the Depression and creating a stable, prosperous economy.

Without a formal political voice, textile workers formed unions that, by default, became the means by which they communicated their notion of just government to those in power. Since the NIRA had also protected the right to form unions, union locals became, in the workers' minds, government-sanctioned vehicles for the exercise of their citizenship rights. Here was the meaning of the New Deal for southern textile workers. By forming unions to protest the stretch-out, millhands were, as one labor leader put it, trying to make the NIRA "a living thing" in the textile mills of the South.

———

The birth of an idea, whether it be as simple as ending the stretch-out or as far-reaching as establishing industrial justice, does not happen in the abstract; it comes out of organization. This account identifies four stages in the development of a regionwide organization of textile unionists. During the first stage, 1901–29, southern textile workers collectively held mill owners accountable, through swift, direct action, for ensuring "customary work practices." Except for a brief foray into unionization during World War I, these protests remained local in scope and temporary in duration.

In the second stage, from 1929 to 1933, the widespread disruption of customary work practices in southern textile factories led mill workers to move toward greater regional organization. Strikers sought not only to put economic pressure on mill owners, but also to challenge public perceptions of mill owners as benevolent paternalists. By thus subjecting the mill owners' ideological posture to local middle-class public scrutiny, workers were able to slow down the installation of dramatic changes to their workloads.[16] But this was not a permanent solution to their predicament, for mill owners ultimately resorted to the exercise of force, through local or state militia, to defeat them.

The third stage began with the election of Franklin Roosevelt as president in 1933. Roosevelt's rhetorical commitment to the rights of working people created a political opening that inspired textile workers to go over the heads of local elites and put their faith in their most powerful potential ally, the federal government.

As it turned out, such faith was premature. Unbenownst to textile workers, the historical legacy of northern reform efforts and the fundamental demands of Washington politics put the New Deal administration at odds with the southern workers' struggle. New Deal reformers and leaders of organized labor championed efficiency measures as "progress" without fully understanding how textile-industry modernization disrupted southern workers' lives and communities. Nor was Roosevelt himself a definite ally; despite the president's desire to cultivate working-class political support, he was simultaneously beholden to the southern branch of the Democratic party—run by the South's economic elites—for passage of his programs in Congress. The strike's fundamental cause remained employer hostility to the rights workers perceived that they had under the NIRA. But its major catalyst was the fact that the institution that the textile workers thought to be their savior—the federal government—was either unable or unwilling to carry out its promises.

The workers' failure to secure the full backing of the New Deal government proved decisive in catapulting them onto the fourth stage, the decision to hold a general strike. By means of the strike, workers hoped to lay a powerful claim on the federal government to enforce justice in the mills. In this sense, the '34 strike resembled a political demonstration.[17] But the '34 strike also reflects a return to workers' traditional methods of direct action. Through the exercise of their economic strength on the ground, textile workers hoped to implement economic reforms that a host of bureaucrats in Washington had been unable to accomplish.

———

The impact of all of these developments on the union that ostensibly led the strike, the UTW, becomes visible almost as an anticlimax, suggesting a final theme: the opportunities and constraints facing unions organizing workers across regional and cultural boundaries. On the one hand, no group had more to gain from supporting the unionization of the southern mills than factory workers in the New England textile mills, for whom the cheap wages of the southern mills were a constant source of instability. Indeed, the mass migration of New England mills to the South throughout the decade preceding the 1934 strike had decimated northern textile workers' communities. A successful alliance between New England and southern workers seemed the key to overcoming the devastating effects of the mobility of capital on textile workers' lives.

Yet the fact that 200,000 northern textile workers joined the 170,000 southerners in this nationwide strike masks the sectional issues that divided the union. From a northern perspective, the South of 1934 was another land. New England's textile workers were Irish or English craftsmen or Italian and Eastern European unskilled immigrants; the South's were poor white farmers in a region characterized by stark racial hierarchies. Largely agrarian and still significantly poorer than the rest of the nation, the South was to the rest of the United States as a developing nation is to the industrialized West today.

Barriers to solidarity between workers in the two regions were also economic. All too often, high-wage northern workers saw lower paid southern workers as their rivals. UTW leaders had historically joined northern employers in seeking to gain an advantage over the southern industry by encouraging efficiency measures in the northern mills, precisely the "modernization" programs against which southern workers were protesting.

But perhaps the most insurmountable barriers to a strong union were not issues dividing the workers of the two regions, but issues that divided the members of the UTW—north and south—from their leaders. Throughout the year leading up to the strike, UTW officials played a complex and ambiguous role as brokers for their members' grievances with the New Deal government. Like organized labor generally, UTW leaders believed so thoroughly that labor progress was inseparable from the progress of the New Deal that the bold challenge of the '34 strikers to the New Deal created an agonizing dilemma. The southern workers' decision to strike forced UTW leaders to choose between their own complicity in New Deal policy making and their desire to represent their constituencies. In one startling, clarifying moment, the UTW put itself on the side of the strikers. But the moment could not last, and the final drama of the strike settlement not only sealed the fate of southern textile workers, but shattered the integrity of the UTW itself.

———

In the narrative that follows, some of the chapters describe the same events from different perspectives. Thus, chapters 1 and 2 explore the years from the turn of the century to 1932 from the perspective of southern workers, while chapter 3 looks at those same years from the perspective of the New England–based United Textile Workers union.

Chapter 4 brings the union, employers, and New Deal liberals to Washington where their perspectives and power relations shaped Roosevelt's New Deal legislative program. The resulting legislation, the NIRA, elevated the scope of conflict between textile workers and employers to the national level, transforming the nature of their struggle. The impact of the NIRA in the southern mills is described in chapter 5.

Chapters 6 and 7 document, from different perspectives, how southern textile organizing put pressure on a reluctant UTW organization to protest publicly the way that the NIRA was being implemented in the southern mills. In chapter 8 southern workers and the UTW leadership achieve a coming-to-terms that produces a measure of union solidarity. But despite this coming-to-terms, the strike means very different things to workers on the ground and individuals in Washington, as chapters 9 and 10 illustrate. Chapter 11 and the conclusion deal with the aftermath of the strike and its legacy for southern cotton mill workers and for American society as a whole.

———

There is much that this account does not do. Most significantly, it does not examine in detail power relations inside individual mill villages: relations between skilled and unskilled workers, between men and women, between supervisors and regular workers, between white workers (the vast majority) and the small number of black sweepers and bale openers and nursemaids who shared in mill life, between longtime residents of mill villages and more transient workers. Intensive local studies that explore these relationships are now emerging.[18] Nor does this account tell of the two hundred thousand northern textile workers who walked out in 1934, another story that needs to be told.[19]

Finally, this account does not explore in detail the psychic cost paid by the thousands of strike participants who had to live silently with the strike's catastrophic failure.[20] The very stereotypes of passivity and irrationality that textile workers struggled to defy in 1934 continued over the generations to contribute to their powerlessness, erasing from popular memory the mere possibility that they could have waged such a protest. Even today, when most Americans imagine southern textile labor protest the example most likely to come to mind is the Communist-influenced Gastonia strike in 1929.[21]

This historical amnesia makes it all the more difficult to retrieve from the past the experiences of thousands for whom 1934 was in fact a beginning, not an end. Only recently have scholars confirmed that a viable union movement flourished in the southern mills for at least a dozen years after 1934.[22] In many instances, local labor conflicts at individual mills had a far greater transformative impact on workers and the conditions of their work than did events at the national level. Because of the large-scale focus of this account, it only hints at the shape and substance of subsequent organizing in individual southern mills.

Yet whatever local victories grew out of textile labor organizing in the twenties and thirties, it remains a reality that textile workers never subsequently achieved the national influence that they did in 1934. The 1934 General Textile Strike, then, needs to be seen for what it was. At a critical moment in American political history—the beginning of the New Deal—a group of geographically far-flung workers built an organization capable of coordination on a regional, even national, scale. To achieve a national voice, they sought to channel their energy through organizations capable of amplifying their grievances, such as the UTW. Through painful experience, they discovered the limitations of other groups in fully embracing their cause. The '34 strike was, finally, an attempt by southern textile workers to be seen and heard on their own terms, not mediated through the eyes and ears of others. Even now, more than sixty years later, we are struggling to hear what they had to say.

1

CUSTOMARY RIGHTS

In the 1880s and 1890s, in the rolling countryside known as the "fall line" of the southern piedmont, ambitious men of the New South harnessed water power, built brick factories, and recruited white farm families—mostly "widow women and girls"—to tend spinning frames and weaving looms that were often imported from the North. At sites far removed from established towns, these mill owners constructed entire villages— houses, churches, and schools. Nearly all the villages were unincorporated, making mill owners' legal power over the use of property absolute. Many of these men also wielded considerable power in local and state politics, either behind the scenes as leaders of the South's all-white Democratic party or in public as county commissioners.[1]

By contrast, the men and women who migrated from the dirt farms of the southern backcountry to the mills had little or no formal power. The women had no right to vote, and the growing minority of men who worked in the early industry found that there was little local government to vote for, since the mill villages were privately owned, and most of the rural South did not have local government at smaller than the county level. In county or state elections, millhands' voices were often dwarfed by the farming majority in the countryside. By the turn of the century, the workers' right to vote was further muted by the poll tax—the law that required every voter to pay money in order to exercise the franchise.[2]

Southern textile workers were not only politically disfranchised, they were also marked by southern elites as culturally inferior. Southern gentry, eager to replace the humiliation of the Civil War defeat with a bright new image, found themselves embarrassed by textile workers' primitive living conditions, their mountain music, their apparent susceptibility to such unrespectable illnesses as pellagra and hookworm, and their teenage boys' disturbing habit of throwing rocks at strangers who entered the mill village. The sociologist Harriet Herring wrote that townspeople "eulogized" textile workers' employers, the mill owners, as builders of the New South, even as the mills' employees were "pretty well ignored" or "positively looked down upon."[3] "The very term mill hands," noted another North Carolina observer, "has seemed to create the impression that textile workers are a different people, and they have been isolated in their community life, never called into conference with other citizens when matters of interest to all citizens are being acted upon, until the textile workers are not looked upon as other citizens of the State."[4]

Despite their diminished status in the eyes of outsiders and their lack of formal power, however, textile workers from the beginning exercised a measure of power over their lives. This power was encoded in a set of work practices, or "customary rights," that textile workers had collectively developed in the years before World War I. Only once this truth is acknowledged can the dynamics that led to the 1934 strike be understood, for the 1934 strike culminated almost a decade of worker protest over management assaults on customary rights.

Family Labor

To appreciate the degree of power that cotton textile workers had, it is necessary to understand that, despite the wealth and political status of early southern industrial leaders, they launched their business ventures under cultural and economic constraints. Cotton mill men needed to reassure local southern community leaders, for example, that factory life would not disrupt the culture or values of a predominantly agrarian society. They also recognized that in the wake of the humiliating defeat of the Civil War and the abolition of slavery, their fellow elites were looking for a way to solidify a culture of white supremacy. To achieve cultural legitimacy, therefore, mill owners characterized their cotton mill campaign as a homegrown enterprise that would uplift both a region and a race. These imperatives in turn shaped the nature of the mill's labor force. Looking for workers that would cost them little and give them the least amount of trouble, mill owners recruited white women and girls from farms where falling cotton prices and the crop-lien system were making it increasingly difficult to eke out a living.

Problems arose immediately, however, for white rural southern culture would not permit a young girl to live independently of her family (as was done, for example, in the textile mills of Lowell, Massachusetts, in the 1830s). Mill owners therefore recruited whole families. While the initial recruiting process favored widows and their children, the mills increasingly hired families headed by men as well, so that by the 1890s one-third of the southern textile labor force was male. To make the best use of this labor force and maintain its "homegrown" quality, mill owners trained male heads of families as low-level supervisors, or "second-hands." Thus fathers and uncles worked alongside or over their wives, children, nieces, and nephews, who worked as doffers, spinners, or other lower-skilled positions. Under the "family labor system," not only did the work involve entire families, but work roles replicated the traditional family hierarchy.[5]

Early cotton mill workers tended spinning frames or weaving looms for eleven- or twelve-hour days in hot, humid, dusty rooms for meager wages. Yet the family labor system also forced mill owners to depart from what modern observers might think of as traditional factory discipline. Rituals of childhood, adolescence, and man- and womanhood were now reproduced within the structure of the factory system. Young children often played in the mill, for example, while their parents worked, causing irritating distractions; older boys and girls exasperated supervisors by taking off work to go play in the nearby brook. Mothers routinely took time off to attend to sickness, nurse babies, or prepare the noon-hour dinner, while men would take a day or two off to hunt or fish. Work and community life were inextricably intertwined, "the one infusing the other," according to I. A. Newby, "in ways that make it impossible to separate their basic elements."[6]

Blood ties were not the only force that linked workers together; these families also hailed from the same rural subculture. On the job, workers covered for each other when one took a break. In the mill village, more prosperous workers shared food from their gardens with those in need and more fortunate workers collectively shouldered the responsibility of caring for the sick. Strong kinship networks reinforced this sense of mutual responsibility.[7]

This set of affairs had benefits and drawbacks. Workers' cooperative spirit could be useful for mill owners looking for a smoothly running factory; but this community spirit could also be directed at the mill owner himself. Through direct and often unannounced confrontation with supervisors, or with the "overseer" of the labor force, mill workers extracted what might be called "swift justice." Workers frequently contested the exploitation by mill supervisors of women and girls whose entrance into "public work" was a new development in southern culture. The historical record is full of such incidents. Burns Cox, who worked at Dwight Mills in Gadsden, Alabama, remembers when his father had to go "up there in the mill and get on the damn man because he slapped one of my sisters." If necessary, workers collectively walked off their jobs. In Cooleemee, North Carolina, in 1914, Dora Cope and her entire family, consisting of more than ten individual families of Copes, walked out of the mill because she was being harrassed by her supervisor. A major strike in Alamance County, North Carolina, in 1901 occurred because a female weaver had been treated "unjustly and rudely" by her supervisor.[8]

Probably the most contested arena was overseers' attempts to "drive" the workers. Workers wanted a work schedule that gave them the flexibility to handle chores at home. Workers resisted pressure to work harder by simply staying home. As late as 1919 an observer noted: "Irregularity at work is common. When an applicant is asked if he works regularly the general reply is, 'Yes, when I am not sick. Of course I stay out about one day a week. No one could stand up under the work if he did not.'"[9] Widely discussed by employers, workers' absenteeism was often attributed to their laziness or tendency to roam. So pervasive was the practice of taking time off that mill owners developed a "spare hand system," consisting of up to 25 percent of the workforce, to replace absent workers.[10]

Unionism in a Conservative Era

By the turn of the century, the power of a culturally homogenous workers' subculture combined with another critical ingredient, a dramatic shortage of skilled labor, to produce a real threat to the mill owners' control of their labor force. When employers attempted to expand the scope of their production to include more weaving, a job requiring considerably greater skill than spinning, they discovered that local supplies of labor had been exhausted. The extreme labor shortage gave workers, especially weavers, new leverage. At the same time, the AFL-affiliated National Union of Textile Workers (NUTW) had begun an organizing campaign in the South.

The NUTW was not the first union to attempt to organize southern cotton mill hands. In the 1880s a few hundred mill workers had joined mixed locals of the Knights of Labor, a national labor movement. But these locals died as the wave of reform retreated.[11] By the time the NUTW had come to organize southern workers in the late 1890s, the construction of a rigid racial and class hierarchy in the South had been almost complete.

Nevertheless, motivated by the leverage that the shortage of labor portended, somewhere over five thousand cotton mill workers out of a total of approximately ninety thousand workers in five southern states joined the

NUTW. In areas where membership was concentrated—Augusta, Columbus, and Atlanta, Georgia, and Columbia, South Carolina—the union became a force to be reckoned with. As strikes by skilled workers won real if limited concessions, mill owners became increasingly wary. "This matter of unionism," one Columbia, South Carolina, manufacturer said, "that is another thing. We are the owners of our mills and we propose to run them. We do all we can for our help, and propose to do much more. We do not propose, however, to have any of this unionism business."[12]

After enduring several strikes, mill owners began employing evictions and lockouts to defeat workers. Their tactics worked, and the NUTW was destroyed. What their tactics failed to do, however, was to maintain a secure pool of skilled labor, as evicted or fired strikers simply moved on to work in other mills. Nor did such repressive measures reassure wary southern townspeople who feared that the coming of factory labor would bring class conflict to the region.[13] As a long-term strategy, then, frequent and unpleasant labor conflicts made little sense.

Desperate to overcome their labor shortage, mill owners tried to hire black workers. But white southern cotton mill workers shared and effectively appropriated the racial ideology of the dominant culture, turning it against their employers for their own purposes. For white textile workers, the offering of industrial work exclusively to them was a means to uplift the white race. Consequently, among their most powerful early expressions of collective solidarity, mill workers refused to work unless their owners promised not to hire black labor, except for the most unpleasant jobs—sweeping or bale opening, for example.[14] However morally problematic these actions are, they underscore how effectively mill workers contested mill-owner power in areas where dominant cultural attitudes framed the behavior of both owners and workers.

By the turn of the century, national movements for economic justice—populism, the Knights of Labor—had been replaced by regional ideologies of southern redemption and white supremacy. For mill workers this proved a double-edged sword. In the racially charged atmosphere of the post-Reconstruction South, textile workers could use race to their advantage. But the repression that southern elites used to maintain that atmosphere made it impossible for millhands to sustain a union movement. Since the shortage of labor continued to give workers leverage, cotton mill workers would continue to exercise their collective power, now, however, through informal acts of resistance unmediated by a union. These factors help explain not only the absence of formal unionism in southern textiles from the turn of the century until World War I, but also why southern millhands turned again to unions when the larger ideological climate changed during World War I and the New Deal.

Customary Rights

After the disastrous attempt to hire black labor, mill owners settled into a successful strategy for retaining not only a stable and secure workforce, but also the goodwill of the southern public. Beginning around the turn of the century, southern mill owners made a conscious decision to improve working and living conditions in the mills. Of course individual employer practices varied widely, leading workers to make distinctions between "a good place to work" and a "hobo" mill. At the worst mills conditions remained primitive, overseers were rude and abusive, work stoppages were frequent, and labor turnover was high. In the better mills, however, owners chose to minimize disruptions by cultivating bonds of personal loyalty. They encouraged the use of kin networks as mediating institutions and promoted respected family members, particularly the increasing number of adult men, in textile families. They walked through the factories, calling workers by name, and led church meetings, presented children with Christmas gifts, gave advice on gardening, and held annual Fourth of July picnics.[15] They also improved conditions in the mill villages, installing toilets, sewage systems, and electricity. For the mill owner, these welfare measures were not only a concession to workers, they were an investment, as the generation raised in the mill village was the mill's future labor force.[16]

Such practices produced what Mary Wingerd calls a "settled cohort" of workers who invested themselves in the betterment of the workplace and the mill village.[17] By no means was this a perfectly harmonious community. The hierarchy of family networks spawned internal tensions, particularly accusations of favoritism regarding promotions and shift positions.[18] Tensions also existed between the settled community and the floating population of migrant mill workers, who tended to undermine the atmosphere of sobriety and moral rectitude the settled community had worked so hard to create (and which many a mill owner sought to reinforce). Gossip, peer pressure, occasional ostracism, and at times collective action could be turned on fellow community members as much as it could be turned on supervisors and overseers. It was, as one witness described, a "tough" culture.[19]

Despite tensions among workers, however, their community power served as a foundation for a broad-based defense of their livelihood. Workers continued to use informal acts of resistance—by individuals, by families, or sometimes by the entire community—to extract concessions in areas important to them. Over a generation, mill workers were able to hammer these small concessions into a set of informally understood "customary rights" that southern mill owners undermined at their peril. "Scarcely a week has passed recently," an editorial in the industry journal, the *Southern Textile Bulletin*, declared in 1911, "that some competent superintendent has not suddenly left his position" because he "got in trouble with a woman."[20] An industry analyst observed in 1916, "We find that the overseers and foremen of these plants have been known to their fellow employes [*sic*] since they were children and any orders to do work in a way different from that which they have been accustomed to do would be looked upon as a curtailment of their rights."[21]

Perhaps most important, given what was to come, workers retained the flexibility they valued on the job. "If they could catch up," remembers one worker, "if they wanted to go to the store, they could go to the store and come back, and like that." "I think we done as we pleased then," recalled another former worker, "cause there weren't no fence around the mills and if we wanted to go home and get a biscuit or anything we'd go home."[22]

The mill village system thus maintained employer dominance while also serving workers' real needs. While many have called this system paternalism, it may more accurately be characterized as a field of force, within which both parties exerted some control. So stable were its larger contours that for decades the mill village system became the standard by which textile labor relations were measured. Only dramatic changes could undermine it.[23]

Industrial Democracy

World War I was one of those forces powerful enough to disrupt the accommodation that workers and owners had made with each other. The government's appeal to the nation to join a "war for democracy" provided textile workers with a new framework for thinking about their own circumstances in the factory and in their community. Pulled into a cause whose scope transcended regional boundaries and regional ideologies, southern textile workers found reason to make a claim, for the first time in at least a generation, to the national political inheritance.[24] James Barrett, the North Carolina textile union leader, later described war veterans as the "leading spirit" behind organizing textile workers in North Carolina during and after the war. "We fought like the devil for democracy over yonder," Barrett reported hearing war veterans say, "and we want a pound or two in this little old North Carolina state."[25] Connection to a national crusade, in turn, made it more likely that textile workers would look favorably on joining a national labor union. Between 1917 and 1919, as many as forty thousand southern textile workers formed local chapters of the AFL-affiliated union, the United Textile Workers of America. It was the most successful union movement the southern mills had ever seen.[26]

While a detailed examination of the union the textile workers joined must wait until chapter 3, it is worth noting here that the UTW was an unlikely vehicle for southern textile worker militancy. An amalgam of craft unions of skilled workers—loom fixers, weavers, and mule spinners—the UTW's form of organization was not easily grafted onto a community of workers in the South whose population crossed gender and occupational lines.[27]

What made unionism in the southern mills viable during the war was the way that southern workers infused their new locals with a structure and organization that fit their needs. In Columbus, Georgia, for example, textile workers transformed a union local consisting of only skilled workers into a broad-based organization, whose membership was large enough to force the closing of the Swift Spinning Mill in 1918. Their numerical strength, combined with wartime government protection of unions, produced a signal victory. By 1919 Columbus had witnessed a walkout of seven thousand people in twelve different mills, representing nearly two-thirds of the Columbus mill population.[28] A similar broad-based organizing effort occured in the North Carolina piedmont, where in the spring of 1919, fifteen hundred workers coordinated a walkout from mills in Concord and North Charlotte to protest the elimination of a wartime bonus. When the protest was resolved on terms favorable to the workers, mill workers in North Carolina joined the UTW so swiftly that "even leaders of the movement could not keep track" of the size of the membership.[29]

These wartime union struggles served as an important incubator for the more full-blown unionism of the 1930s.[30] They also generated indigenous southern union leaders that went on, in at least some cases, to become union leaders in 1934.[31] Neal Bass, a textile worker who led a protest at his mill in Piedmont, South Carolina, in 1934, first led a controversy there in 1914. John Dean, a UTW organizer in Charlotte during the war, was the lead organizer in Alabama in 1934. Tom Crow, a Dalton, Georgia, textile worker and 1934 labor leader, had gained wartime experience in the longshoreman's union.[32] Workers from World War I craft unions in Gadsden, Alabama, helped to organize a textile union there in the 1930s.[33] In 1927, six years after the World War I movement had been defeated, the historian George Mitchell presciently reported: "Something is left of the network of partially trained leaders and the thousands of union sympathizers. Not a few villages have charters waiting in the attics until reorganization comes."[34]

A Doctrine of Hate

The strikes of the war years may have revealed the potential for southern textile unionism, but once the war ended, textile unions were again exposed to the full power of their employers, unrestrained by federal wartime mandates.

Southern mill owners universally viewed the UTW as an agent of northern firms attempting to sabotage the southern competitive advantage in the textile industry.[35] Either sincerely or disingenuously, southern mill owners expressed "astonishment" that their workers would join such an alien movement. In Charlotte, North Carolina, mill owners described the union's message as a "Doctrine of Hate."[36] Fiercely independent, southern textile manufacturers were unwilling to concede any autonomy to what they perceived to be an "outside" interest. They were determined to operate their industry, as one Columbus, Georgia, mill owner put it, "on a non-union basis—closed non-union, if that will make it any stronger. Closed hermetically, climatically, sectionally, or any way you want it."[37]

Southern employers had an additional asset on their side: local public opinion. Ever since the beginning of the cotton mill campaign, townspeople had viewed mill owners not as exploiters of labor but as uplifters and civilizers of the South's poor whites.[38] Because mill workers were generally isolated from town culture in their mill villages, it was easy for townspeople to forget that there even was an industrial working class. "About the only time textile workers are noticed," one North Carolina observer noted wryly, "is when they are forced to strike against unbearable conditions, and this notice usually comes in the way of bitter criticism."[39]

Even before the federal government had withdrawn its support for unions at the end of the war, mill owners had counted on the southern middle classes to support the use of state power to supress labor unrest. Their confidence was not misplaced. In South Carolina, mill owners succeeded in securing the use of the state militia in 1916, ending a pivotal strike at the Gluck and Equinox Mills and consolidating the position of that state as a nonunion fortress. This preemptory action was so successful that in 1919, the peak of worker unrest, South Carolina textile workers needed only cautionary reminders that unionism was not for them.[40] In Anderson, South Carolina, for example, a UTW organizer in 1919 was whipped, robbed of his clothes, and escorted out of town by a gang of thugs.[41] Meanwhile, in LaGrange, Georgia, north of Columbus, the local Chamber of Commerce campaigned against the "union menace," describing the UTW as a "silent, slimy, and treacherous monster in sheep's clothing," and predicting that a successful union campaign would make LaGrange "a veritable Hell on Earth." The campaign proved so effective that a pro-union sympathizer remarked that the mere mention of the word "union" now made the town hysterical.[42] In North Carolina, where the UTW was the strongest and lasted the longest, unionism also died the hardest. In 1921, when nine thousand workers in the final UTW stronghold in the Charlotte area of North Carolina left their jobs to protest massive wage cuts, Governor Cameron Morrison used troops to drive them back to their jobs. No one, not even longstanding craft union organizations in North Carolina, raised a word of protest.[43]

The dynamics of World War I southern textile labor struggles thus suggested that workers would willingly join unions if afforded the opportunity. In the absence of some countervailing power, such as that of the federal government or wider public support for the workers, however, state officials did not hesitate to use state militia to eliminate the presence of an "outside" union. That no voices were raised in opposition to the use of force to break strikes suggests just how much the "better" classes in the South continued to see the mill owners as benefactors, and mill workers as a liability and an embarrassment in need of control and supervision. If southern textile unions were to succeed it would be necessary for the balance of power to shift. Textile workers needed allies, constituencies in the larger society who would be willing to weigh in against the power of the mill owners.

Exhaustion and Nervous Stress

In the mid-1920s, the way of life in the cotton mill villages of the southern piedmont was about to change. Textile owners were about to begin an organized efficiency campaign that would end the customary patterns of work that had been negotiated between southern cotton mill workers and their employers over generations. Guided by "efficiency experts" and "time-study men," textile manufacturers began a massive restructuring of the workplace through mechanization, speedup, and increased supervisory discipline. The nature and degree of these changes varied from region to region, indeed, from mill to mill. But all variations had in common the increased machine load for some workers followed by the laying off of others.

Some textile manufacturers divided existing jobs into their component parts, creating out of one complex job several jobs, each involving only one task. The weaver, for example, no longer filled batteries, that is, put the spools of yarn needed to make cloth onto the loom frame. This job was given to battery hands, freeing up the weaver to handle more looms. Others—particularly mill owners in western Georgia, Tennessee, and Alabama, the site of the new mills built in the 1920s—simply purchased more efficient looms and increased the number of looms per weaver. "A few years ago a worker was expected to look after 30 or 36 looms," noted a U.S. labor official in 1929. "Now quotas are 90 to 110."[44] In the older textile mills in the North and South Carolina piedmont, however, the new efficiency was a simple speedup. Overseers switched workers from hourly wages to piece rates, timed them by newly installed timepieces on each machine, and told them they had to keep up a faster pace if they wanted to keep their job.[45] Workers called it the "stretch-out."

Zelleree Donnahoo, a retired millhand, describes the weeding-out of workers at her mill in Inman, South Carolina: "The mill had about thirty weavers. They'd lay 'em off, stretch 'em out, lay 'em off, till they didn't have but about twelve." Zelleree's sister-in-law filled batteries, "and she had about 180-something batteries to fill. They used to have, oh, about twelve or thirteen battery hands. And then, [by the time] they took those looms out, they didn't have but about five or six hands."[46]

The stretch-out restructured not only the nature of work but workers' social world. During the workday, millhands had no time to help each other, tend to family affairs, socialize, or even eat. "People were not given the consideration that they had been before," remembered one worker. "You were pushed as a worker. More was put on you. More looms. More than you could run."[47] Instead of working in a cooperative setting, millhands now found themselves in daily competition with each other. Donnahoo noted that her husband, Vance, would often come home and say, "Well, they stretched out again today, I don't know if they'll get me next or not." Those over the age of thirty were particularly vulnerable to dismissal because they were not nimble enough to work at the speed required by the new machines or the new work rules. Even if workers weren't fired, "exhaustion and nervous stress" would push them out of their jobs.[48] Their work was speeded up so fast that "you was always in a hole, trying to catch up."[49] "We cannot stand the load they've put on us," complained women at the Cone Mills in Greensboro, North Carolina.[50] A Greenville, South Carolina, worker compared the stretch-out to "Egyptians making slaves of the children of Israel."[51]

Equally important, the new efficiency campaign threatened the integration of community and work life that was the essence of the family labor system. Even before 1925, mill owners had begun to consider the family labor system a drag on efficient shop-floor practices. During the war, for example, quietly and without fanfare they had begun to eliminate young children from the mills, replacing them with more efficient adult men.[52] Of course, now that young children were not in the mill, an increasing minority of female workers began hiring nannies to tend to the children at home.[53] By the mid-1920s, such domestic help appeared to be a necessity; with more streamlined operations in the mills, it was getting harder and harder for workers to run home during the workday to tend to chores.

Perhaps the most graphic portent that manufacturers were severing the intimate connection between work and community were the fences that began appearing around some factories. When a fence was built around the Harriet and Henderson Mills in 1925, reported one observer, "women going home to cook hurried meals for their sons and daughters and husbands were forced to walk as much as a quarter mile farther around mill property to get home."[54] Two years later, the owners of Henderson Mill ordered that the mill gates be locked; they also stationed guards at the gates to take the names of "operatives" leaving the premises and the length of time they were absent. The Loray Mill, the scene of the famous 1929 Gastonia strike, erected its own fence in 1927 and began locking the doors during working hours.[55] Clearly the stretch-out was only one facet of a much broader effort on the part of management to impose a stricter discipline on work inside the factory walls.

To understand why the stretch-out occurred requires a look at the changing nature of competitive pressures on southern manufacturers themselves. One of the reasons that employers in the early years of the industry had permitted a relaxed pace of work was that it was not necessary for southern textile factories to perform at top efficiency to make handsome profits. Because wages in the southern industry were up to 40 percent lower than those in the North, southern manufacturers maintained a distinct advantage over their northern competitors for most of their early history. Early mills had routinely reported profits of 15 to 20 percent on invested capital; in the booming 1890s, it was said that southern cotton manufacturers experienced "exceeding prosperity."[56]

But by the 1920s, changes in the economics of cotton manufacturing had caused southern employers to reexamine the terms of their informal bargain. For one thing, the shortage of textile labor during World War I had driven southern wages up over 100 percent. While mill owners engaged in wage cuts of up to 50 percent after war's end, wages never went back to their prewar levels. By this time, southern employers had weeded most children out of the mill; they were now relying increasingly on experienced adult workers, who cost more to employ. Higher wage costs in turn put southern employers under increasing pressure to cut costs elsewhere.[57]

A second influence on employers' behavior was the surplus of production in the cotton textile industry. Unlike other major U.S. industries, like coal or steel, the textile industry consisted of hundreds of small factories that were relatively easy to move. The industry became an early lesson in the logic of mobile capital: it constantly sought to locate in areas with lower costs and cheaper labor. The opportunity to employ cheaper methods of production drove competitive manufacturers to produce even when worldwide demand for textiles was saturated, as it was by the end of World War I. Analysts repeatedly observed the industry's "constant tendency to build up surpluses with the resulting price depressions more or less chronic."[58] As profit margins became razor thin, competition became cutthroat, leading mills to even further step up their search for lower production costs.

The third and most dramatic influence on manufacturers' behavior was the end of southern millhands' traditional lever for ensuring that their needs were addressed: the southern labor shortage. Beginning in the early 1920s, thousands of former tenant farmers and sharecroppers, casualties of the failed crop-lien system and the infestation of boll weevils into the cotton crops, began migrating to nearby mill villages and towns in search of a new life. It did not take textile manufacturers long to understand the opportunity this labor surplus created for them. "If the people leave the mills they have no where else to go," wrote one industry analyst in 1925. "The southern mill workers cannot go on strike even if they would."[59] For the first time, employers could alter work practices, and if a worker objected the supervisor responded: "if you don't like it there's a barefoot boy waitin' at the gate for your job."[60]

Socially Minded People

The newfound power of mill owners to enforce their will on the factory floor forced textile workers to rethink their traditional strategies for claiming shop-floor control. In contrast to the situation before the war, the smallest attempt to protest was now met with swift discharge.[61] Without their historic shortage of labor, what power did workers have?

In these difficult circumstances, two important developments helped lay the foundation for a new strategy. The first was a refreshing new wave of public criticism of the mill "system." Ironically, the trigger for this public criticism was the very victory that mill owners had won over textile unions at the end of World War I. To at least some observers, manufacturer repression had revealed that coercion as well as uplift shaped the relationship between mill owners and their workers. As these critics saw it, mill owners had undermined their self-proclaimed virtue by using violence to suppress workers' grievances. James Myers, a northern observer of the southern industrial scene, wrote acidly: "The company's wishes prevail in every phase of the life of the people who live in subjection under a complete industrial feudalism. This feudalism may be paternal and kindly. It usually is so *until its authority is questioned or its will is threatened by a show of independence on the part of the workers* . . . . In such industrial crises, the entire machinery of autocracy goes into action. The workers are evicted from their houses, intimidated by the police, or deported from town."[62] Though still critical of mill workers' "primitive" culture, an increasing number of observers blamed not the mill worker but the mill owner for the degradation of life in the mill villages.[63] The cynical explanation of the writer Broadus Mitchell is typical: "They do not have an emotional attitude toward their workers. They are not burdened with a sense of *noblesse oblige*. They are not aristocrats, but bourgeois. They are class-conscious and money wise."[64] Thus even as manufacturers were acquiring greater power within the walls of the factory, they were losing ground in their campaign for the allegience of the southern middle classes.

Public attitudes changed not only about mill owners but about mill workers as well. Southern textile workers' emergence into public light during the war—even as disrupters of the social order—had brought into being a new generation of social scientists and journalists willing to actually visit mill villages and to survey and interview mill workers.[65] Their reports gave human dimension to a people often caricatured and, as Daniel Singal writes, "often brought [the writers] to challenge the region's most treasured values."[66]

These developments led to what the journalist Paul Blanshard called a "rapidly growing minority of socially minded poeple" concerned about the rights of textile workers in the South.[67] Southern-based groups began to make public statements. A 1927 Southern Industrial Conference spoke out against low wages and poor working conditions.[68] That same year, forty-one southern bishops and ministers penned an "appeal" to industrial leaders of the South to improve labor conditions. Signed by "leading pastors in practically all communities in the South," the appeal called upon southern manufacturers to build their industry "upon good-will and cooperation, higher wages, shorter hours, labor representation and the absorption of the mill village by the larger community."[69]

But the shift in middle-class opinion was only one development laying the foundation for a new strategy. The second was the changes in the cultural attitudes of mill workers themselves. The 1920s witnessed a dramatic expansion of southern textile workers' worldview, as radio, movies, streetcars, and most importantly, the automobile drew them out of their mill villages and into a more urban material culture.[70] Their incomes boosted by the dramatic wage increases during World War I, the new generation bought cheap used cars "on time" and drove to town on the highways that were part of a massive road-building campaign in the South in the 1920s. Some even came to town to live, commuting to work at the new mills close to town, the mills having been freed by electricity from the need to locate in remote areas along falling water.[71]

These young adults experienced after World War I the sense that "the world had somehow shifted under their feet."[72] As Fielding Burke describes in her novel about the young mill worker Ishma, the encounter with the new consumer culture could be dazzling. Trinkets and beads—"she could bury her *soul* in them"—awakened in Ishma not material acquisitiveness but a yearning for a culturally fuller life than she had been able to lead either in the mountaintop home of her birth or in the drab mill village in which she now lived. Harriet Herring's more scholarly assessment in 1934 echoes Burke. Consumer goods, she wrote, were "more than mere silk stockings and automobiles and movies. They were more than a new way of living. They were physical proof of a new life."[73] Healthier and better educated than their predecessors, the new generation appeared at least to one observer to be wholly different from the "docile creatures of twenty years ago that came down from the little farms and mountains satisfied to earn a few meagre dollars under any conditions."[74]

The sense of heightened expectations was so palpable that it frankly worried members of southern society who saw the potential for social unrest. Churches in the mill villages bemoaned the younger generation's attraction to worldly interests.[75] "The world has been turned upside down," an editorial in the *Charlotte Observer* complained. One could sense a certain "excitement in the air," a "craving for something new." The source of this new optimism? "There is too much money now in the pockets of the people."[76]

By the late twenties, workers found themselves between two worlds, still deriving sustenance from the rural-based community traditions that bound residents of a mill village together, yet possessing an "awareness of the outside world which did not exist ten or fifteen years ago."[77] Their exposure to mass society through radio and movies and their new presence as consumers in the town stores were potential building blocks of a new cultural assertiveness. Thanks to this increased awareness, thought one observer, workers were "ready to contest the stretching system in spite of the unemployment which exists in this section."[78] Both forward-looking and defensive, the textile culture of the late twenties was potent and dynamic.

Southern millhands would ultimately fail to prevent the stretch-out from being implemented across the South. But they would succeed in making its implementation difficult to accomplish. Workers would draw on their heritage of mutual aid, their fragmented but existing heritage of union organizing, and their new access to the larger culture to wage a campaign of significant dimension. As the union organizer John Dean said in 1934, "This is not alone a strike. It is a revolt against the stretch-out system."[79]

2

HOMEGROWN UNIONS

The year 1929 was one of the most sensational in U.S. labor history. Workers at the Loray Mill in Gastonia, North Carolina, staged a dramatic walkout against the stretch-out system. Led by the Communist-affiliated National Textile Workers' Union, the conflict subjected the entire town to a clash of ideological slogans that elevated the event into the national limelight.

Unlike the World War I era, however, in 1929 there was no nationwide clamor for "industrial democracy" to legitimize labor protest, no federal support for organized labor, and certainly little public sympathy for Communism. The nation watched as the strike was met with swift repression: the state called the National Guard and the mill evicted the Gastonia strikers from their village homes. Following the killing of the Gastonia police chief, union members were tried for murder in an atmosphere so charged with sensationalism that one of the jurors appeared to go insane. So absorbing were the ideological fireworks and the accompanying violence that the stretch-out system, the original target of workers' anger, vanished from public consciousness.[1]

The violence and rhetorical intensity of the Gastonia strike so dominated the media that few noted that the strike was not in fact typical of the workers' protests. In dozens of other southern textile towns in 1929, workers had engaged in walkouts unaffiliated with any national union. Although organized labor had participated in some of the southern protests (particularly the strikes at Marion, North Carolina, and Elizabethton, Tennessee), workers generally ignored the power of national unions, seeking instead to use local resources. Increasingly comfortable traveling outside the boundaries of their own villages, mill workers built networks of resistance that linked workers from different mills together. And they actively cultivated the sympathy and support of the surrounding local population. The result was a series of "leaderless" strikes that, unlike the strike in Gastonia, succeeded in getting employers to slow down or even halt the stretch-out in their mills. The North Carolina labor leader James Barrett called their organizations "homegrown" unions.[2]

Like so many walkouts in the past, these local strikes were waged to restore customary work arrangements. Workers wanted, they told South Carolina Labor Commissioner J. W. Shealy, to go back to the "old" system that had been in effect before the stretch-out occurred. They were even "willing to take a cut in wages to have the 'old' system again operative."[3] Innovative in their organization, yet traditional in their objectives, the 1929 strikes represented the coming of age of a new generation of textile workers.

South Carolina

South Carolina workers were perhaps best prepared to utilize a "homegrown" strategy because of their unique history of influencing local opinion by flexing their collective voting power. Unlike other southern textile states, where the poll tax disfranchised most of the poor, South Carolina posed no barrier to voting in the so-called white primary, in which Democratic party candidates competed against each other for the privilege of representing the party in the general election. In a one-party state, of course, the primary was for all intents and purposes the general election. Since the turn of the century, therefore, workers in South Carolina textile towns had had experience in the art of gaining local public support for a cause. In Ware Shoals, Pelzer, Greenville, and other mill towns, "homegrown" protests emerged in 1929 in response to the stretch-out.

Possibly the best example of homegrown organization in 1929 was in Greenville. Instead of provoking a coordinated response from the mills by waving the flag of organized labor, South Carolina mill workers chose to speak to their potential supporters simply as local citizens. When James Myers, a Federation of Churches representative, asked the strikers if union organizers had approached them, "they said, 'We don't want that 'til after this is over.' They said that the mills in this district have a common treasury to fight unions. 'So long as we have no union, the other mills won't help the Brandon, but the 'hands' in neighboring mills are helping us anyway!'"[4]

To support their campaign against the stretch-out, these workers not only walked off their jobs, they also held mass meetings, organized fund-raising committees, and courted the support of local politicians. State representatives came to the mill towns to speak on the workers' behalf.[5] Strike leaders also staved off possible negative publicity by keeping peace on the picket line, putting drunk or rowdy picketers in their own makeshift jail.[6] James Myers reported that public sympathy "was very largely with the strikers."[7] Newspapers reported "a considerable amount of community giving to the strike funds."[8] Mill owners were put on the defensive to such an extent that they "dared not" evict workers from their homes.[9]

This was not a narrow test of economic strength between workers and their employers; now the moral authority of the community was to be added to the exercise of the workers' economic muscle. Textile workers construed their 1929 protests as a public campaign to contest the southern mythology that progress depended solely on the prosperity of the mill and its stockholders. Before the war, the public had seen workers as a drain on community morality and progress, and looked to the mill owner as their benefactor. But in 1929, it was the mill owner who failed the test of enhancing community welfare. If mill owners claimed that they needed to stretch out workers for their own economic survival, it was an admission that they had abandoned their own historic posture as benevolent institutions, the very basis for the community support they had enjoyed in the past.

Textile manufacturers responded to this shifting public opinion by embarking on what one labor leader called a "stupendous advertising campaign" to persuade the community that the stretch-out was in fact "progress."[10] But few bought the argument. Instead, the *Spartanburg Herald* chided employers for "oppression" and "the assignment of tasks that are unreasonable," especially when the workers were "lifelong residents of the region, natives of the South, making their contribution to the South's progress with a pride in their labor and a sense of devotion to the industry." It was a remarkable departure from the usual subservience of the local press to business interests.[11] The cloak of progress and civilization, under which southern industry had operated in the past, was becoming frayed and tattered.

The result was a victory for the workers that is remarkable given the traditional power of mills in the region. In the Greenville-Spartanburg section of South Carolina, textile workers managed to halt the implementation of the stretch-out system, at least temporarily. At the American Spinning Company, management permitted workers to vote on whether they wished to continue the stretch-out or return to former work arrangements. The vote was overwhelmingly in favor of a return to the old ways. The Ware Shoals Mill granted strikers' demands to return to the former number of looms.

Permanent grievance committees were formed in both the Ware Shoals and the Pelzer Mills. Pro-worker sentiment was so widespread that the South Carolina mills agreed as a body to an across-the-board wage increase.[12]

Not all of the 1929 strikes were victories and, indeed, many of their gains were eroded once their cause was out of the limelight. Nevertheless, textile workers could not have helped noticing that the outcome of these strikes differed dramatically from a strike supported by an "outside" union.[13] The ideological and organizational ground these "homegrown unionists" cultivated in 1929 nourished what turned out to be a much longer-term campaign to have a say in work arrangements in the southern mills.

Alabama and Georgia

Cotton mill workers organized in the late 1920s not only in the Carolinas, but also in the southwestern piedmont—western Georgia, eastern Tennessee, and northern Alabama. This was the site of much of the new growth in the textile industry. But here the unionism that developed was not hostile to organized labor. Many of the mills were run by northerners, men with less of a tradition of personal control over their workers. Such individuals proved less concerned than the old-style autocrats in the Carolinas about the presence of national labor unions in their mills. There was another difference: unlike mills constructed in North and South Carolina at the turn of the century, the newer mills contained more modern equipment. Thus, mill owners had less of an economic incentive to institute stretch-out measures. Protests against heavy workloads did not appear in these mills in 1929.[14]

Culturally, too, Alabama's textile workers were in a better position than workers in any other southern textile state to welcome organized labor into its mills. Since the turn of the century, Alabama had witnessed the development of an industrial union culture based on heavy industry in Birmingham, and surrounding mines and mills in the mountains to the north. Union presence was strong enough that Alabama Governor Bibb Graves actively sought the support of organized labor in his 1928 campaign.

By 1930, UTW locals in Huntsville, Gadsden, and Anniston, Alabama, and Columbus, Georgia, were growing "in leaps and bounds."[15] The Huntsville local alone boasted four thousand members, while in Columbus a speech by UTW Vice President Francis Gorman generated an audience of over a thousand.[16] But even when textile workers organized under the banner of the United Textile Workers, they still sought local support. They built alliances with independent local merchants who wished to see higher wages for their customers, the mill workers. "We are sick of the whole business," moaned an Alabama store owner in 1930, "the open shop plan has been disastrous; the workers have no money to spend; therefore our goods lie on the shelves and bankruptcy stares us in the face. . . . Better wages is the answer if we are to have prosperity."[17] Merchants in Huntsville publicly supported the trade union movement.[18] In Anniston, local merchants even lent organizers their trucks to help transport workers to open-air meetings conducted outside town.[19] In Elizabethton, Tennessee, farmers and small merchants supported the women who walked off their jobs at the Bemberg and Galanzstoff rayon plants because they, the local businesspeople, resented the high-handed attitude of the owners—outsiders who thought they could do what they pleased. The controversy even resulted in the formation of a citizens' committee that criticized the plant's owners for misusing tax dollars and mistreating its employees.[20]

The Coming of the Great Depression

The 1929 mobilization of southern cotton mill workers had won a short-term reprieve from the stretch-out. Yet workers' experiences from 1930 to 1932 demonstrated that their troubles were only just beginning. With the nation plunged into a nationwide depression, workers now faced layoffs due not only to the stretch-out but also to a depressed market. By 1930, one out of every five mill workers was unemployed.[21] According to one UTW organizer, textile mills "all over the South" were "curtailing more" than he had ever known. "Some are not running at all," he reported, "and many only have about 1/4 or 1/2 their machinery running."[22] Some mills closed altogether during the summer.[23]

In this precarious environment, millhands found themselves vulnerable not only to management strategies such as speedups, but also to instances of favored treatment for bosses' "pets." Earl Richardson from Cordova, Alabama, joined his local union after his boss hired a man "over the weekend that had never been in the mill," and then gave him the "overallers" job, "next to the highest paying job."[24] Abusive treatment of women also increased. In Gadsden, retired worker Laura Beard remembers: "The women were taken advantage of, terrible advantage of . . . . People just don't admit it because it's too embarrassing." Future southern UTW leader Paul Christopher joined the union in Shelby in 1932 because of the abuse of a female worker by a supervisor in his mill.[25]

By the summer of 1932, the southern piedmont was the stage for another round of scattered local strikes that continued to make use only of local resources.[26] Workers in High Point and Rockingham, North Carolina, built local unions, expressly forbidding national labor unions from rendering assistance. In Arcadia Mills, South Carolina, strikers who were ordered to leave their homes appealed their evictions in court, demanding a different jury for each eviction trial, "so that as many people as possible will see just how the laws of the state are administered."[27]

Perhaps the best example of the strategy of courting local support was the 1932 strike at the Horse Creek Valley mills in South Carolina. The Horse Creek Valley area was brilliantly organized by Paul Fuller, the AFL labor education director, whose work won the support of local business groups, fraternal organizations, churches, and radio stations.[28] In 1932 they protested depression-inspired layoffs and severe wage cuts. Workers sought the support of the town by proclaiming their identity as members of the local community, a position that had local resonance because the mill had recently been bought by a northern firm. Appealing for support "at the bar of public opinion," strikers asked their community to side with them instead of the people "into whose hands" the mill had fallen. "Here is our home," they wrote, "here, we and our fathers were born, and our affections for generations have been rooted in this soil; we love our village and its mill."[29] Characteristically, local politicians mediated the disputes in all the above instances.

But while the strategy of courting only local support had its advantages, it also had its limits. In cases where the mill village was farther removed from the town and the eye of the press, workers could not easily leverage the support of their local community. In the 1930 Marion strike, for example, not even local store owners supported the workers; the conflict ended in disaster when sheriff's deputies shot and killed six strikers.[30] In the dispute between workers and owners in rural Rockingham, North Carolina, in 1932, mill managers refused arbitration despite the direct intervention of Governor O. Max Gardner. Workers returned to work signing yellow-dog contracts.[31] In other places workers lost their nerve. When managers of the Cone Mills in Greensboro installed a particularly onerous efficiency system in February 1932, workers walked out in protest, but were persuaded to go back to work agreeing to a pay cut.[32] Even the 1929 South Carolina local union organizations were thrown into disarray in 1931 when the mills reduced workers' wages, violating the promise to raise them that they had made after the 1929 strikes.[33] As long as the majority of mills in the South remained unorganized, progress at a local level was uneven, and victories precarious.

Public Opinion

If the results of the 1929 strikes in the workplace were ambiguous, their impact on public perception was decisive, producing what one historian has called "a watershed . . . in the development of public opinion."[34] In South Carolina, for example, the state legislature issued a highly critical report, charging "gross negligence on the part of the mill owners maintaining decent and adequate living standards in their villages."[35] State labor agencies were "in a state of inertia and lethargy . . . always ready to suppress and excuse practically every violation of the labor laws."[36] Manufacturers lost stature even when they decisively defeated the workers, as occurred in Gastonia and Marion. "Southern middle class opinion about labor matters has been remarkably changed," wrote George Mitchell. "The harshness of the repression used in the big textile strikes angered many."[37] Meanwhile, labor organization increasingly achieved the status of a positive good. In 1929, 415 North Carolinians headed by Frank Porter Graham, future president of the University of North Carolina, adopted a "Statement on North Carolina Industry," approving the principle of collective bargaining.[38] Months later, the Southern Council on Women and Children in Industry issued a "Statement by Some North Carolina Citizens" asking for a nationwide investigation into textile mill conditions and that collective bargaining rights be recognized.[39] Following the Gastonia strike, Josephus Daniels, editor of the *Raleigh News and Observer*, predicted: "Unionism will eventually come, and so long as mill owners refuse to let it come peaceably and reasonably they may not be surprised if it comes violently and unreasonably."[40]

Even in mainstream southern churches, institutions generally known for their "extremely limited" social conscience, the 1929 strikes planted seeds of a new social awareness.[41] One of the most remarkable developments occurred at the Mulberry Methodist Church in Macon, Georgia. Macon was home to Bibb Mills, one of the largest and most antiunion cotton manufacturers in the South. The Mulberry Church was the "wealthiest and most influential church" in the South Georgia Conference of the Methodist Church. Many chief officials of the Bibb Mills were, in turn, powerful laymen in the South Georgia Conference. Bibb owner William Anderson was called "the Bishop of Georgia." Trade publications lauded Anderson for having "a deep, abiding concern for the enrichment of the lives" of his workers.[42] But in 1932 the pastor of Mulberry Church attacked the company, citing the testimony before the U.S. Senate that the wages in the Bibb Mills were "below the minimum required for health and decency." The sermon was such an affront to Anderson's authority that the vice president of the Bibb Mills in Macon resigned as steward and left the church.[43]

While these examples are not conclusive, they suggest that textile workers had made some progress in connecting their own welfare to the local public good. Mill owners, put on the defensive, were forced to regroup. It would take the New Deal to create the opportunity for southern mill owners to find a context for claiming public support for their role as benevolent employers besieged by unreasonable union leaders.

Conclusion

Approximately eighteen thousand southern workers had been involved in walkouts between 1929 and 1932, less than half the number who struck during the war ten years earlier.[44] Yet despite the limited scope of the 1929–32 strikes, they helped southern textile workers prepare for the larger challenge of working together for change. Although victories were local and scattered, successful protests occurred frequently enough to convince at least some observers that a loose federation of local unions was possible in the South. In early 1933, hosiery and textile workers in High Point, North Carolina, formed the Piedmont Textile Council, which they later renamed the North Carolina Textile Federation and which played a critical role in the events leading up to the 1934 strike. Even South Carolina workers briefly experimented with a short-lived group called the Palmetto Organizing Council. The beginnings of a region-wide organization of textile workers were thus present even before the New Deal.[45]

The labor conflicts of these years also prepared workers in each state to play different roles in the 1934 strike. In northern Alabama, for example, thanks to the presence of sympathetic local merchants and the union experience of nearby coal miners and iron ore workers, textile workers had a deeper base of social and economic support than millhands in other southern states had. In this sense, northern Alabama workers possessed a great advantage over the workers in North and South Carolina. On the other hand, because the stretch-out had not hit Alabama mills as hard as it did the older mills in the Carolinas, Alabama workers had less experience in strikes and negotiations.

By contrast, North and South Carolina workers had endured a number of daunting strikes both during the war years and from 1929 to 1932, strikes that gave them experience confronting and negotiating with management. They had pulled local legislators and community leaders into the role of mediating settlements, giving them a greater stake in promoting industrial stability. While the north Alabama textile workers perhaps had a capacity for greater endurance, the North and South Carolina workers were better prepared to evaluate power and to develop strategy.

Suddenly, in 1933, everything changed. The election of Franklin Roosevelt and the inauguration of the New Deal legitimized—for the first time since World War I—southern textile workers' open affiliation with a national union. The New Deal would force southern textile workers to wage their campaigns not only locally and regionally, but also at the national level. As will be seen in chapter 5, somewhere between 80,000 and 135,000 southern millhands, at least one-third of the southern textile labor force, would join the AFL-affiliated United Textile Workers.[46] Southern textile workers' message would now be mediated through the institution of the UTW, a union whose history had been shaped by New England craft workers. How the "homegrown" community basis of worker power in the South would mesh with the goals, strategies, and leadership of the UTW would decisively shape the outcome of the labor conflicts to follow.

3

UNION-MANAGEMENT COOPERATION

There were important reasons why the United Textile Workers of America historically did not serve the needs of southern cotton millhands. The unionism of the UTW had been nourished by circumstances that lay far from the mill villages of the southern piedmont. At the same time that textile workers in the South were learning to navigate an emerging industrial economy, members of the northern-based UTW faced a declining industry struggling to stay afloat. Southern millhands were attempting to extract concessions from highly competitive and individualistic firms, while in the North the UTW was attempting to negotiate with a coordinated body of employers. The South's economic leaders found the very notion of unionism antithetical to their professed notions of civilized society; by contrast, progressive New England mills saw cooperation with unions as a means to create desired common goals: stablity and prosperity for both parties. While southern textile workers used the moral voice of the community to enforce understandings (often expressed only through oral commitments), and put a premium on theater and public opinion, the UTW worked with methods of negotiation—collective bargaining—that put a premium on rational discourse, formal proclamations, and precision of language. While southern protest was a direct expression of workers' grievances, the UTW sought a niche within the world of industry as a mediator between the workers and owners.

To understand what happened when southern workers joined the UTW in massive numbers in 1933–34, then, it is thus necessary to examine the roots of the UTW's own structure and ideology in its native setting, the New England mills, going back to its origins in 1901.

National Standards

Unions like the UTW performed a valuable service for liberal New England employers. By extracting higher wages from the small, fly-by-night, cutthroat competitors who undermined the profitability of the larger firms, the union served to discipline members of the employers' own ranks. Especially in competitive industries like textiles, liberal employers favored strong unions as a convenient vehicle for establishing national industry standards.[1] The first UTW president, John Golden, was an active participant in the National Civic Federation, the famous turn-of-the-century organization of large employers and union leaders committed to eliminating cutthroat competition and sweatshop wages and to creating national standards in industry. In an era of often chaotic labor-management relations punctuated by radicalism, violence, and brutal repression, cooperation between union leaders and large employers in these highly competitive industries formed a vital center.

The emphasis on national agreements, however, required that the UTW be willing to discipline not only the employers through the threat of strike, but also workers in the textile plants. When necessary, UTW leaders acted to contain militancy on the part of less "responsible" elements of the labor force. The UTW adopted a highly centralized organizational structure to ensure, for example, that members at the plant level would have to petition the executive council for approval of a strike. So heavily did the UTW emphasize its role as a disciplinarian of its own ranks that employers in Paterson, New Jersey, actually invited the UTW into their plants during World War I to prevent the continuation of a rash of "local disturbances" by the workers.[2]

The UTW also had been built from a workplace culture decisively different from that in the South. Since in the South skilled and unskilled workers came from the same culture, often the same family, southern textile protest tended to be inclusive of all members of the textile workforce. By contrast, in the North, the ethnic makeup of the skilled workers—Irish, English, and German—distinguished them culturally from largely Italian and Eastern European semiskilled workers. The UTW based its strength on the leverage of craft workers such as mule spinners, loom fixers, and weavers, often sacrificing the well-being of the semiskilled workers. Understandably, large numbers of northern immigrant textile workers joined the more radical union, the IWW, as an alternative. So hostile were relations between the UTW and the IWW that at the famous Lawrence, Massachusetts, IWW strike in 1912, UTW President Golden "exceed[ed] some manufactures in his condemnation of the immigrants' union tactics" and "did all in his limited power" to weaken the workers' position. "For a price—company recognition of the skilled workers," writes Melvyn Dubofsky, Golden "practically offered to break the strike."[3]

World War I changed the UTW briefly; even in the North, the union responded to worker pressure by becoming increasingly militant and more inclusive.[4] But this militancy was short-lived. By 1920, the UTW had fallen back into its prewar practice of opposing "radicalism." Golden's successor Thomas McMahon, despite his experience in the Knights of Labor in his youth, returned the union to its traditional practice of selling the UTW to employers as a responsible alternative to militant rabble-rousers.

This history shaped the UTW response to the southern labor insurgency in 1929. The southern industry, which paid wages up to 40 percent lower than those in the North, posed a threat to the stability that northern employer and union had attempted to achieve. The result was a durable coalition of interests. Even before the founding of the UTW in 1901, some northern employers were publicly urging leaders of the American Federation of Labor to use the organization's power to raise southern labor standards.[5]

Yet the challenge of organizing the South had divided the UTW membership. Conservative northern unionists opposed sending their resources to another region. As late as 1921, an editorial in the *New Bedford (Mass.) Morning Mercury* admitted that most New Englanders held "the common belief that Southern operatives are 'poor whites,' which to the New England mind means sloth and illiteracy and the evils arising from them."[6] Ironically, in light of future events, it was UTW President McMahon who championed the more progressive position. McMahon warned: "if we do not try to lift these workers up to the standards existing in the North . . . they will drag us down to their conditions as naturally as it is for water to find its own level."[7]

The UTW was finally galvanized into action by the acceleration of plant closings in the North in the mid-1920s. In a development Louis Adamic called "pathetic, not to say appalling," northern workers watched helplessly as manufacturers of fifty-one northern factories moved to southern locations between 1921 and 1929. About two-and-a-half million cotton spindles in New England were scrapped, a development George Mitchell called "momentous for the American labor movement." The issue of southern competition was so important that the American Federation of Labor devoted the entire November 1928 issue of its magazine, the *American Federationist*, to an assessment of labor's strength in the South.[8]

The southern textile walkouts in 1929 would appear to have presented organized labor with the opportunity it had been waiting for to raise southern labor standards. Yet the UTW was never able to capitalize on southern

In the May 1919 issue of *The Textile Worker,* UTW Vice President Thomas McMahon stands between worried Rhode Island manufacturers and workers being organized by a "bolshevik" labor organizer. The caption that accompanied this cartoon read: "Do you want this riffraff, or do you want to do business with lawabiding labor?" The following year McMahon succeeded John Golden as president of the UTW.

textile worker militancy. UTW leaders were fearful that the "poor white" culture of southern millhands would make impossible the respectable, accommodationist brand of unionism they had forged with New England employers. The UTW followed the lead of its parent organization, the AFL, which denounced southern worker militancy and urged instead the "assimilation" of southern workers into existing AFL unions. If textile workers were left to their own devices, argued the *Atlanta Journal of Labor*, they would become "a more dangerous menace to the progress of the organized workers than can be found in any other economic obstacle now confronting them."[9] Instead of a union led by the concerns of southern workers, AFL President William Green proposed in 1930 a "Southern Organizing Campaign" that appealed directly to employers. Green spoke of the "refining influence" that the AFL brand of unionism could bring to both "the factory and its community."[10] Through a "quiet, businesslike procedure by which the union idea is first sold to the boss in the office," Green announced, AFL unions could "clear up misunderstandings," and thereby "prevent such strikes as are now harrassing the South."[11]

The AFL's conviction that organized labor could appeal to employers to accept their services as mediators put the UTW into a series of untenable positions during the strikes of 1929 in the South. The UTW repeatedly found itself used as a pawn in mill owners' strategy to sap the power of mill workers' protests. In both Elizabethton and Marion, for example, management negotiated backroom agreements with the UTW. These agreements became the basis for workers abandoning their picket lines and returning to work, but were immediately followed by management's discharge of the main strike leaders.[12] The strikes fell apart or, worse, descended into violence, as workers, confused and internally divided, could no longer maintain solidarity.

The AFL's quiet, backroom method of unionizing also directly undercut the strategy of textile workers during the '29 strikes: amassing community support by bringing their concerns to the public light. Nor did it take into account the intense hostility of southern manufacturers toward unions. At the same time that the AFL was proposing union-management cooperation, for example, the sheriff of Ware Shoals, South Carolina, had run George Googe, AFL representative, out of town.[13] No matter how much the union redefined itself to represent the interests of the employer, textile mill manufacturers continued to see organized labor in no other terms but as a challenge to their absolute control over the labor force.

Efficiency

The structure of the UTW was not the only obstacle hindering its usefulness as a basis for an organization of southern textile workers. Another obstacle was its historical unwillingness to make the stretch-out an issue. The cries of southern workers against the stretch-out in 1929 had been uttered a generation earlier by Italian and Eastern European immigrant women in

Passaic and Paterson, New Jersey, and Lawrence, Massachusetts. The tes-
timonies of these workers could have been uttered by any southern stretched-
out worker: "It is drive, drive, drive, every minute of the day," complained
one Passaic worker in 1915. Workers described exhaustion and clothes "ring-
ing wet with sweat." "We have to work like dogs," reported another; "I hate
my boss now, and he was one fine boss, but no more."[14] The famous IWW
strike in Paterson, New Jersey, in 1913 was triggered by manufacturers'
decisions to introduce what was called the "four loom system" in silk mills
where one or two looms had been the normal workload. While workers
protested that "it was becoming a physical impossibility" to run four looms,
they were even more distressed by the resulting unemployment. "One man
would do the work of two and the other man would be eliminated," explained
Adolph Lessing, leader of the strike. "The weavers realized that if the thing
became general throughout the trade, the three and four looms, it meant
the filling of the streets with unemployed, which would mean a general reduction in wages, and that is what all the weavers realized, all the workers."[15]
The essential arguments of southern textile workers twenty-five years later
were already formed in the immigrant cultures of the northern mills.

The response of UTW President John Golden in 1914 set the stage for
the UTW's encounter with stretched-out workers in the South in 1929. At
first, this outpouring of protest from ordinary workers forced Golden to
condemn the new efficiency schemes.[16] But Golden was reluctant to strain
the foundation of the UTW's power: the alliance between UTW leaders and
progressive northern employers. He therefore welcomed arguments from
employers and their allies in Progressive-era reform movements that scientific management was a positive change for workers. By making plants more
efficient, employers argued, they could compete with cheap southern plants
without cutting northern workers' wages. As for the stretch-out, Golden was
counseled by liberals like Louis Brandeis that scientific management, when
properly applied, did not exploit workers. Far from hurting the worker,
Golden said in 1915, efficiency schemes eliminated "waste" created by
"inefficient and incompetent management," thus freeing up resources to
increase workers' wages.[17] Accustomed to collaboration with employers and
cultually removed from the daily reality of semiskilled immigrant workers,
Golden agreed in 1914 to compromise the union's opposition to speedups
in Brighton, Passaic, and Paterson, New Jersey.[18]

UTW President Thomas McMahon continued Golden's policy in favor
of high-wage, scientifically managed firms. In 1926 the UTW president
supported the new "multiple-loom system," suggesting that cost savings
could be used to increase workers' wages. The potential elimination of jobs

did not bother McMahon much. "If the introduction of modern machinery means a reduction of the number of employees in this industry," he wrote, "this, to my mind, will be the better for all concerned, because those remaining in the industry will receive a wage that will bring their condition closer to the American standard of living."[19]

These developments may have reconciled the union and northern employers, but they caused increasing tension between the union and parts of its membership who were exhausted or unemployed as a result of the stretch-out. The seeds of a complete break between the UTW and many northern workers were sown in 1928 when McMahon met with representatives of northern textile interests and state legislators in New Bedford, Massachusetts, to discuss the instability of the industry.[20] At this meeting the northern textile manufacturer Ernest Hood, owner of the Pequot Mills in Salem, Massachusetts, sought UTW support for the introduction of efficiency measures into his plant. Hood was a member of the Taylor Society, a group of industrial engineers, social reformers, and personnel managers who supported the principles of scientific management as the means of providing an objective basis for the organization of work to which both worker and employer could agree. Hood therefore proposed an experiment in "joint research," wherein union and management would join together in introducing scientific management procedures into his mill.

UTW leaders and industrial engineers plunged into the experiment with energy and enthusiasm, convinced that it would demonstrate the rationality of scientifically determined workloads and dispel worker suspicion of them once and for all. Instead, they found themselves opposing their own members as they entreated them to submit to workloads to which the union-management committee had agreed. Workers complained the new work assignments were "unjust, heavily burdensome, and nerve-racking."[21] As fewer employees took on increased workloads, those considered surplus were let go. By late fall 1931, upwards of two hundred workers had lost their jobs.[22] The UTW local officers were by this time under so much attack from their own members for permitting increased workloads that they changed the constitution to reelect themselves as the only means of retaining control.[23] When workers finally called a strike against any further stretch-out measures, the UTW declared the strike illegal. By 1933 the entire labor force had rebelled against the UTW and formed an independent union.

The Pequot experiment appeared to blast the notion that "science" was an objective and neutral approach wherein union and management could find common ground. Yet despite explosive opposition to scientific management from northern and southern textile workers, the UTW could not break from its chosen path. Convinced that efficiency measures were "progressive," the UTW found itself on the wrong side of the southern workers' campaign to redefine "progress" in the southern mills. Ignoring completely the fact that South Carolina mill workers had run the mill's "efficiency expert" out of town during its own local battles against the stretch-out, the UTW sent the AFL's own industrial engineer, Geoff Brown, to visit the heads of southern textile mills, "to gain the consent of other textile mills to union participation in the introduction of the stretch-out system."[24] Needless to say, no approach could have alienated workers more. It would take a revolution of textile workers in 1934 to force the UTW to come to a reckoning with its fateful embrace of scientific management.

On the Eve of the New Deal

By the early 1930s, UTW President McMahon concluded that the UTW campaign to raise southern labor standards by union organizing had been a complete failure. McMahon therefore turned to the only other vehicle he knew for establishing national wage standards: the industry trade association. According to McMahon, labor would only be secure when the industry found a way to discipline the "small group of unfair employers" who undercut the wages and prices of more honorable employers, forcing the latter to reduce wages to compete. McMahon supported any measures that would bring "stability out of chaos."[25] Oblivious to the threat to workers' unions posed by a broad-based employer alliance, by 1932 McMahon was openly calling for a "strong, militant Textile Manufacturers' Association!"[26]

The situation by 1933 was filled with apparent ironies. Never had the UTW been so weak. It had, at most, thirty-two thousand members nationally. Its base was eroding in the North, and it was failing to establish a significant presence in the South. And yet never had southern textile workers been so restless. While the UTW had cultivated the cooperation of industry on the basis of their common interests, southern workers had never been more disillusioned with their employers. McMahon was focusing on a national solution to the union's problems, while southern workers were determinedly seeking to win their demands by building local support.

Yet it would be a mistake to assume that the UTW sunk no roots in southern soil. The experiences of four key union leaders provides evidence for assessing the union's base in the South even before the New Deal.

Among the UTW leaders with the greatest experience in the South was the English-born UTW vice president from Rhode Island, Francis Gorman. Educated in the principles of trade unionism through his family's close association with wool workers in Bradford, England, Gorman was brought to Providence in 1903 at the age of thirteen, where he got work as a sweeper in a woolen mill. The UTW made him an organizer when he was thirty-two and vice president in 1928 when he was thirty-eight.[27]

Gorman first came to the South in September 1929 to call together southern organizers of textile workers and leaders of southern state federations to a meeting in Rock Hill, South Carolina, to plan a campaign to organize textile workers in the South. Then at Marion, North Carolina, he collaborated briefly with union organizers trained in the progressive Brookwood Labor College.[28] Possibly because of this early association, Gorman appeared to be more interested than other UTW national officers in organizing southern workers.

But Gorman became frustrated by the extraordinary power of southern mill owners to squash labor militancy. Not only did six workers die in the Marion strike, but the UTW also lost a critical strike in 1930 in Danville, North Carolina, under Gorman's leadership. This was an especially bitter defeat. All conditions had seemed positive: workers had greeted the UTW with enthusiasm even after massive discharges of union members; the local public supported the workers even after the union was backed into a strike. Indeed, the strength of the strike could be measured by the fact that the mill had to travel out of state to find strikebreakers. The strike began to weaken, however, when the mill succeeded in provoking violence, which in turn became the justification for calling out the National Guard. From that point forward, workers could no longer prevent strikebreakers from taking their jobs.[29] By February 1931 the union was forced to end the walkout with only vague promises from management that strikers would be rehired.[30]

The Danville failure profoundly demoralized Gorman, leading him to consider the possibility that to raise southern wage standards it might not be necessary that the southern worker be organized. By 1932 the entire UTW leadership had changed its strategy from organizing the southern worker to seeking industry regulation, either through a strong trade association, the option championed by McMahon, or government regulation. As Gorman was to say in 1934, it was a "matter of indifference" to the UTW whether workers got higher wages by negotiating collectively with the management, or by other means, such as strong wage-and-hour laws.[31] The UTW ideologically committed itself to the path the industry would follow under the New Deal.

If the Danville strike led Gorman to become disillusioned with organizing southern millhands, the UTW gained support in the South when national organizers departed from tradition to experiment with methods of organizing that were more compatible with southern textile worker culture. One such organizer was Paul Fuller, the director of the AFL Education Department, who worked under UTW supervision in the Augusta, Georgia/Horse Creek Valley, South Carolina area following the 1929 strikes (see chapter 2). Fuller was a minister who had been trained in worker eductation at Brookwood Labor College and with the progressive miners' union in Pennsylvania.[32] After visiting Marion and Elizabethton during the labor turmoil there, he was sent to the Augusta area in the fall of 1930 by the AFL's Worker Education Bureau. By March 1931, he had managed to organize 90 percent of the textile workers of the Augusta area into the UTW, using community-based methods quite unusual for an AFL staff member.[33] Although a strike of the Horse Creek Valley workers in 1932 failed, Fuller remained in the area and continued to build the organization. While UTW membership in the rest of the South languished, Augusta/Horse Creek Valley remained a stronghold of union support.

Gorman and Fuller were northerners who acquired valuable experience on the ground in the South before the New Deal. But a few southern UTW leaders also emerged in the early 1930s. One was John Peel, vice president of the North Carolina Federation of Labor in 1929. Peel had participated in the Marion strike before becoming the UTW's southern vice president. His experiences caused him to reject entirely the UTW's union-management cooperation approach. "The past two years," he wrote in 1931, "have shown definitely that the manufacturers of the South have no intention of dealing with their employees in a humane manner . . . but that they intend to stick to 1860 paternalistic slave driving methods of 'run nigger run, or the Patty-roll will get'cha.' While the textile workers do not plan a blood and thunder campaign, yet it is to be a more aggressive one, in which pacifism will not be the watch word."[34]

The most important southern UTW leader generated by the 1929–32 strikes was North Carolina's Paul Christopher. Christopher's parents were both skilled textile workers who, like many millhands, had moved about several times during their careers. When Christopher's mother was made to work for six weeks as an apprentice weaver without pay at a mill in Greenville, South Carolina, his father joined the UTW. He was promptly fired and forced to find work under an assumed name. Meanwhile, Paul trained as a weaver. Like many of his generation, he attempted in 1930 to leave mill work for an education, enrolling for three semesters at Clemson Agricultural College. Financial difficulties forced him to return to the mills, however, and in 1932 he became a weaver at the Cleveland Cloth Mill in Shelby, North Carolina, owned by the governor of North Carolina, O. Max

Gardner. Christopher joined the local union after learning that female workers at his mill had been sexually abused by a supervisor. He became president of his local, then president of the Piedmont Textile Council. By 1934, he would be the most important spokesperson for southern textile workers in the UTW.[35]

Given the strategic and cultural chasms between the UTW and southern textile workers, the commitments of southerners like Peel and Christopher to the UTW at this early stage were unusual. Indeed, had the New Deal not come about, it is doubtful whether a broad-based commitment to the UTW among southern millhands could have been achieved. In 1933, however, the climate for unions changed nationwide. The election of Franklin Roosevelt and the inauguration of the New Deal legitimized—even in southern communities—textile workers' open affiliation with a national union. The passage of the famous Section 7(a) of the National Industrial Recovery Act of 1933, granting workers the right to join a union free from interference from their employers, would stimulate a groundswell of union participation on a scale not seen in the United States since the end of the First World War.

But Section 7(a)'s legitimation of unions did not occur only in the abstract. New Deal policies became midwife not only to unionism, but to a specific brand of unionism whose shape would be determined by how it was used by workers, union leaders, and government policy makers. Groups like the UTW sought to make government support of unionism reinforce their own institutional and organizational commitments. As we shall see, New Deal policies wed the UTW even more tightly to the goals, strategies, and methods that undermined the community basis of worker power in the South.

4

NEW RULES

Had the country not been on the verge of a profound economic crisis, the revolts of southern textile workers over the stretch-out in 1929 might have assumed at most regional significance. However, with the coming of the Great Depression and then the New Deal, southern textile workers and southern manufacturers operated in a new context. President Franklin Roosevelt's call for a recovery program to end the depression staked out a national battleground for a struggle that, until now, had taken place only in the mill towns of the South.

By 1933, 15 million persons were out of work nationwide. Everywhere one saw haunting scenes of poverty amidst plenty, of goods on the shelves and no one to buy them. The laws of supply and demand seemed no longer able to "invisibly" create a balanced and healthy economy. It appeared that unless the whole economy was managed, the country would remain in chaos. No longer could either workers or employers conduct their business ignorant of the impact of their actions on the larger economy.

For textile employers, this political climate presented a unique opportunity. Using the political muscle exercised by their national trade association, the Cotton Textile Institute (CTI), they sought New Deal legislation that would enable them to achieve a long-term industry goal: the elimination of cutthroat competition through nationwide price and production standards. But textile manufacturers' political agenda was constrained by national sympathy for the unemployed worker. In order for mill owners' economic recovery program to be politically viable, it had to at least appear to address the dire needs of America's working people.

In truth, manufacturers' private agenda to modernize their factories directly contradicted the public's insistence that the New Deal address the problem of unemployment. Yet manufacturers could gain access to the power of the New Deal only by posing as advocates of reform. Present at the moment of the New Deal's conception was a contradiction between rhetoric and reality that would eventually explode into massive conflict in the southern mills in 1934.

Early New Deal Reformers

Southern textile workers had only an indirect voice in the federal legislative debate over economic recovery. Despite the presence textile workers had achieved in mill towns and in the hearts of southern reformers, they had almost no political voice at the national level. Instead, southerners were almost universally represented in Congress by members of the southern elite.

By default, the welfare of southern workers fell into the hands of liberal policymakers in the Roosevelt administration, whose job it was to reconcile competing interests into a coherent and politically viable recovery program. These men and women, arriving in Washington in March 1933, had themselves been shaped by a generation of national debate over the proper place of "labor" in modern society. Haunted by memories of the explosion in labor protest after the end of the First World War, these reformers were determined that Roosevelt's presidency would forge a permanent resolution to the constant labor upheaval that had characterized the industrial sector since the end of the Civil War.[1]

Four major influences shaped policymakers' thinking. First, they understood, realistically, that any solution to the "labor question" must acknowledge and contain the disruptive power of labor by recognizing the right of workers to have their collective voice represented in the workplace through unionization. This led to the inclusion of the famous Section 7(a) of the recovery legislation, guaranteeing workers the right to form unions free from interference by their employer. For southern textile workers, as for all workers, this was a great gift.

Second, policymakers endorsed "market unionism," the notion that unions played a positive role in stabilizing industry by achieving national labor standards. "It is simply impossible," declared the general counsel of the National Recovery Administration, "to maintain satisfactory labor relations in modern enterprises, or fair competition between industrial units without some form of labor organization."[2] Their support for national labor standards jibed with the view of northern textile employers and the

UTW, both of whom felt their own well-being was being undermined by cutthroat competition.

Third, policymakers sought to address labor welfare issues through economic strategies designed to end the Depression. As Frances Perkins wrote in early 1933: "As a nation, we are recognizing that programs long thought of as merely labor welfare, such as shorter hours, higher wages, and a voice in the terms and conditions of work, are really essential economic factors for recovery."[3] This analysis especially privileged higher wages, a cornerstone of Keynesian economic policies, which favored increased purchasing power to stimulate economic growth.

Keynesian economics would prove an enduring foundation for the rise of the labor movement of the 1930s; but Keynesian economics defined the limits as well as the extent of government concern over labor issues. In return for raising wages and recognizing unions, most policymakers were also willing to acknowledge the legitimacy of management's drive for efficiency. This was the fourth influence on New Deal labor policy. Many New Dealers shared the Progressive-era belief that efficient management practices were the mark of liberal thinking. They believed that labor conflict was more likely to occur in the the old-fashioned "autocratic" firms, such as the steel industry, whose management was not based on scientific principles. Firms with "modern" business practices, they believed, were more likely to have a cooperative relationship with labor. In the context of the Depression, these policymakers also championed efficiency measures as a means of keeping consumer prices low without sacrificing workers' wages. Policies based on these beliefs had been advocated for over a decade by the Taylor Society, a group of reformers and industrial engineers committed to both efficiency and labor harmony. But belief in efficiency was even more widespread than this; so completely did it permeate the thinking of even the most sympathetic and courageous reformers that it was almost unquestioned.[4] In a statement that would have made little sense to textile workers suffering from stretch-out, Senator Robert Wagner, a dedicated worker's advocate, explained that under Roosevelt's New Deal, "efficiency, rather than the ability to sweat labor . . . will be the determining factor in business success."[5]

Putting People Back to Work

Southern textile workers simply did not see the world in this way. For them, the critical issue was not inefficiency but the fact that workers were losing their jobs. The onset of the Depression simply intensified the connection workers made between management restructuring and unemployment. "The stretch-out system is the cause of the whole trouble," said one South Carolina millhand in 1930, "we wouldn't have the depression if it were not for it." These sentiments were echoed by a worker at the Cone Mills in Greensboro, North Carolina: "I could look out there in the years and see the awful misery ahead for working people. Thousands throwed out of jobs and the rest drove like machines till they died before their life was half over."[6] Convinced that the solution to the Depression was job creation, the Greenville, South Carolina, Trades and Labor Council proposed that the rules for stockholder dividends be altered so that a firm's value was based not on how much they produced, but according to the "number of producers employed." Meanwhile South Carolina mill workers lobbied the state legislature for countless bills to abolish the stretch-out.[7]

Textile workers had identified a real problem of national proportions. From 1919 to 1927, the productivity of labor in U.S. manufacturing overall had increased by 53.5 percent while the number of workers employed in industry had actually declined 2.9 percent.[8] This development was not entirely ignored in the national debate over New Deal policy. Mary Anderson, head of the Women's Bureau in Washington, D.C., spoke about it at a meeting of the Piedmont Organizing Council, a UTW-led group that enjoyed a brief existence in the wake of the '29 strikes. "We find ourselves with a grave problem," she began, "the increased use of machinery and the need of fewer hands because of this expansion." The dimensions of the impact on workers were vast: "No one knows today how many persons are out of employment because of this change. . . . no one knows what happens to the workers so displaced, how long they remain out of work . . . nor whether the older workers secure any job at all or are permanently left out as wage earners." Although she had no concrete solutions, Anderson called for a policy that would ensure "that the workers do not pay the price in heavier work and increased unemployment."[9]

But it was workers in other industries who managed to make technological unemployment a live political issue in Washington. Thrown out of work or seeing friends and relatives lose their jobs, rank and file union members raised a cry against the evils of technological unemployment at the 1932 AFL Convention in Cincinnati. Seizing the moment, AFL leaders channeled this sentiment into a campaign for shorter hours that would culminate in the Black thirty-hour bill in 1933.[10] "Back of it all," testified AFL President William Green to a House Committee on technological unemployment, "is the mechanization of industry that has been going on for two decades and gradually men have been displaced and thrown out of work."[11] In a rare moment, UTW President Thomas McMahon reported to a House Committee on

Labor that the stretch-out had thrown 750,000—about one of every two textile workers in the country—partially or completely out of work.[12]

Although technological unemployment was not a foremost concern in the thinking of New Deal policymakers, there is evidence that they would not have objected to reforms in this area as long as they were consistent with a consumer-based recovery program. Secretary of Labor Frances Perkins responded to the AFL's proposed Black Bill, for example, by suggesting that a minimum wage provision be added to it, so that shorter work hours would not result in reduced purchasing power. This incipient alliance between Keynesian liberals and workers, however, never got off the ground, because Perkins and the House Committee on Labor were overwhelmed with the objections of industry. Rather than alienate business, Roosevelt called together policymakers in his administration to devise a policy that would have greater business support.[13]

Yet despite Roosevelt's rejection of the thirty-hour bill, the popular sentiment behind it made clear that even a pro-business bill would have to at least engage in the rhetoric of a crusade against the scourge of joblessness. As Roosevelt himself had said in his inaugural address: "Our greatest primary task is to put people to work."[14] Here was the first inkling of a possible underlying tension between the reality and the rhetoric of Roosevelt's New Deal policies.

The Cotton Textile Institute

While southern textile workers had to rely on New Deal reformers to take their concerns into account, southern textile manufacturers had constructed a powerful independent platform for their views in Washington. These men sought a strategy that would advance their agenda while taking into account growing nationwide sympathy for the plight of labor. This was a lesson that southern manufacturers had learned earlier, for the labor upheaval of 1929 had given the southern industry a black eye. Beginning in 1929, therefore, a minority of southern textile manufacturers had already begun to propose terms for a peaceful accommodation with labor. So successfully did southern manufacturers reconcile their goals with those of liberal reformers that by 1933 they found themselves in the very center of the halls of power in Washington. The cornerstone of their new institutional power was the National Industrial Recovery Act (NIRA). To understand the importance of this new law for southern textile manufacturers, it is helpful to follow the thinking of a few key southern textile industry leaders as they strategized how to proceed following the 1929 labor unrest.

Among the most important leaders of textile manufacturers' political efforts in 1933 was former North Carolina governor O. Max Gardner, owner of the Cleveland Cloth Mills in Shelby, North Carolina. Unlike mills committed to cheap goods using cheap labor, Cleveland Cloth was a good example of a "medium-size best practice firm."[15] Owners of such firms were willing to pay higher wages because they hoped that the introduction of the latest management and labor relations techniques would afford them cost advantages over low-wage competitors. Because the mill contained up-to-date machinery, Gardner was also less interested than others in using the stretch-out to increase production. As a new businessman (his mill was built in 1925), Gardner was not steeped in the traditional labor relations of prewar mill owners. As a politician, Gardner also maintained a deep interest in industrial harmony. Thus Gardner came to believe in the "high wage thinking" so prevalent among newer, more consumer-oriented businesses. "We cannot build a prosperous citizenship on low wages," he wrote in 1929.[16] Wages at Cleveland Cloth Mill were the highest in the area. Finally, Gardner believed that the government had a role in facilitating industrial peace, a role he himself had played as governor of North Carolina in 1932 when he successfully mediated a general strike led by hosiery workers in High Point. "I am fully convinced," he wrote in September of that year, "that the wise employer will recognize that there is a new deal coming in industrial disputes."[17] If any southern textile employer embodied the aspirations of efficiency-minded labor reformers, it was Gardner.

Gardner's statement was not intended to indicate, however, that he agreed with labor's demand to end the stretch-out. Like his fellow manufacturers, he believed in the creation of "an efficient labor force;" and like so many of the era's reformers, he saw no incompatibility between being pro-efficiency and pro-labor. To the contrary, Gardner believed that management could persuade workers to agree to use the latest efficiency techniques because the average millhand was a more educated and therefore a more "reasonable person than he was twenty or thirty years ago."[18]

Gardner was supported by his colleague B. B. Gossett, president of the Chadwick Hoskins Mill in Charlotte, North Carolina. Gossett also felt that mill owners had suffered a bad public relations defeat in 1929. Writing in the *Southern Textile Bulletin* in 1929, Gossett expressed his frank annoyance that the clumsy implementation of the stretch-out system in Gastonia had made possible the exploitation of the situation by organized labor, alienating reformers—who once saw mill owners as "uplifters" of their workers— from mill owners. Gossett counseled his fellow manufacturers to be more tactful in the future, suggesting that "nothing of the nature of a radical departure from usual working conditions. . . should be undertaken without fully first consulting one's employees. . . .We have reached the time when employer and employee must closely work together on a basis of mutual good faith and understanding," he wrote, "in all matters effecting [*sic*] their mutual welfare."

But while Gossett suggested some form of accommodation with textile workers, he insisted that manufacturers' goal be to squeeze out organized labor and leave management firmly in control. Indeed, the very purpose of consulting with one's employees was to make sure that no "outside agencies" would "come into the picture." Gossett also believed that manufacturers needed to adhere to their long-term goal of increasing production quotas for their workers. He acknowledged that efficiency measures involved "the elimination of the unfit and the reduction of the employees per unit of product"; but, he added, "in this mechanical age, such practices are necessary."[19] Thus, although Gossett was less willing than Gardner to cooperate with unions, both were in essential agreement: however tactful the industry might be, the "rationalization" of the textile industry must continue.

To advance their agenda, southern manufacturers became active in the industry association, the Cotton Textile Institute (CTI). Originally founded in 1925, the CTI was not formed specifically to deal with labor issues, but rather to stabilize a volatile textile market created by an intensely competitive industry. The CTI was also the first national cotton textile association supported not only by northern mills, but also by the sector of southern textile manufacturers who likewise found their profits eroded by declining prices, overproduction, and unpredictable markets.

Southern manufacturers such as Gossett saw in the CTI a way to cultivate political goodwill among reformers and stabilize the industry at the same time. The CTI therefore focused its energies on night work—the practice, increasingly common in southern mills, of running the mills twenty-four hours per day in an attempt to minimize overhead costs and thus sell goods more cheaply than their competitors. The consequent overproduction in the industry drove prices down even farther, leading to bankruptcy in less aggressive mills.[20]

Gossett proposed that textile manufacturers voluntarily eliminate night work for women and limit weekly production on the other two shifts to 105 hours. The proposal would go into effect if 80 percent of the mills agreed to it. If the percentage of the industry participating in self-regulation fell below 80 percent, then the CTI could no longer require compliance.[21] To please reformers, textile industry leaders consciously stressed the advantages of eliminating night work for mothers of young children. Not incidentally, industry leaders like Gardner of the Cleveland Cloth Mill and Ernest Hood of Pequot Mills in Salem, Massachusetts, also publicly endorsed higher wages for mill workers. Altogether, the package was a shrewd move.[22]

But while the proposal may have improved the industry's image among its major detractors, it failed to accomplish the goals of limiting production. For a brief period in 1931, the CTI managed to recruit over 80 percent of textile manufacturers to the hours-limitation proposal. However, a brief surge in demand for textiles in 1932 ended the willingness of many manufacturers to comply and dashed the hopes of industry leaders for coherence and direction in an unstable industry. Twenty-four-hour operations in southern mills again became common, and the industry appeared to be headed for another cycle of overproduction.[23]

The NIRA

As it became clear that no amount of self-regulation was going to create stability in the industry, the CTI turned to Roosevelt's industrial recovery legislation for help. The CTI now wanted Congress to grant it the authority to regulate production, hours, and wages in the textile industry. For the CTI to seek a political solution under the conditions that existed in 1933 involved some risk: sympathy for workers made it inevitable that any industrial recovery legislation would necessarily involve some recognition of the rights of labor. Yet, in the final analysis, CTI leaders concluded that, given the enormous need for government authority to regulate production, labor legislation was only a minor liability. In a letter to fellow mill owner William Anderson, Donald Comer, among the most sophisticated antiunion mill owners, described how he imagined the resulting legislation would work: "The more nearly we can settle these points . . . in Washington . . . the less need there will be for union labor organization in the plants themselves because if Washington is going to fix the wages and the tasks, that is all organized labor could promise to do and thereby industry will be better off as a result."[24] Southern textile leaders thus fused into a single strategy the goal of eliminating overproduction in the industry and that of deflecting labor dissatisfaction in their factories. The government would in essence perform the same function that nationwide unions performed, with the difference, however, being that industry would have a much greater say in wage and production policies.

These ideas all came together in the National Industrial Recovery Act. The NIRA authorized not only the cotton textile industry but every industry in the country to draw up "codes" of fair competition. Each industry code entitled industry assocations like the CTI to limit production levels in their own industries and to set standards for wages and hours; and although industry leaders were not too happy about it, each code also included Section 7(a), the protection of workers' rights to form unions. The NIRA also included a modest public works program.

Together these provisions would have a powerful and wrenching impact on the southern mills in the year to follow, an impact that will be explored in the next chapter. What is important to note here, however, is the political context within which the bill was passed. Although the increased powers given to industry trade associations was one of the more remarkable features of the new recovery act, leading sponsors of the NIRA soft-pedaled these provisions. Instead, the act was hailed as the centerpiece of Roosevelt's program to help solve the unemployment problem.[25] The new administrator of the National Recovery Administration (NRA), Hugh Johnson, emphasized the point: "It is the purpose of the National Recovery Act to put people back to work promptly."[26] As a further rhetorical flourish, the NIRA provision that set standards for wages and hours in industy was called the president's "re-employment agreement."

CTI representatives beat the drum of full-fledged cooperation with the goals of the recovery program, particularly the rhetorical goal of ending unemployment. CTI President George Sloan publicly predicted that if the code were implemented, one hundred thousand people could be put back to work. Stuart Cramerton, a North Carolina owner, estimated that an additional fifty thousand southern workers would be hired when the code went into effect. Bibb Mills owner William Anderson suggested that such a program would be so successful that there would be an actual shortage of labor in the South.[27]

To further improve its public image, the industry also granted concessions designed to please liberal reformers. At the public hearings, for example, reformers expressed concern about the persistent problem of child labor. Industry spokespersons argued in response that the new higher wage levels mandated by the Code would make the cost of child labor so prohibitive that it would be effectively outlawed, but reformers were not satisfied. So, in a gesture that won the industry a round of applause, the industry offered to end child labor in the mills. The industry's public relations efforts could not have been better executed.

Ironically, the final ominous note during the hearings came from the ranks of the industry itself. One witness, Robert Johnson, was the owner of Johnson and Johnson Company, maker of cotton bandages. The firm's textile mills were wholly owned, vertically integrated into its operations. Thus the company was not affected by the volatility of the industry as a whole; Johnson therefore was not invested in the fate of the NIRA the way that other manufacturers were. In a statement completely out of step with the orchestrated performance of the CTI, Johnson looked at the reduction in machine hours mandated by the Code and concluded that the result could be a layoff of some five thousand workers in textile plants around the country.[28] Could this be true? Johnson's comments were quickly forgotten in the rounds of mutual congratulations between NRA administrators and textile industry leaders over their successful completion of the first code ever to be established under the new recovery program.[29]

Prohibiting the Stretch-out

The passage of the NIRA and the creation of the Cotton Textile Code did not, however, go entirely smoothly for the textile industry. The industrial recovery bill had been rapidly making its way through Congress when, apparently out of nowhere, Congressman John Clarence Taylor of South Carolina proposed an amendment to abolish the stretch-out.

This action spoke volumes about the nature of southern workers' political power, for South Carolina was the only state in the textile South where textile workers' votes mattered. Congressman Taylor had been elected in 1933 to represent the textile district of Anderson, South Carolina, one of the most active regions of labor protest in the South. Co-owner of the *Anderson Independent*, Taylor had worked in textile mills as a child, and had earned a law degree from University of South Carolina in 1919. Along with South Carolina Senator James Byrnes, Taylor became the political voice of South Carolina labor, and by default, of all of southern textile labor.[30]

"I know mill life," Taylor said in 1933. "I have worked in mills and when I did, a weaver attended to twenty or thirty looms. Now it is 100 to 150. Machinery has improved, it is true. But I am not objecting to that." Rather, Taylor wanted provisions in the Code "whereby a man will not have to drag himself home at night worn to frazzle, and trudge back next day unable to enjoy life and with nothing to look forward to and to shoulder the same machine load every day that wears him down under the stretchout system."[31]

The wording of Taylor's amendment was remarkably straightforward: "that in any agreement entered into by employers and employees under the industrial recovery act, in addition to a minimum wage and the hours of labor there should be an agreement as to the maximum machine load of employees." Although the amendment was killed in a House-Senate conference, Taylor sought to keep the idea of an anti-stretch-out provision alive. He got additional help from Senator Byrnes, who called the stretch-out system a "running sore" in relations between workers and manufacturers.[32] Finally, Hugh Johnson, the administrator of Roosevelt's new recovery agency, the National Recovery Administration, promised Taylor that the intent of his amendment could be carried out in the implementation of the newly enacted legislation in the language of the Cotton Textile Code.[33]

Johnson proposed a provision of the Cotton Textile Code known as Section 15. The wording of Section 15 was significant: "no employee of any mill in the cotton textile industry shall be required to do any work in excess of the practices . . . prevailing on July 1, 1933, unless such increase is submitted to and approved by the [new cotton textile industry committee] and by the National Recovery Administration."[34] If Section 15 survived the Code hearings and became part of the Cotton Textile Code signed by President Roosevelt, the U.S. government would be regulating the stretch-out in cotton mills.

This was a component of the New Deal that cotton textile manufacturers had not bargained for. CTI president George Sloan and members of the Cotton Textile Industry Committee Thomas Marchant and Ernest Hood immediately implored Administrator Johnson not to to discourage "improvements" in machinery as a way to end unemployment. Sloan acknowledged that the industry's "efficiency" measures had exacerbated the unemployment problem. "In times of depression such as these," Sloan conceded, "employees whose services become unnecessary by reason of such improvements cannot readily be reabsorbed through increased operations in the industry itself or into other industries." But he urged Johnson to attack the problem not by limiting "the development and use of improved mechanical devices and technique." Instead the government should decrease a worker's hours of labor "with accompanying adjustment in wages." Their appeal concluded with praise for the "American instinct for inventiveness and efficiency" and a hope that the upcoming legislation would "avoid the hardship to the individual which may otherwise avail in times like these."[35] The conflict between southern textile workers and their employers thus was joined at the national level. Largely ignored by reformers and the public, the debate over Section 15 contained the seeds of a larger conflict over the role of efficiency measures in New Deal government labor policy.

The Stretch-out Committee

The UTW played almost no role in the debate over Section 15. It was not that the textile union lacked a voice in the Code-formation process. UTW leaders did intervene in those areas of traditional UTW concern: elimination of wage differentials and maintenance of wage levels of skilled workers. At the Code hearings, UTW representatives argued that the proposed minimum wage—$10 per week for southern workers and $11 per week for northern workers—was too low. It was raised to $12 and $13 per week, respectively. They objected to the Code's definition of "employee" as too narrow, encompassing only machine tenders. The UTW wanted sweepers, balers, learners (new employees), and other non-machine workers to be covered by the Code's minimum wage, while industry leaders did not want to include these workers at all. A compromise was reached: the Code would guarantee outside workers and learners a minimum wage that amounted to three-fourths of the minimum to be granted to other workers. This distinction was critical to maintaining a wage differential between white and black workers in the southern mills.[36] Finally, the UTW was concerned that nothing in the Code protected skilled workers' wages, which were traditionally considerably higher than the minimum wage. At the last minute, after the hearings had been concluded, President Roosevelt agreed to add a provision indicating that the differential between skilled and unskilled workers' wages would be maintained. Industry leaders cried foul, arguing that this provision had not been discussed during the hearings, but the president's word was final, and the provision became part of the Code.

These interventions were significant. Nevertheless, the UTW's historic alliance with scientific management prevented it from becoming a force shaping the outcome of the debate over the stretch-out. The crucial turning point came when, under pressure from both the industry and the South Carolina Congressmen, NRA Administrator Hugh Johnson agreed to suspend implementation of Section 15 until an "investigation" of the stretch-out was carried out by a committee to be appointed by Johnson himself.[37] So politically charged was the question of the stretch-out that the membership of this "investigating committee" became the all-important question. Immediately, behind-the-scenes jockeying began, as Johnson's attempt to appoint two South Carolina textile manufacturers to constitute the entire committee met with vehement objections from the South Carolina Federation of Labor. Finally, Johnson agreed to a three-person committee with one representative of labor, one of industry, and one from the government. This was a conscious duplication of the composition of the labor-management committees formed inside the federal government during World War I.

The identities of the three men who were chosen to determine the fate of Section 15 paints a vivid picture of the political influences shaping decisions about southern textile labor in Washington in 1933. For the labor representative, Johnson chose not a southern textile worker, or even a member of the UTW, but George Berry, president of the Printing Pressman's Union, from Knoxville, Tennessee.[38] Johnson's choice of Berry was not entirely illogical: in 1929 he had been a government-appointed mediator during the strike of textile workers in Elizabethton, Tennessee. After a few attempts at mediation, Berry had resigned his post when management refused to negotiate, calling the position of the mill owners "scandalous and indefensible."[39] But Berry was also a conservative AFL leader who criticized textile workers for their frequent tendency to resort to strikes. He advocated "proper leadership" and "constructive trade unionism," and he encouraged unions to "realize their responsibility to industry and to society."[40] As for the stretch-out, Berry acknowledged that while it existed "in some mills," in "many" cases he thought it was really a problem in workers' "state of mind."[41] Textile workers who looked to Berry for a vigorous defense of Section 15 would be sadly disappointed.

For the industry representative, Johnson appointed Benjamin Geer, of Greenville, South Carolina. Unlike moderates such as Gardner, Geer adamantly opposed textile unions, believing them to be a "contentious and troublesome element."[42] He also opposed a shorter workday, claiming it would only give textile workers more time to get into mischief.[43] Pressed to support the concept of collective bargaining as mandated by Section 7(a), Geer insisted that if workers wanted the union to represent them, then every worker in the unit had to be a member of the union.[44] If moderates such as Gardner and Gossett reassured reformers and government that the industry was in full cooperation with the recovery program, Geer represented the hard-line position behind the scenes.

But it was the choice of Robert W. Bruere as chair of the stretch-out committee that revealed most starkly how unprepared New Deal administrators were to give a fair hearing to southern workers' opposition to the stretch-out. Bruere had been involved in the negotiations in the mid-1920s that led the AFL to accept the offer of the industrial engineer Geoff Brown to work for unions as their "expert" in the implementation of scientific management in the textile industry.[45] Both a member of the pro-efficiency Taylor Society and a contributing editor to the reform-minded *Survey* magazine, Bruere genuinely believed it was possible to bring employer and employee together to effect "the elimination of waste through efficient production."[46] Now Bruere was appointed to head a committee to investigate the stretch-out. It was probably Bruere who suggested that the investigating committee be aided in its work by two "engineers"; one of them was none other than Geoffry Brown.[47] If Taylor and Byrnes thought that this committee would validate workers' concerns about stretch-out, they were mistaken.

Conclusion

A lot had changed in four years. In 1929, southern cotton mill workers who protested their labor conditions needed only to be strong enough to influence the attitudes of local citizens. By contrast, in 1933 southern textile workers needed enough power to shape the parameters of national policy. Congressman Taylor's amendment abolishing the stretch-out, now Section 15 of the Code, provided textile workers with a most tenuous foothold in the new law. By contrast, textile employers had a much greater advantage. Their industry association, the CTI, was now in charge of enforcing the Code. It was now called the Code Authority.

Yet if cotton textile manufacturers had acquired a new political weapon in the Code Authority, textile workers had a new economic weapon in Section 7(a) of the NIRA, guaranteeing workers the right to form unions. This new right was an unprecedented boon to textile workers. In short, with the enactment of the NIRA, the rules for engagement between workers and their employers had completely changed. How each side would use their new powers would ultimately determine the shape of work relations in the textile mills in the South.

5

DIRTY DEAL

Stabilization, what crimes are to be committed in thy name!
—Senator William E. Borah of Idaho, June 1933

The New Deal was far more than the intricate skirmishes behind the scenes that occurred in the battle over Section 15 of the Cotton Textile Code. It also was a rallying cry for a public looking for hope in the midst of despair. As one piece of legislation followed another at breakneck pace, the New Deal lifted the country out of its state of near paralysis and enabled it to act. Eula McGill, a retired textile organizer, remembers: "When Roosevelt took office . . . newspapers and everything were very quick to publish everything, because everyone wanted to get the country back on its feet. So consequently, these people were expecting, they were ready to do something."[1] Hugh Johnson, administrator of the NRA, encouraged this sense of mass participation with his slogan, "We Do Our Part."

Southern textile workers were among Roosevelt's most enthusiastic recruits. Throughout the first year of the New Deal, thousands of southern millhands wrote to the president, his wife, or Hugh Johnson, giving advice, expressing gratitude, or describing problems. All expressed a remarkable outpouring of affection and gratitude to the new president for his sympathies for what they called the "laboring classes of people." Here was a federal law that was going to give southern workers an eight-hour day, a minimum wage of $12 a week, an end to the stretch-out, and the right to organize a union. "I wished when I knew you had signed the NIRA that I could send you a message," wrote a woman from the Avondale Mills in Alexander City, Alabama, "so grateful was I that at last we had a President who was interested in the laboring class of people."[2] "It is impossible to emphasize the faith [southern mill workers] had in the Code," the *New Republic* said a year later. "When the Code went into effect there were dances and celebrations."[3] The Code, proclaimed Alfred Hoffman, a veteran of the 1929 strikes, was "the greatest Declaration of Independence that any president has ever signed since the one in 1776."[4] "When we first received word about the Textile Code, the Blue Eagle, and our right to bargain collectively, it was too good to be true," said J. P. Holland, a textile union leader from Gadsden, Alabama, also a year later. "It was a real new deal for us."[5]

It was, indeed, too good to be true.

"The Jobs Are So Bad Stretched Out"

Perhaps it was naive to have imagined that the government could have implemented both higher wages and limits on production hours in a highly competitive, decentralized industry such as textiles. Low-wage mills, whose very existence depended on their ability to undercut the "better class" of employers, were simply unwilling to pay the higher "Code wages," unless, that is, they could get greater production out of their existing workforce. Or, as the veteran hosiery organizer and union education director Lawrence Rogin put it, "Always a stretch-out when you get a wage increase in textiles."[6]

But workers judged the codes not by the logic of the market but by Roosevelt's and the industry's own promise: that the codes would put people back to work. And here the Textile Code would prove a cruel joke, for rather than increase production, it prompted employers to lay even more people off.

Ironically, in light of what was to follow, the spring of 1933 did witness a temporary increase in textile employment. Between April and July—that is, between the enactment of the NRA and the implementation of the industry codes—many mill owners began a feverish increase in production of cloth. Fearing that the Code provisions would raise production costs, they ran their mills "full blast" to build up as much cheaply made stock as possible. Some mills instituted second or even third shifts, hiring hundreds of additional employees. Some even raised wages to keep their workforces as productive as possible during the short time before the Code went into effect.[7] Such anticipatory production occurred not only in textiles but in many industries throughout the country. Called the "boomlet" of the spring of 1933, this production increase brought the textile industry up to pre-Depression standards of production.[8]

All this came to a halt on July 17, 1933, the day that the new Cotton Textile Code went into effect. The elation of the mill workers in having a president who was for the working person evaporated as they confronted the actual practices of the southern mills under the new code. "The jobs are so bad stretched out," complained Ellis Covan from Pelzer, South Carolina, "that they are not using near all the people around here."[9] "We understand you was supposed to get the unemployed to work," wrote an angry textile worker from Merrimack Mills. "Now it's the other way. People are getting out of work instead of getting work."[10]

The job cuts went deep into the core of the mill community with layoffs ranging from dozens to hundreds in one mill. At mills with good employee relations, workers reported that their overseers hated to dismiss them because their work had been satisfactory. At Samoset Cotton Mill, many of the two hundred laid off "were skilled laborers, men and women with years of experience."[11] In other cases, layoff practices were combined with the worst aspects of favoritism. At Dwight Mills in Gadsden, Alabama, the mill "dropped 650 employees from payroll" due to stretch-out, giving what jobs remained to members of the supervisors' "families, their wives and their children."[12] "After discarding the ones that really need the work," wrote union organizer Margaret Pearson, "they are now working girls that have good homes . . . also . . . young married women with husbands . . . . there are scores of people that are now confused over being unemployed."[13]

Those remaining on the job were asked to do more work in eight hours than they had done in ten or twelve. "Before the Code first class spoolers could make 300 spools in eleven hours," reported *The Textile Worker* magazine, the official publication of the United Textile Workers union. "Now they are required to make 400 in eight hours or 350 in seven hours."[14] "There are literally hundreds of employees out at the Springs mills," wrote a distraught Monroe Jordan to NRA Administrator Hugh Johnson, "and the ones who are Still at Work are Being Treated as Bad or Worse that the Slaves were in Slavery times."[15]

A mill worker of eleven years from Gastonia lamented that she had once been considered "one of the best of spinners," but that now "the load has almost got the best of me, for the machinery has been speeded to the highest notch, more cleaning up has been put on us, till we can't hardly bear any more." She added, "I've seen women so wet from perspiration that it could be wrung from their clothes. I've seen them go to a window for a fresh breath of air only to be whistled at by a section hand and made to get away from the window, and he would threaten to discharge the next one who opened a window . . . . The work is speeded so high since the short hours began that the mill men are getting off more production in six and eight hours than they got off in eleven hours per day."[16] A worker from the Sanford Cotton Mill in Sanford, North Carolina, reported similar speedups, concluding, "It will kill anybody the way they have to work in this mill now."[17]

The truth of these anecdotal reports was confirmed by systematic studies. The Bureau of Labor Statistics reported that from August 1933 to August 1934, employment in textiles fell 12.7 percent, a number representing perhaps fifty thousand workers nationwide.[18] At the same time, the trade magazine *Textile Notes* reported, "a large amount of additional equipment, other than for replacement purposes, was installed in southern mills." The increase in machinery in 1934, in fact, was the largest such increase in the southern mills since 1929.[19]

What about wages? Here results were mixed. According to workers' letters, the wages of the unskilled were often raised up to the minimum standard required by the Code. The Bureau of Labor Statistics also reported that southern women, who comprised the bulk of unskilled labor in the cotton mills, experienced a 25 percent increase in earnings between July 1933 and August 1934. But the worst fears of the skilled workers were confirmed. The UTW's own informal study of wages under the Code concluded that the unskilled workers were "the only group of workers who have benefitted under the Cotton Textile Code." For semiskilled and skilled workers, "in numerous instances wage reductions have taken place."[20] The BLS similarly reported that men, generally higher paid than women, received on average only one-half of 1 percent increase in wages.[21]

Mills devised other, more blatantly illegal methods to decrease labor costs after the Code went into effect. Mrs. Reaves, from the Samoset Cotton Mill in Talledega, Alabama, wrote to Washington: "I have been working in a cotton mill over 15 years and they put *learner* on my pay envelope."[22] Under the Code, learners received only three-fourths of the minimum wage. From the Aragon Cotton Mill, Ester Steel wrote to Roosevelt that her employers were doubling up the workload and signing up workers as learners, "saying they wasn't going to abide by the law." Steel conveyed the intimidation used to reduce the status of longtime workers to that of beginners. The mill supervisors "were so cruel to the hands," she wrote, "talks so mean to them, tells us if we don't do what they tell us to do get out of their mill."[23] In Macon, Georgia, L. J. Kines also spoke of intimidation: "They are hiring hands off of the farms, causing them to leave their crops, working them three or four weeks as learners and then some of them are let go. And that isn't all. They are having a paper carried throught [*sic*] the mill getting the hands to sign it as learners so they can work them at low price." Kines went on to explain that those who refused to sign the paper were laid off.[24] A millhand in Pell City, Alabama, wrote that his supervisors marked him as a sweeper to keep from paying him the higher wages. "They don't intend to pay some of us the high wages until they are made to do it," he concluded.[25]

"Of the sixty textile mills I know of in the Carolinas," reported organizer Lawrence Hogan to the North Carolina State Federation of Labor, "only two are anywhere near living up to the provisions of the Code."[26] The workers at the Eagle and Phenix Mills in Columbus, Georgia, wrote that their employers were "striving by every conceivable means at their command to defeat all the plans and policies laid down by this administration."[27] At the Lincoln Mills in Huntsville, Alabama, the supervisor allegedly threatened the workers if they gave him trouble for violating the Code: "Im tired of this damn bunch any way and when you all think Im going to pay you 30 [cents per] hour you are certainly mistaken for I am not going to do it. If you fool with me I will fire every damn one of you and get a new set of hands."[28] "Employers in the South are sure as not going to do [whatever they want] until they are forced" to abide by the Code, wrote W. L. Hilton, from Dwight Mills in Gadsden, Alabama. "Conditions are worse now than Before. There is more dissatisfaction among labor now than I have ever seen."[29] Thirteen people from Albertville, Alabama, signed and sent a plea to Washington: "Please do something. There is many here that will give you a glad welcome and tell you of the Dirty Deal this eight hour law has give us."[30]

Fear

During the year following the Code's enactment, the Cotton Textile Code Authority received over four thousand letters of complaint such as these.[31] But these letters represented only a fraction of the discontent. What was not present in the complaint pile were the grievances of hundreds of textile workers too intimidated to write a letter to Washington. The act of writing a letter of complaint required such courage, in fact, that many of those who wrote letters were destined to become leaders of the union movement among textile workers.

Two major fortresses of nonunionism were the Cannon Mills in Concord, North Carolina, and Donald Comer's Avondale Mills in central Alabama. These huge complexes had plants and villages comprising several unincorporated cities and towns in the area. Both mill owners also had a reputation for extreme paternalism. Charlie Cannon was reported to have been "a man with a big heart."[32] As for Donald Comer, "My daddy liked Comer," remembered the son of a Sylacauga textile worker. "He said he was one of the best people he ever worked for. He was good to those people down in Sylacauga . . . . If some of your people had to go in the hospital, he would go down to the hospital and write that check. If you wanted to buy a house, he'd buy the house, then he'd ask how much you can pay back. If you say $2.00 a week, he cuts $2.00 a week out of your pay."[33] Comer was said to have so strongly opposed night work on humanitarian grounds that he refused to employ a second shift in his own mill in the 1920s despite financial difficulties.[34] He even owned a vacation resort that workers could visit during their holiday as part of the reward for working in his mill.

This sense of generosity on the surface seemed to account for the startling absence of protest among workers from Cannon and Avondale Mills. Indeed, not a single letter of complaint from a textile worker in the Concord division of Cannon Mills found its way into the files of the Code Authority.

The evidence, however, suggests a different explanation. Although no Concord worker wrote a letter of complaint to Washington, the "Cannon, Concord" file does contain two letters from individuals who were not employed by Cannon. S. J. Gwyn was not a textile worker but described himself as "in sympathy with them." Gwyn not only described the familiar sequence of wage cuts, stretch-out, and layoffs that took place after July 17, but also spies and people being fired for speaking up. "Please do not send anyone to the Overseer," he begged in conclusion, "but to the hands."[35]

A few workers at the Avondale Mills, a degree bolder than those in Concord, wrote their own letters. But these letters described similar fears. "I am writing you this," wrote one Avondale worker, "knowing if my name is know[n] I will loose my Job hoping you will not let it be know[n] I work in Avondale mills Sylacauga . . . . please don't make my name known for I have a wife and four children depending on me for a living and work is scarce."[36] According to another Avondale textile worker in Childersburg, the boss had raised the rent and cut workers' wages on July 17, telling them that "if we didn't keep our lips closed he would discharge all of us."[37] An anonymous Avondale worker in Alexander City wrote that it was "my duty to report this but if they find out that I did it it will cost me my job."[38] A man in Pell City, Alabama, wrote a letter representing "at least three hundred persons here in Pell City, Ala.," begging the government: "Please do not let this company here have this letter for they would . . . fire the man who wrote to you."[39]

If the simple act of writing a letter could result in an employee's dismissal, the act of joining a union more assuredly would lead to to being fired. Some workers in the Avondale Mills in Sylacauga nevertheless attempted to form a union. They were fired routinely. Many were frankly told that the mill would "not work union labor." In Alexander City the workers found a local doctor to speak for them rather than risk identifying themselves by joining a union.[40]

Workers in the mills surrounding Greenville, South Carolina, expressed similar fears. Here nearly all the textile mills had been gerrymandered out of the city limits. Labor relations, despite workers' proximity to a city, more closely resembled mills in remote villages.[41] Among the few groups of workers to even attempt to organize were those at the Dunean Mills. Yet their meetings were monitored by two deputy sheriffs instructed to keep a "careful watch" on the workers; the overseers warned employees to stay away from the meetings. Three employees had already been discharged "for talking organization among the employees," and "the matter of unionization of the workers" was now being mentioned at Klan meetings, "to which the overseers and pimps and a few good people belong."[42]

Most workers in these highly restrictive environments chose to bear their burdens quietly. In Cannon Mills in Concord, in Avondale and Cone Mills, in most of the mills in Greenville, in some of the mills that experienced devastating defeats in 1929 (such as in Marion, or in Henderson, where a strike in 1927 failed), the repressive atmosphere was so strong that no outsider would have known what went on within.

Resistance

But in mills with less repressive environments, the enactment of the NIRA, the Cotton Textile Code, and Section 7(a) legitimized unions for the first time since World War I. AFL representative George Googe claimed 150,000 union members in various southern industries by the beginning of August 1933.[43] A former UTW organizer estimated that workers in 75 percent of the South Carolina mills had formed a union local by the fall of 1933. Vance Donnahoo, a retired textile worker from Inman, South Carolina, thought even that estimate low: "Oh it was 100%, just about all the mills! I'd say every mill was 90–95 percent union, every mill then."[44]

That workers in some mills dared not even mention the word "union," while in others unionization was "almost 100 percent," reflects in part the divided mindset among southern manufacturers about how to respond to Section 7(a) of the NIRA. While many mills brazenly ignored 7(a), others did not attempt to interfere with union organizing; some even explicitly recognized their workers' unions.[45]

An equally important component of strong union building under the Code, however, was workers' connection with pre–New Deal organizing. By September 1933, workers in Walker County, Alabama, for example, had held large open-air meetings and established six locals of textile workers.[46] By February 1934, Huntsville claimed over twenty-six hundred union members, leading a labor newspaper to brag that "labor union history" was being made in this "formerly untouchable 'open shop' town."[47] In both these places textile union organizing had also thrived in 1930–32. Here also coal miners had a tradition of union organizing and forming farmer-labor alliances.[48]

In North Carolina, union organizing had begun to snowball in February 1933, even before the Code had gone into effect. Building on their previous year of successful organization, hosiery workers from High Point had joined with textile workers from nearby towns to form the Piedmont Textile Council.[49] By May 1933, UTW organizer C. W. Bolick was bragging that the Piedmont Textile Council was the "best ever organized in this section."[50] By October 1933, one thousand millhands had joined the central labor union formed to serve the several mills in Shelby, North Carolina.[51] In the Charlotte area, railroad machinist George Kendall recruited local mill workers and developed them into union leaders.[52] By February 1934, fifty-five thousand North Carolina textile workers had signed union cards.[53] In South Carolina, by September 1933 more than six thousand mill workers in the state had formed UTW locals.[54]

All of these activities contrast sharply with the situation in Georgia, where workers in 1933 had little foundation on which to build a union. Indeed, the climate against unions in Georgia was so hostile that the major historian of Georgia labor could learn of only one textile union in the state in 1929, and its location and identity was a secret.[55] By 1933 things were not much better. As the president of the Cotton Manufacturers Association of Georgia revealed years later, the mills in his state had "no intention of abiding by the Code."[56] The most forbidding antiunion territory was the Chattahoochee Valley, in towns like Newnan, Sargeant, Hogansville, and LaGrange. With the consistent exception of Columbus, on the Alabama state line, Augusta, on the South Carolina state line, and Macon, farther south, few strong union locals emerged out of Georgia.

Scant records provide only the most rudimentary glimpse into the makeup of these southern textile union locals. Although most UTW presidents were men, women were highly visible union officials and local organizers. Women were secretaries of at least eight of the North Carolina locals. Mrs. B. M. Miller, union secretary at the Chadwick Hoskins Mill in Charlotte, North Carolina, was also appointed by the Charlotte Central Labor Union to investigate and report on all violations of the Textile Code in the Charlotte area.[57] Lucille Thornburgh of Knoxville, Tennessee, and Eula McGill of Birmingham, Alabama, not only served as dynamic leaders in their state in 1934, but became notable southern union leaders in the decades after 1934 as well.[58]

Less visible but also present were black textile union members. The New Deal organizing of 1933–34 was midwife to the creation of approximately a dozen "colored" locals in places like Huntsville, Alabama; Macon, Georgia; Spartanburg, Union, and Columbia, South Carolina; and Durham, North Carolina.[59] Sprinkled throughout the records of complaints of textile workers to the NIRA were also complaints by black workers that they were fired unjustly or that they were receiving less than the minimum wage.[60] The relationship between these black workers and white textile unionists remains unclear.[61] Yet the mere presence of "colored" locals suggests at the very least a willingness by the UTW to acknowledge the right of black workers to make demands for their own just treatment.

The Meaning of Southern Textile Unionism

Unionism in southern textiles in 1933 emerged out of a sense that for the first time in generations southern workers were being included in the national interest. The hope offered by the federal government caused more workers than ever before to "muster up the courage," as one worker put it, to take action themselves.[62] Yet unionism did not only represent southern cotton mill workers' hope that federal intervention would bring justice to the southern mills. It was also an expression of their belief that the success of the New Deal depended on them and on their willingness to courageously take action to support a vision of justice in which they believed.

An outstanding example of this symbiotic relationship between the NIRA and indigenous organizing was J. R. "Jim" Foster, president of UTW Local 1918 of the Merrimack Mill in Huntsville, Alabama. Nicknamed the "grand old man," Foster was so respected by the workers that when he died many years later the mill closed down for his funeral.[63] In July 1933, Foster was laid off from the mill at the age of fifty-seven, "just prior to the mill going on shorter hours." He used his own firing to write to Roosevelt, to bring to light conditions in the mill. Foster described "young girls worked and young boys worked and underfed and housed in terrible places, underfed, undernourished, underpaid," of "bullying overseers" who would "press their attentions and autocratic beastly selves on those whom they had in their control." Foster noted that many overseers required a payoff from workers who wanted to keep their jobs. The mill also required workers in the weave room to begin working their machinery fifteen minutes before starting time.

Like thousands of workers, Foster wrote to Washington because he believed that the Roosevelt administration intended to do something about these conditions. But textile workers knew better than the government itself what a dangerous task the federal government had committed itself to by taking on the southern mills. To succeed, the government needed all the help it could get, and yet many dared not become involved. But the government could count on Foster. "I HAVE THE GUTS TO SEE IT THROUGH," he wrote, "if your department really wants to help correct local and national conditions . . . . I will work with you, not from a standpoint of spite but of human decency, and anybody who knows Jim Foster will tell you he has never backed off of a job before."[64] For Foster and others, unions were the means by which ordinary people could not only participate in government, but also make the New Deal vision a concrete reality in their communities.

The Cotton Textile Code Authority

The spinning and weaving rooms of the southern mills were both physically and culturally a long distance from the National Recovery Administration offices and the editing rooms of the *New York Times*. In the North, NRA administrators and northern journalists heard a very different story from the one told in letters coming from the southern millhands. Their information came not from handwritten letters from ordinary people, but from typewritten reports from the Cotton Textile Code Authority, the industry body now endowed with the power to enforce the regulations of the cotton textile industry under the new Code. All letters of complaint, whether addressed to Hugh Johnson, Frances Perkins, or President Roosevelt, were referred to the Code Authority for action. And here lay a problem. The Code Authority was for all intents and purposes identical with the Cotton Textile Institute. It even claimed the same leader, the New York lawyer George Sloan.[65] The way that the Code Authority ignored, dismissed, or sanitized textile workers' complaints serves as a classic example of the use of bureaucracy to kill dissent.

In retrospect it hardly seems likely that the Code Authority would have authorized investigations that would have impinged on the activities of CTI members. But even if the investigators had acted in good faith, they would have been hard put to expose Code violators. Investigators found themselves handcuffed by lack of information and resources. It took several months for the procedure to address employee complaints to begin. By September 1933, the Code Authority had hired only two field examiners to investigate a bulging file of complaints. (It never hired any more.) It was December before a final procedure was established.[66] The lack of direction and resources produced delays as long as five weeks between receipt of the complaint and its investigation.[67] After a year had passed, of 1,724 allegations that wage and hour provisions had been violated, the Code Authority had investigated only ninety-six.[68]

There were other problems. To protect workers from reprisal, investigators were not given names of complainants. Usually investigators spoke only to the mill supervisor about the problem; "in many cases a mere denial by the management cannot be traced further," UTW President McMahon complained later.[69] Sometimes employers would receive advance word that an investigator was coming to the plant, causing them to "cut the speed and have it in good shape" before the investigator arrived.[70] When investigators actually found a case of noncompliance, the employer simply promised to make the changes necessary to conform to the Code. There is no evidence of follow-up. The results of the investigations were supposedly sent to a committee called the "NRA Planning and Supervisory Committee of the Cotton Textile Industry," what James Hodges has called "a nonfunctioning committee chaired by Hugh Johnson."[71] Only one Code violation, that of the Atlantic Cotton Mills, was ever referred to the NRA Compliance Division for further action.[72]

Meanwhile the Code Authority moved to capitalize on the new powers given to industry. One of its functions was to collect data measuring how well the Code was fulfilling the purpose of the Recovery Act: reemployment. This role was vigorously protested by Frances Perkins. At one of the first meetings of the Special Industrial Recovery Board in late summer 1933, she said: "I think we are in deep water if we allow trade associations to handle our statistics."[73] But Hugh Johnson dismissed Perkins' concerns, voicing his support instead for government noninterference in this new experiment in industry self-government. Free to handle its statistics as it wished, the Code Authority quickly moved to shield its activities from public view. At the first meeting of the Code Authority, the group decided to end its previous practice of making its data public.[74]

The result of the Code Authority's ability to manipulate its own statistics borders on farce. At least some of the data from mill managers were falsified to give the appearance of increased employment when in fact workers were being dismissed. While it is not clear how widespread this practice was, evidence suggests that false reporting was no small problem. At the Eagle and Phenix Mills in Columbus, Georgia, for example, the work was "divided among many people to make the impression that their payrolls has been greatly increased, when the fact is only a small portion of their help actually get to work forty hours per week."[75] In Newnan, Georgia, at the Hogansville Mills, payrolls were "vastly padded," with some of the mills keeping "two distinct payrolls covering the same week's work." The second payroll, "often containing names of persons who are not actually employed in the mills," indicated "much higher wages payments than the actual payments made to the workers."[76] Similar practices occured at the Cannon Mills in Concord, North Carolina, where, according to one source, the second shift had been almost completely laid off since July 17, and the first shift had been employed only part-time, but "all are retained on the pay rolls in order to maintain an appearance of full employment to be exhibited to the recovery administration."[77]

If reports of such violations ever made it to the Code Authority's desk, they were ignored. Instead, Sloan used his new position as a government spokesman to issue public statements that the industry was making glowing progress in fulfilling the purposes of the Recovery Act. Sloan reported, for example, that from March to September 1933, the industry had employed 145,515 new workers, bringing the total number employed in textiles to an all-time high of 465,915 workers.[78] Six months later Donald Comer used these same statistics to make the claim that the cotton textile industry was a leader in the "NRA program of putting people back to work."[79]

Even if the processes by which Sloan had collected his data were not suspect, such figures were highly misleading. A careful observer would have noted that Sloan began counting new employees in March 1933—when the industry had engaged in stockpiling in anticipation of the Code—not in July, when the Code went into effect. Sloan's statistics were largely a description of what had happened during the "boomlet" of the spring of '33. These statistics did not say much at all about what had happened because of the Code.

Yet Sloan was so successful in using the Code Authority to disseminate misinformation that his statistics were subsequently cited as evidence that the Cotton Textile Code was a model for the president's reemployment program. No one in Washington questioned the conclusion that the Code was a model of compliance with the spirit of reemployment mandated by the Recovery Act. Observers were so thoroughly convinced that the Textile Code had increased employment that this conclusion has been accepted to this day.[80]

Containing Future Protest

The Code Authority worked quickly to solidify its position within the government. It had produced an investigatory procedure that all but sanctioned manufacturers' stretch-out and layoff practices. It cranked out congratulatory statistics to reinforce the message that the cotton textile industry was cooperating with the recovery program. It was on its way to creating a private sphere within which it could handle industry affairs as it wished, shielded from the "meddlesome" interference of the public or the government.

But the Code Authority could not prevent textile workers from leaking information directly to the public about conditions within the mills. Despite the competing voice of the Code Authority, southern textile workers' voices were not entirely muzzled. The hundreds of letters they wrote to New Deal administrators in June and July, combined with scattered local strikes in southern mill towns throughout these same months, caused the NRA's newly formed "Labor Advisory Board" to take notice.[81] In response, the Labor Advisory Board requested that Hugh Johnson authorize a special investigation of southern textile mills' violations of the labor provisions of the Code.[82]

The possibility that other government agencies would become involved in labor disputes in the textile industry constituted a serious obstacle to the Code Authority's complete control over its own affairs. In July 1933, the possiblity of greater government regulation of the industry's labor management relations grew with each passing day. The summer of discontent was not limited to southern textiles. Workers in the hosiery, mining, and motion picture industries were also claiming their new right to organize. Over two hundred strikes involving 125,000 workers took place in July 1933. Section 7(a) became what observers called the "storm center" of unrest.[83]

The strikes and the apparent ambiguity of the language of Section 7(a) prompted nervous administrators at every government level to seek as quickly as possible some mechanism for establishing labor peace. The Brookings Institute claimed that "there was serious danger that the whole re-employment campaign would collapse under the growing pressure of labor disputes."[84] To respond to this crisis, NRA administrators proposed a labor relations board for each industry composed of representatives of labor, manufacturers, and government. But liberals like Senator Robert Wagner felt that the country could not wait for each individual industry to develop its own labor-management board. Wagner favored instead an umbrella national labor board to handle disputes in all industries.

It was against this background of growing interest in federal oversight of labor disputes that the new Cotton Textile Code Authority worked out a plan for dealing with its own labor unrest. The Code Authority received a good deal of help in this matter from, of all places, the stretch-out investigation committee formed by Hugh Johnson back in June.[85] This committee had held its own hearings on the prevalence of the stretch-out on July 13 and 14, 1933, in Greenville, South Carolina. If workers hoped these hearings would increase public awareness of the stretch-out, they were disappointed. Its chairman, Robert Bruere, and the industry representative, Benjamin Geer, drew up a report concluding that the stretch-out was "sound in principle," although it had been abused "through hasty and ill-considered installations with resultant overload on the employees."[86] The report did not suggest specific ways of regulating or controlling the stretch-out, but instead treated it as a matter of misunderstanding between worker and owner. To resolve these "misunderstandings," Bruere's committee suggested that the Cotton Textile Code be amended to create a complex mediation process. Mill workers and owners would be required to attempt to resolve disputes over the stretch-out on their own; if this failed, either party could appeal the case to a specially created "Cotton Textile Industrial Relations Board," to be set up under NRA authority. The committee's final recommendation was as misleading as it was dramatic: "in accordance with article 15, no cotton textile employee shall be required to do any work in excess of the practices prevailing on July 1, 1933," until the mediation process described in the report could be incorporated into the Code as a new section, Section 17. In other words, if the committee's recommendations were accepted, Section 15 would be nullified. It would no longer be a Code violation to stretch out workers.[87] As the Bruere Board itself was to state a year later as a clarification of its role: "Section 17 superceded Section 15 of the code and the stretch-out or specialization ceased to be a code violation and was made a subject of investigation, conference, and adjustment."[88]

From the workers' perspective, Burere's recommendations were a giant step backward from the language already in the approved Code. Employers could admit that they were stretching out the workers and it would not be wrong. Bruere had made the ability of employers to institute the stretch-out in each case a question of political and economic power, rather than a technical question or even a legal matter. Workers could prevent the imposition of the extra load only if they organized and negotiated with their employers to stop it. If the issue was appealed, workers had no guarantee that their complaints about stretch-out would have any merit even if they could prove it was taking place.

But in July 1933 none of this was clear to textile workers, the UTW, or the public. George Berry, the only labor representative on the committee, was not involved in writing up the report. No textile union officials were informed of the proposed amendment to the Code.[89] The report was merely approved by Hugh Johnson and sent to the Cotton Textile Code Authority for action. The Code Authority, understandably pleased, accepted the committee's report as its first major action. At its August 1 meeting, the Code Authority voted to incorporate the elaborate set of boards recommended by Bruere into the Code. The new Code provision became known as Section 17.

The Final Step

By replacing Section 15 with Section 17, the Code Authority had gotten rid of the hated prohibition of the stretch-out. It had not, however, gotten rid of the oversight and public scrutiny of Senator Wagner and the NLB. To carve out yet additional industry autonomy, Code Authority Chair Sloan recommended extending the authority of the new Cotton Textile Industrial Relations Boards to cover arbitration not only of stretch-out issues, but of "any other problems of working conditions in the cotton textile industry."[90] The next day, August 2, NRA Administrator Hugh Johnson announced that the stretch-out committee itself was to become the permanent Cotton Textile National Industrial Relations Board (CTNIRB). Its charge was broad: to "guarantee a peaceful settlement of all disputes in the cotton textile industry." Indeed, it was to serve as a model for all industries attempting to develop their own processes for peaceful resolution of disputes.[91] It became known as the Bruere Board.

The Bruere Board was created just in time. The following day, August 3, members of the Industrial Advisory Board and the Labor Advisory Board met to determine the shape of a new agency that would oversee the resolution of labor disputes in all American industries.[92] Two days later, on August 5, President Roosevelt announced the formation of the National Labor Board (NLB), consisting of seven members, three from labor and three from industry, with Senator Wagner at its head. In determining its jurisdiction, the National Labor Board decided that any industry that already had a board to resolve labor-management disputes would be exempt from the oversight of the National Labor Board. The Bruere Board clearly satisfied this requirement. In this way, cotton textile workers became exempt from the rulings of the National Labor Board. The Code Authority had thus removed labor disputes in the cotton textile industry from the oversight of other agencies of the NRA. It had now successfully shielded its activities from federal oversight in all areas of its operation. For the workers it was to be a devastating blow.[93]

Conclusion

It is impossible to overestimate the sense of hope mill workers felt because of the Code. It legitimized their sense of place in society. It also created an intense loyalty to the New Deal and to President and Mrs. Roosevelt. Mrs. C. A. Morgan from Bath, South Carolina, wrote to Mrs. Roosevelt: "I am telling you these companys is no friend to Mr. Roosevelt, but we poor people are his friends and we are going to stick by him till we die."[94]

Energized by the NIRA and confronted by blatant disregard of Code provisions by southern manufacturers, workers formed local chapters of the United Textile Workers Union. Their decision to join the UTW had less to do with the structure, goals, or history of the UTW than with their belief that through unionism they could make the New Deal a reality in the southern mills.

Behind the scenes, leaders of the cotton textile industry had transformed the Cotton Textile Code Authority into a nearly autonomous fortress inside the government working on behalf of the interests of employers. To cope with the possibility of labor unrest, the Code Authority had constructed as its front line of defense the Bruere Board. A mediation board rather than an agency of enforcement, the Bruere Board would have no power to resolve worker grievances. Textile workers were about to embark on a long and painful journey during which they would engage in battle with their employers over the true nature of the New Deal.

6

A BATTLE OF RIGHTEOUSNESS

The enactment of the NIRA and the creation of the Cotton Textile National Industrial Relations Board fundamentally altered the nature of textile workers' campaign to achieve justice in the mills. In the years 1929–33, protesting millhands had eschewed national unions, attempting to minimize brutal employer retaliation by forming instead "homegrown" unions that appealed to local public opinion. With the creation of the CTNIRB, or Bruere Board, in August 1933, however, this organizing task was shunted aside. Now textile workers were being asked to pursue redress of grievances within a narrow bureaucratic structure. Section 17 removed textile workers' disputes from the public eye, preventing workers from exercising their central tactical lever: exposure.

To be sure, the Bruere Board did create new opportunities. Section 17 proposed that workers and employers who had a conflict would each send three representatives to a "mill committee" that would meet and attempt to resolve the dispute. In requiring workers and mill managers to sit down face to face and talk, Section 17 represented a new advance for southern textile workers and their unions.

But Section 17 did not require collective bargaining. Instead, if the mill committee failed to resolve a dispute, either side could then appeal its case to a newly created state cotton textile industrial relations board. Like the Cotton Textile National Industrial Relations Board (the Bruere Board), these state boards would be composed of a labor representative, an employer representative, and a public member. If the controversy could not be settled at that level, the National Board would make a final "decision."

As will be seen, this cumbersome appeals process effectively deflected worker unrest. At the same time, however, the Bruere Board accelerated the construction of a national textile workers' union. The Bruere Board became the school in which southern workers were educated about the true nature of the New Deal bureaucracy. This chapter chronicles workers' tumultuous experiences over the nine months from September 1933 through May 1934, as they became first hopeful, then disillusioned, and finally, mobilized to confront a New Deal bureaucracy unresponsive to their grievances.

Southern millhands' experiences with the Bruere Board varied widely depending upon the specific nature of labor-management relations in any given mill. In mills where workers had never had strong organization, employers used the Bruere Board structure to nearly destroy a union presence there. In places where unions were strong, however, the Bruere Board's involvement galvanized worker energies and helped build a regionwide union movement. To illustrate the dynamics of this roller-coaster ride requires exploring southern workers' experiences with four different state boards. Out of the hundreds of labor controversies that emerged during this time, however, two were crucial. The first was at the Horse Creek Valley Mills on the border of South Carolina and Georgia, and the second was at the Cleveland Cloth Mills of Shelby, North Carolina.

Disillusionment: The Lower South

The Horse Creek Valley mills were the first southern mills to attempt to make use of the Bruere Board structure to resolve a labor controversy. The area was ripe for union organizing. It had a history of working-class political strength and union organizing going back to at least 1901.[1] Workers in the Horse Creek Valley also benefited from their proximity to Augusta, Georgia, home to a half-dozen cotton mills, several of which had incipient union locals. Augusta unions also had a long history, extending back to the days of the Knights of Labor in the 1880s; and Augusta textile workers were well integrated into the city's community of organized labor.[2] The strength of craft labor in Augusta helped buffer Augusta textile workers from blatant discrimination, and by March 1931, 90 percent of the workers in Augusta had been unionized. When a wave of organizing in the Horse Creek Valley resulted in a strike of twelve hundred workers in 1932, the Augusta Central Labor Union contributed money to their support.[3]

While this special combination of circumstances nurtured a tradition of union activism in the Horse Creek Valley, workers there also suffered from the tactical problem of strikebreakers coming from nearby farms. Job security for union members was so tenuous, in fact, and public endorsement of a union by the workers so suicidal, that no mill worker was willing to act as leader in the 1932 strike. Instead, a sympathetic lawyer acted as their spokesperson. The 1932 strike failed, and a sizeable number of fired union members experienced persistent blacklisting and returned to the countryside for lack of a job.[4]

That the failure of the 1932 strike did not completely break the back of unionism in the Horse Creek Valley can be at least partly attributed to the presence of AFL Education Director Paul Fuller. Fuller and his wife had been stationed in Augusta since 1930 when the AFL's southern organizing drive began. Together they developed activities to build unity, confidence, and organizational skills among local textile workers, including drama, craft, and public speaking activities. When it came to strikes, Fuller remained discretely in the background. As an education worker rather than organizer, Fuller did not understand his role to be a strike leader.[5]

Fuller's low profile and careful program work proved to be exactly what was necessary to prepare Horse Creek Valley workers for the long and difficult struggle confronting them. Despite heavy repercussions from the 1932 strike, the union retained a presence in the Valley, symbolized by a labor temple erected there in the fall of 1932. By the time the NIRA was enacted, workers had built an organization they felt could sustain them during a strike, and had found in Fuller a leader they could trust.[6]

The day the Code was put into effect, Horse Creek Valley workers felt its impact. As hundreds were dismissed from their jobs, L. James Johnson, head of the local union, encouraged workers to take advantage of their new opportunity. "The organized workers in the Valley have the best chance they have ever had," Johnson announced, to make a difference in their working conditions, "and it is left entirely up to them."[7]

But as the union grew, so did the harrassment of union members. Leaders were fired; lower-echelon members were harrassed on the job and paid less than nonunion help. And the stretch-out—the reason for the union organizing in the first place—continued. Workers complained to Washington so insistently that the Code Authority sent down at least two investigators during the fall to look into allegations of speedups, layoffs, and discrimination. In both cases management denied the charges and no further inquiry took place.[8]

It was not until September 1933 that Fuller learned of the existence of the labor mediation procedure set up under the Bruere Board.[9] Attempting to act according to procedure, Fuller tried to get a meeting with management. Failing this, he sent word of the union's grievances to the newly appointed chairman of South Carolina's State Industrial Relations Board, H. H. Willis.[10] But nothing happened. Appeals to Wagner's new National Labor Board were also unavailing. So, on October 20, about three thousand workers from Augusta and the Horse Creek Valley walked off their jobs. Within two weeks the number had grown to over six thousand.[11]

The workers perceived the strike as their chance to "center national attention on the local situation." Fuller called the strike "an act of self-defense and fully justified under the law." Drawing upon his training as a minister, he announced that workers were "fighting for human rights in this battle—a battle of righteousness if there ever was one. We are striking to have the National Industrial Recovery Act made a living thing instead of a dead letter in the cotton mills of Augusta."[12]

Even the cautious AFL southern representative George Googe supported the strike. Claiming that no one was paying attention to the workers' grievances, Googe insisted that "it was necessary for labor to create a major situation" to compel the attention of federal agencies.[13] Within days, the governors and U.S. senators of South Carolina and Georgia were asking the NLB to accept jurisdiction over the dispute.[14]

It was at this point that the real function of the Bruere Board became clear. Until the Horse Creek Valley workers walked out on October 20, the Bruere Board had not even been functioning. The state boards had not been organized, and industry representative Benjamin Geer was maintaining his vehement opposition to the board's involvement in labor controversies.[15] No sooner had the NLB agreed to adjudicate the dispute, however, than Geer, in a remarkable about-face from his earlier position, agreed that the intervention of the CTNIRB was appropriate after all. By November 1, ten days after the strike began, Bruere and Geer had arrived at the scene to investigate the dispute. Curiously, boardmember Berry was nowhere to be seen. According to press reports, Berry had "pressing duties elsewhere."[16]

The decisions made by this hastily called and incomplete "board" set the precedent for the CTNIRB's method of resolving subsequent disputes in the textile industry, and were a major step down the road to the general strike. The board announced that its job was not to resolve issues of substance but to bring all strikes to an end and encourage both sides to utilize the grievance procedures established under Section 17. The Bruere Board ended the walkout of the Augusta/Horse Creek Valley workers, however, through the questionable process of effecting a division between workers on either side of the state line. First, Bruere convinced workers to return to work if the mill managements would promise not to discriminate against strikers. The board then secured the agreement of the three mills in Augusta whose workers had struck not to discriminate against the strikers. No such assurances were given, however, by the Horse Creek Valley mills. The board then announced that all employees should report back to work on Monday, November 6. While Augusta workers found themselves back at work, "not a single man on strike" in the Horse Creek Valley had been allowed to work. Over one thousand workers remained unemployed. In Graniteville, one of the mill towns in the valley, management began evicting strikers from their homes. As one union member later reported, management was bringing in strikebreakers from the agricultural sections "by the truckload."[17] Reported Fuller, "so far as the solution is concerned now it has turned from a strike to a lockout."[18]

In keeping with the procedures outlined in Section 17, Horse Creek Valley workers appealed their new situation to the State Cotton Textile Industrial Relations Board. But the State Board would not require the mills to take back the strikers. Instead, it recommended that the strikers "re-apply" for their jobs. A disgusted Fuller turned to Assistant Secretary of Labor Edward McGrady for help. "The Cotton Textile State Industrial Relations Board recommends in effect that strikers of the Horse Creek Valley get back their jobs as best they can," Fuller wrote. "These workers have been organized for four years as it now stands none of them will be reemployed unless they give up their union affiliations. All rights given them under industrial recovery act and textile code have been denied."[19]

On December 2, 1933, only a month after the initial National Board decision to end the strike, strikers traveled to Washington to appeal matters to the National Board. But the National Board accepted industry's terminology of the strikers as "former employees" and insisted that the board had no authority to tell the mill to fire the replacement workers. The board did, however, require the mills to "rehire" the strikers "unconditionally" and "without discrimination as to either rehiring or assignment of work." Management was to draw up a list of "former employees" for workers to examine to determine who was eligible for reemployment. The State Board would be the final arbiter of the names on the list. The mill agreed to begin rehiring January 1. How the mill was going to rehire strikers without firing the strikebreakers was left unexplained.[20]

As the new year dawned, hundreds of workers, now unemployed for over two months, lined up to be reemployed by the mills. Owners of the Horse Creek Valley mills, claiming they were abiding by the Bruere Board decision, insisted that the only jobs available were jobs paying less than what the workers had made prior to the strike. Some former skilled workers were offered jobs as sweepers paying eight or nine dollars a week, less than half their original pay.[21] The outcry began anew. State Senator John F. Williams of Aiken wrote: "Those mills aren't carrying out the orders of the National Board, and the state industrial relations board does not seem to be functioning at all." The strikers, he complained, had been "treated like cattle."[22]

The momentum of the Bruere Board's decisions was now clear. While the board did not openly embrace the mill managements' position, it would not reverse any actions already taken by the mills. Once the mills had taken in strikebreakers, for example, the board tried to mitigate the impact on the strikers. But by requiring the workers to reapply nonetheless, the board legitimized a practice that was not articulated as legal under the Code. Now the issue was being pressed one step further. Could the strikers who were rehired be forced to accept jobs below their skill level? Was this not to be considered discrimination? Once again the National Board was called to the scene to investigate. It was the workers' last hope for a fair response from the Bruere Board structure.

Inexplicably, UTW President McMahon chose this moment to ask the AFL to transfer Labor Education Director Paul Fuller from Augusta to Philadelphia, where McMahon claimed he was urgently needed.[23] The besieged strikers' morale, already tested to the limit, gave way altogether before this final blow. J. Ralph Gay, a local union leader, would later remember that they had lost Fuller "right at the time we needed him most," a turn of events that "left a hard place in some of the people's hearts." Since that time, Gay lamented, "the mill management has been doing whatever they took a notion to do and get by with it."[24]

Not until March 1934 did the State and National Boards finally rule. Strikers were to be rehired "as rapidly as they present themselves and work is available."[25] The mills, the State Board added, were not relieved of their responsibility to offer a skilled worker a skilled job when it was available, but no deadline was given to the mills to move a worker out of a job "below his level" back into his regular job.[26] The boards, aware that they could not effect a change in mill practice simply by declaring that it needed to take place, sanctioned the mills' evasions of the presumed intent of their rulings, and declared as a "ruling" only what the mills had already agreed to do in any case. Bruere's entire board structure was a charade.[27]

Throughout the lower South, workers in mill after mill found their hopes dashed by their experiences with the Bruere Board structure. In north Alabama, for example, mills would not engage in any formal meeting with local textile unions.[28] Workers who appealed to the Alabama State Board confronted inaction or, on occasion, referrals back to their employers. In only two cases was a dispute even brought before the State Board. The life of the

Alabama State Board effectively ended in December 1933 when its labor member, V. C. Finch, refused to put his name to decisions he felt were unfair to the workers.[29] Presumably such results were the reason CTNIRB staffperson L. R. Gilbert later spoke "very highly" of the results of the Alabama Board.[30]

In Georgia the State Board showed a refreshing willingness to take employee complaints seriously. But their decisions were ignored by employers, or even worse, undermined by the National Board. At the East Newnan Mills, for example, the State Board ordered the employer to reinstate eighteen workers discharged for union activity. But when the mill failed to reinstate the workers, nothing happened. At the Arnall Mills in Sargeant, Georgia, the State Board attempted to address workers' complains about stretch-out by asking for and receiving assurances from Bruere that an engineer would be sent into the mill to evaluate the workloads in each department. The National Board, however, failed to send an engineer, and conditions deteriorated. When workers finally returned to work under assurances from the National Board that an engineer would be sent, forty union members discovered they were out of jobs. Needless to say, the State Board could not persuade the mill to give workers back their jobs. Fed up with the entire board structure, State Board Chair Thomas Quigley resigned. The labor member O. E. Petry followed suit shortly thereafter, convinced, as he said, that the boards were "worse than useless."[31]

The failure of the Bruere Board to address worker grievances caused outrage. "Where can we get lawful action when the NRA law is violated?" complained one union leader from Rome, Georgia. "Who has authority to enforce same? Why can't we have the right to organize without interference by mill officials here in Rome Georgia?"[32] "Is the NIRA a bona-fide law?" asked UTW organizer Albert Cox of a Washington official. "Or is it a farce?"[33]

As it became clear that these boards had no power, employers became more bold, spreading fear among leaders of textile unions in the lower South that their unions would collapse. "We have never had a decision from the Cotton Textile Industrial Relations Board fair to the workers," declared a UTW member from LaGrange, Georgia, at a meeting of the Georgia-Carolina Textile Council. "We have plenty of grievances and we need them straightened out and if something isn't done our organization is going to weaken."[34] Union members at the Dwight Mills in Gadsden, Alabama, suffering from blatant "discrimination" by mill managers, could get no help from the State Board.[35] Finally, in January J. P. Holland, president of UTW Local 1878, wrote to Secretary of Labor Frances Perkins: "If the union is to succeed we must have something done at once . . . . If you will write to us showing that the Labor Department and the government is going to stand by us and urging our people to organize and stand together, we feel that it will be a great help to us here."

Like most southern workers, Holland continued to operate on the assumption that the people of Washington *wanted* the union to succeed. How else could government leaders be guaranteed that their laws were being enforced at the local level? Of course, Perkins did not respond the way Holland requested. Instead, as procedure dictated, she forwarded the letter to the Cotton Textile National Industrial Relations Board, which wrote to Holland that it would look into the matter if Holland would write with details about the case. It is likely that this final bureaucratic rerouting finally wore Holland down, for no further record of his correspondence exists.[36]

It would take several more months for the Gadsden union to give up entirely on the NIRA, for Dwight workers did not strike until July 1934. It was their decision to leave their jobs that triggered the chain of walkouts across the South. These walkouts, in turn, snowballed into the general strike. In the middle of the winter of 1933–34, however, most workers still held out hope, even as the reality of government inaction was pushing them to abandon it, that the government would come through. John Peel, UTW director of southern organizing, probably spoke for many when he said, "I believe the NIRA will be enforced. What a terrible thing it would be if we were to learn that it was only a farce. There is no greater crime I can think of than to destroy the confidence of the American people in this 'New Deal.' . . . Well, it will be just too bad."[37]

Agitation: The Upper South

In areas where unions were strong, southern cotton mill workers faced a problem of a different order. Workers in North and South Carolina faced the same intransigence of the Bruere Board as workers in Alabama and Georgia. In the Carolinas, however, workers had stronger organization. Here their task was to mobilize the national leaders of their new union, the UTW, to become an instrument of southern workers' collective will. Given the historic reluctance of the UTW to engage in confrontational tactics, this was no small task. By November 1933, UTW President Thomas McMahon was already bemoaning the "thousands of appeals" from workers North and South, "demanding that they be allowed to strike."[38]

If this incipient southern insurgency was to survive as part of the UTW, it was critical that the national union develop a way to serve and nurture it.

But the UTW leadership was eyeing another role for itself: that of partner in the bold new experiment in industry self-regulation represented by the NRA and the Code. To achieve this coveted position, leaders of organized labor knew that they needed to demonstrate labor's willingness to cooperate with the recovery effort.

Pressure on unions like the UTW to "cooperate" with the NIRA came from friends and foes of labor alike. Government officials warned labor leaders that it was going to be necessary for unions to educate workers to channel their grievances through the new NRA structures. As a practical matter, this meant that labor should not strike. Even Senator Wagner, an unflagging supporter of labor, conceded that there was a problem with strikes if they were used "as an instrument of first resort." "Industry and labor cannot co-operate by means of the strike," he said in a radio speech in October 1933.[39]

Bent on retaining organized labor's foothold as a partner in economic self-government, national union leaders willingly counseled their own members to resist striking and attempt to work through the existing governmental agencies. They reminded workers that Wagner's new board, the NLB, was proving itself to be an honorable mediator of labor management disputes. Rather than stir up discord at the bottom, workers should place their trust in the efforts of the AFL leadership to influence policy at the top.[40]

It was in this context that UTW national leaders responded to the creation of the CTNIRB, or Bruere Board. The officers of the UTW did not discover the existence of the CTNIRB until September 1933, and did not fully understand the existence or meaning of Section 17 until November. At first, UTW President McMahon expressed a healthy suspicion of the boards, particularly the individuals who had been selected to sit on them. "It is not to be expected," he wrote, "that justice can be done to the workers by such committees."[41] But McMahon's harsh words softened as pressure for labor cooperation increased during the fall. The UTW president even responded favorably to Bruere's suggestion that many complaints now being "investigated" by the Code Authority could be resolved more quickly and fairly if they were treated as labor disputes and channeled through Bruere's structure of mill committees and state boards. McMahon had become so certain Bruere's new National Board would be fair and impartial that he suggested that the wool and silk branches of the industry, now covered by the NLB, should also be brought under the oversight of the Bruere Board.[42]

As fall settled into winter, however, tension increased between the rank and file and the union's policy of cooperation. As the southern textile region became the scene of more scattered strikes, McMahon came under renewed pressure to rein in his workers. In January 1934, the National Board's labor representative, George Berry, upbraided McMahon for running an organization that encouraged members to behave irresponsibly; clearly the UTW had no "appreciation of the value of collective bargaining." Insisting that there was "an inescapable community of interests between employers and employees," Berry argued that unions should "seek friendly co-operation and the exhaustion of every recourse to prevent trouble rather than to invite discord and confusion." Berry encouraged McMahon to embrace "some new process, some new deal" in the way his union did business.[43]

The impact of attitudes like Berry's forced McMahon to redouble his efforts to encourage his increasingly restless membership to use the complaint process outlined in Section 17. Increasingly defensive, McMahon lashed out at complaining union members as the "great big army of Gimmies," and implored them to more fully "appreciate what our government is trying to do for industry."[44] Even the disastrous outcome of the Horse Creek Valley case did not shake McMahon's confidence in the Board. The problem was not with the Board itself, but with its lack of enforcement powers. "We have appealed to the Board to enforce, if possible, its finding, but they cannot, because of lack of power in the law as now written in the NRA." McMahon emphasized not any injustice of Board decisions but the disregard for the decisions of the Board by the owners of the mills.[45]

By early 1934, the union and the local southern membership had arrived at two different positions regarding the federal government. Union locals, seeing their strength undermined by the inaction of the federal government and bad Board decisions, were growing increasingly angry and impatient with the NRA machinery. UTW leaders, meanwhile, were promising to use the union's influence in Washington to strengthen the Board's enforcement powers, while encouraging workers to continue to use the Board machinery, "hoping and believing that it will bring about more peaceful and orderly industrial relations."[46]

The effect of the UTW's cooperation with the Bruere Board could not have been worse for workers, or better for manufacturers. Confident that worker discontent had been deflected, industry leaders showered NRA administrators with assurances that relations between employer and employee in the southern mills were completely harmonious. "There is more cooperation and understanding between the employer and the employee in the South" than there was in New England, reported the *American Wool and Cotton Reporter*.[47] Thomas Marchant, president of the southern-based American Cotton Manufacturers' Association, wrote to officials in Washington that "not in my thirty-odd years of mill experience have I ever seen the textile workers as happy and contented as they are today."[48]

It fell to the leaders of the southern organizing effort to break through the wall of silence and create a public voice for the UTW's disenchanted southern membership. The tension between local union insurgency and the national union posture of cooperation came to its first climax in a controversy between workers and owners at the Cleveland Cloth Mills of Shelby, North Carolina, in the western part of the state. Newly opened in 1925, the Cleveland Cloth Mill possessed few of the trappings of old-style paternalism that characterized mills built before the war. There was no mill village. The weavers of the mill were among the highest-paid textile workers in the entire South. These were the aristocrats of southern textile labor. Indeed, workers attracted by the high wages flocked to the Cleveland Cloth Mill from many South Carolina mill towns.[49]

The mill was not averse, however, to introducing the same speedup procedures experienced by workers in mills across the South.[50] After months of resentment, workers called for a strike in January 1934, after management announced a new system of weaving that increased the number of looms each weaver worked from five to six, displacing sixteen weavers.[51]

The workers at Cleveland Cloth were in a unique position to test the Cotton Textile National Industrial Relations Board machinery. The mill was owned by two prominent members of the North Carolina Democratic party, former Governor O. Max Gardner and O. M. Mull, former chairman of the state Democratic party.[52] As governor, Gardner had made his political reputation as a moderate and a conciliator of labor disputes. He continued to be a public figure in Washington after he left the governor's office. Understandably, Gardner and Mull wished to maintain at least the appearance of satisfactory labor relationships in their own mill. Gardner was fully aware of the political implications of the workers' protest for him and for the Roosevelt administration, "Whatever happens [at CCM] is going to happen here to five or six others," he told Bruere Board staffperson L. R. Gilbert. "It's important to the administration."[53]

Eager to demonstrate the workability of the NRA's labor dispute machinery, Gardner instructed Mull to follow Bruere's board process to the letter. Mull formed a mill committee and met with the union representatives twice.[54] When employer and union could come to no agreement, the dispute was duly appealed to the State Board. A strike nearly ensued over whether the mill would institute its new system immediately or delay its implementation pending a final decision by the Board. Speaking for Bruere, Gilbert insisted to both parties that a strike would in no way affect the decision of the State Board, but workers persisted in their strike threat. Faced with an imminent walkout, Mull gave in. The new work system was not implemented and workers stayed on the job. Mull's action brought assurances from the Shelby union members that they would indeed abide by a decision of the State Board. Although both sides had nearly balked, each had demonstrated the willingness to make compromises in the interests of labor peace. Here, perhaps, was a model for effective labor relations.

Two weeks later, the State Board decided in favor of management. The weavers would be required to work six looms. As they had agreed to do, the workers accepted the Board's decision.[55] They nevertheless felt that it was unfair, and said so the day after the State Board ruling at a meeting of the North Carolina State Federation of Textile Workers, an outgrowth of the Central North Carolina Textile Council that had been formed in 1932 after the strike in High Point.[56] Over one hundred delegates claiming to represent twelve thousand workers from fifteen locals across the state listened to the federation's new president, Paul Christopher, a weaver at the Cleveland Cloth Mills and leader of the Shelby workers, as he condemned the boards as ineffective tools for improving wages and working conditions. On behalf of the Textile Council, Christopher sent a formal resolution of protest to Bruere.[57]

National UTW leaders chose this moment to remind their members that they needed to continue to cooperate with the boards. If workers wanted reforms, counseled UTW leader McMahon and hosiery leader Emil Rieve at the North Carolina Textile Federation meeting, they should not boycott the complaint process by resorting to strikes. Instead, they should push for influence at the top by seeking labor representation on the Code Authority.[58] The Shelby leaders backed down. A second crisis had been averted.

Union-management cooperation, however, had not yet been achieved in Shelby. A period of uneasy peace on the shop floor followed. Workers feared management would take advantage of its victory to push them even farther. On or around February 20, the mill management, fearing unrest, issued a ban on talking during work. Two days later the weave shop superintendent fired Rodney Wilson, a weaver and union leader.[59] This act convinced local union leaders that Gardner had only appeared to be more tolerant than other mill owners of dissent among his workers. Thirty minutes after Wilson was fired, all 494 workers in the Cleveland Cloth Mill walked off their jobs. This time the workers picketed the mill with "religious fervor."[60] The mill tried and failed to bring in enough strikebreakers to start up the plant. Five days later the mill officially shut down.[61]

The controversy gathered considerable negative publicity for Gardner and, by implication, for New Deal labor policies. The *Raleigh News and Observer* blamed Gardner personally for the prolonged nature of the dispute, calling upon him to "show no less statesmanship than he showed as Governor when he sought peace in industry in North Carolina."[62]

The controversy acquired such public visibility, in fact, that it threatened to spill outside the purview of the Bruere Board and capture the attention of the NLB. This had potentially serious consequences, for on March 1, only days after the Shelby workers struck, the NLB had articulated its strongest endorsement yet of the principle of majority rule. By this they meant that if a majority of a plant's workers voted for a union by secret ballot election, then the union had the right to represent all the workers in the plant.[63] To members of the NLB, the Shelby case was a situation where the workers should clearly hold an election to determine whether the union represented a majority of the workers.

Since its beginning, the Bruere Board had altogether avoided using elections in labor-management disputes, choosing instead, as Bruere had said in another context, to "keep it under Section 17."[64] But now Gardner himself suspected that, given developments at the national level, an election would have to take place at his mill after all.[65] The magnitude of such a breakthrough for the cotton textile workers can not be underestimated. If the NLB ruled that an election should be held, workers would bypass the bureaucracy of the Cotton Textile National Industrial Relations Board.[66]

To prevent such a course of action, the Cotton Textile National Industrial Relations Board simply delayed responding at all to the news of the strike for a full month. While the resolve of the picketers did not weaken, the momentum of the NLB fizzled due to events completely unrelated to textiles. A showdown between workers and employers in the auto industry had caused President Roosevelt to articulate a weakened version of labor's rights under the NIRA, strengthening the hand of employers in all industries. This action paved the way for the NRA Legal Division to rule that the textile industry was exempt from the NLB's rulings regarding union elections.[67] As Bruere was to write to Alabama mill owner Donald Comer on March 27, "Developments here in Washington during the past week have tended to clear the atmosphere and to simplify the problem of our Board in proceeding under Section 17 of the Code."[68]

These national developments were a turning point in the Shelby dispute, for they led to the eclipse of moderate textile manufacturers like Gardner and the emergence into public light of vitriolic antiunion spokespersons for southern mill owners. One such spokesperson was the editor of the *Southern Textile Bulletin*, David Clark. The previous fall, Clark had handpicked his colleague, Theodore Johnson (no relation to Hugh Johnson, head of the NRA), as the chair of the North Carolina State Textile Industrial Relations Board. Dubbed by one labor official "the most radical anti-labor man I have ever known," Johnson served as Clark's puppet. "He owes his job to David Clark and his faction," AFL Southern representative George Google reported, "he won't render any decision they don't approve . . . . he goes to David Clark with all decisions before they are rendered. I can't prove that, but I can prove that he spends hours in D. Clark's office before they are rendered and that Clark got him his job and can have him fired."[69]

Until March 20, Gardner had managed to avoid involving the North Carolina State Board in the Shelby dispute, thus ensuring that the labor dispute process maintained at least the appearance of fairness. But now Bruere put the resolution of the strike in the hands of Johnson's State Board. At the hearing on March 22, Chairman Johnson, reported Googe, "served to all effects in our opinion as counsel to the employer rather than as impartial chairman of the board." Johnson had such contempt for the process that he did not even write down the State Board's decision or deliver it formally to either party. Instead he issued it by simply stating it to a newspaper reporter. The strike was to be declared over. The mill would rehire the strikebreakers who had been hired for the one or two days before the mill closed, and then would reemploy the strikers "as nearly as possible in their original status." Some strikers, therefore, would not get their jobs back.[70]

The decision was a conscious replication of the decision made for the Horse Creek Valley strikers. Indeed, Googe later protested that the Cleveland Cloth Mills case should not be based on the decision made in the Horse Creek Valley case because the situations were totally different. In the Horse Creek Valley the union had been weak and could not prevent the importation of strikebreakers. But at the Cleveland Cloth Mills the union had managed to close the mill down. At issue, of course, was whether the Board was issuing legal rulings that applied to all cases regardless of the power relationships, or whether the Board was an arbitrator sensitive to the power relationships involved. In fact, what the Board had done was to set a precedent based on the power relationships in a case where the union was too weak to prevent the importation of strikebreakers and apply that precedent to a situation where the union was strong. The union was outraged, not only at the decision but at Johnson's arrogance and the manner in which he had reported his decision to the press. Workers now appealed to the National Board.[71]

In Washington, Gardner watched the discontent within the ranks of his mill over the rehiring of the strikers with growing apprehension and concluded that, given the storm of protest over the State Board's decision, it would be best to rehire all of the strikers without discrimination. But Gardner was opposed by the National Board's industry representative Benjamin Geer, who, according to the Board's secretary L. R. Gilbert, was "hellbent on making the strikers wait until they were sent for."[72] This division of opinion initially led Bruere to issue an ambiguous decision upholding the workers' seniority but not overturning the State Board decision that strikebreakers would keep their jobs. Confusion reigned for nearly two weeks. Finally Bruere issued a clarifying statement, referring the Shelby workers to the Horse Creek Valley decision, concluding that by striking, the Cleveland Cloth Mill employees had "broke[n] their continuous service record and thereby lost such seniority of employment as they had." Geer had won.[73]

The anger of the textile workers could not be contained. If the workers lost their seniority because they went on strike, Googe explained to Bruere, then "every union member has no seniority and Mull can lay off our main leaders." Googe continued, "Everything is in a terrible mess. I was under the impression from Governor Gardner that everything that happened was forgotten. This is discrimination to take their length of service from them."[74] For the Horse Creek Valley workers, rural, weak, and poorly paid, to have been so treated was one thing; for the Shelby workers, the aristocrats of the southern textile workforce, the employees of one of the most liberal manufacturers in the South, to be issued such a blow was far more serious. If the Shelby workers were to be defeated it would mean the end of unionism among textile workers in the South.

Theodore Johnson's decision did not in fact end the controversy, but catapulted the local conflict into a statewide campaign. Shelby workers began a petition drive demanding Theodore Johnson's resignation. The signatures of several thousand workers across the state were not hard to secure. Although the Cleveland Cloth Mills was the flagship mill, workers in other mills had also suffered from delays and bad decisions from the State Board.[75] By April 20, seventy textile union locals had passed a resolution demanding that Johnson be fired from his position as chair. "If Johnson is not removed from office within two weeks," declared Paul Christopher at a meeting of the North Carolina Federation of Labor, "members of the textile workers in this state cannot any longer hold their patience, and will resort to every resource at their command to bring about relief from this abominable condition in North Carolina."[76] "The textile workers down here are going to march all over the state and hang [Johnson] in effigy," reported Googe.[77] The momentum created by the petition drive had given birth to a statewide movement.[78]

A Regionwide Textile Union Movement

The North Carolina unionists' public campaign to oust Theodore Johnson influenced textile workers in South Carolina. Workers and union leaders there had encountered a familiar onslaught of delays, discriminations, and bad decisions, all of which weakened local unions and permitted abuses to continue. To make matters worse, National Board member Benjamin Geer had picked out South Carolina as his special area of purview, provoking the ire of union leaders across the state for interfering with their organizing efforts.[79] South Carolina unionists also suffered from the tradition, borne of too many local union efforts that eschewed outside help, that South Carolinians could take care of their own problems "in house." The South Carolina State Board had encouraged both workers and owners to engage in quiet negotiations, away from newspaper reporters and the glare of photographers' flashbulbs. John Peel, the UTW vice president and statewide organizer for South Carolina, maintained as late as April 1934 a posture of active cooperation with the State Board.

But the accumulation of grievances and the example of North Carolina's workers made it impossible for South Carolina's textile unionists to stay quiet any longer. On April 11, only one day after Bruere informed the Shelby strikers that they had lost their jobs, Peel broke his silence. "We have been patient and co-operative in our efforts to establish harmonious relations between employer and employee," Peel wrote South Carolina Board Chair Willis. "Our efforts have been in vain, and daily the manufacturers, or agents of the manufacturers, are giving interviews to reporters of the press of how well the cotton manufacturers are complying with the provisions of the Code. We do not intend to sit quietly by and permit this to continue without letting the public know the facts."[80] Eleven days later in Greenville, South Carolina, seven hundred men and women representing forty-four thousand of the state's eighty thousand textile workers formed the South Carolina Federation of Textile Workers and "clamored" to the International Union to permit them to strike.[81] When the group met again in May, it demanded Willis's resignation as chairman of the South Carolina State Board.[82]

Peel lashed out at the idea that the problem with the Bruere Board was that it had lacked the power to enforce its decisions. Sarcastically, Peel noted the Board's complete inconsistency of private and public postures: "Dr. Bruere says the Board has no power to act. Dr. Geer comes right back in the columns of the Press and says the Board does have power. Whom shall we believe? Thimble, thimble, who has the thimble?" The truth, declared Peel, was that the Board continued to claim it had no power to enforce its decisions until it came time to declare a strike "off." To Peel, nothing made the Board's function as a strikebreaking agency more transparent than this.

Peel then turned to the Board's method of handling reports of Code violations, many of which the Board had never even sent on to the Code Authority for investigation since, in their judgment, no violation of the Code had taken place. Indeed, the sad truth was that nothing in the Code prevented the mills from reclassifying workers to a lower skill level and paying them less; nothing prevented the mills from laying off workers who could not keep up; nothing in the Code prevented mills from abusing their workers, sexually or otherwise. "Dr. Bruere says that they have received more than 3,000 complaints, but they were not complaints, or cases, they were misunderstandings of the Code. Yes," remarked Peel, describing the workers' awareness of the loopholes in the Code, "the workers understand the Code too well."[83]

South Carolina workers picked up where Peel left off. At the April gathering of workers to form the South Carolina State Federation of Textile Workers, months of quiet anger exploded into a "fiery bombardment" cataloging the crimes perpetrated by the State Board on the state's workers. In Anderson, "Willis sat idly by" until the management of Appleton Mill in Anderson, South Carolina, had "completely destroyed" the local union. In Pelzer, Willis took more than two months to even make a visit, and five months to render a recommendation. Workers in Newberry had been waiting for action for almost a year. In the Lonsdale Mill in Seneca, Willis sanctioned a dramatic speedup of machinery in the carding and spinning rooms.[84]

The "coming out" of the South Carolina textile workers brought the southern movement to a new height of power. They were joined by workers in Alabama and Georgia, who, though much weaker organizationally, willingly added their voices to the movement by forming their own state textile councils. In Alabama, in fact, only the intervention of George Googe prevented the State Textile Council from taking "drastic censoring action" against the boards.[85] Christopher and Peel, the two leaders of North and South Carolina, respectively, could now speak for workers not only in their own state, but in the entire South. Their power derived not from some abstract personal militancy, but because their unions possessed new organizational strength.

Fired by the passion expressed at the meeting of the South Carolina Textile Federation, Christopher wrote to UTW Treasurer James Starr that the time for cooperation with the boards had come to an end:

Our workers are suffering, and are being treated worse than dumb animals. Exploitation continues without slack of pace, and maybe at an increased rapidity now, and the only way we are ever going to stop it is to have the strength to take our rights by main force and never give up until we do get what is coming to us, boards or no boards, agencies or no agencies, etc., etc., It has been proven to us that very few things are going to be given us by the Textile boards and agencies that have been set up. It's different with those who come under the National Labor Board, but we are not so fortunate as

some are, and we are, it appears to me, going to have to use other methods.
The workers have got to exercise their power, and do it unflinchingly, so long
as they are within the bounds of reason.[86]

It was time for the national leadership to get on board.

Conclusion

From 1933 to 1934, the course of textile organizing in the South was altered
sharply by the formation of labor-management dispute mechanisms under
the NRA. The "homegrown" unions that eschewed affiliation with the
UTW—or, opting for affiliation, nonetheless continued to stake their claims
to legitimacy on the sympathy of the local population—were eclipsed by the
presence of the Code Authority and the Bruere Board. Workers now found
that they had to appeal for justice not to the local populace, but to state and
federal tribunals.

The assault on work practices from these regional and national tribunals in turn impelled the workers to join organizations that extended beyond
the confines of their own mill. By May 1934, in each of the four textile states,
union members had organized state councils to speak on their behalf. To be
sure, these state organizations represented varying degrees of cohesion and
effectiveness. Their simple existence, however, reflected textile workers'
increasing awareness that theirs was a regional problem, demanding a regional solution. Through the state councils, workers could speak in unison
about their disparate grievances, until gradually the string of local voices of
protest could jell into a coherent regional set of demands.

But by the spring of 1934 southern workers were not only creating a crisis
within the New Deal administration; they were creating a crisis within their
own union. By attacking the board structure, the southern workers were
undermining the policy of accommodation to which national UTW leaders had subscribed to demonstrate their cooperation with the recovery program. How the UTW was to handle this insurgency from within its ranks
would determine whether or not southern textile workers would truly gain
a national voice.

7

WE MUST GET TOGETHER IN OUR ORGANIZATION

The story of the general strike is in part an institutional history, for it illustrates how the UTW was reluctantly transformed into a voice of southern cotton mill workers' discontent by the infusion of massive energy from the South. How successfully would UTW leaders and southern workers wed their cultures, their organizing styles, and their visions of workplace justice? Answering these questions takes us on a journey from the halls of Washington to the South and back.

The UTW Organizes Workers

Until the spring of 1934, UTW leaders like McMahon and Gorman had been so eager to win the favor of government officials that they had squelched rather than encouraged workers' expression of dissatisfaction. As late as March 1934 McMahon was lamenting that, "in all the years I have been connected with the industry, and that is practically my entire life, I have never had so many telegrams and letters importuning me to endorse strikes. Our men on the road are engaged more in stopping our people from walking out and striking and have little time for organizing."[1]

Despite McMahon's distaste for grassroots mobilization, however, the UTW president discovered that he sorely needed it in his own battles for credibility in Washington. Lack of UTW representation on the Cotton Textile Code Authority fundamentally abridged union influence, a reality made unmistakably clear in December 1933, when the Code Authority cut production hours in the cotton mills 25 percent without consulting the union. At that time, McMahon had demanded union representation on the Code Boards, going so far as to ask the AFL to consider a general strike for the thirty-hour week to get it.[2] But he was ignored. Lacking power and uncomfortable with militancy, McMahon was stymied. The UTW president was not destined to lead textile workers through this tumultuous period.

The mantle instead fell to his chief vice president, Francis Gorman. A staunch believer in the need for skilled workers to exercise their power on the shop floor, Gorman was more interested than McMahon in the opportunity for union revitalization presented by the new militancy of its rank and file. At a conference in March 1934 called by NRA Administrator Hugh Johnson to evaluate the performance of the Code Authorities, Gorman accused employers of not adhering to the wage differentials for skilled workers and blasted the Code for its exemptions from the minimum wage for learners and sweepers. Gorman also raised two of the union's traditional demands: an end to the North-South differential and a thirty-hour week.

Although the tone of Gorman's speech represented a new aggressiveness, its content indicated how different the demands of the union leadership were from the demands of its southern membership. The union made its standard response to the government's failure to look out for the workers' interests: a demand for labor representation on the Cotton Textile Code Authority. Gorman also called for an expanded Industrial Relations Board that would handle complaints of workers in all divisions of the textile industry, not only cotton textiles, a proposal that appeared to ignore the Bruere Board's own recent history of union busting in the cotton textile industry. Gorman's final proposals—for better industry reporting and enforcement of the collective bargaining provision in Section 7(a)—certainly began to address some of the problems workers had been having in the field. Noticeably absent from his list of complaints, however, was any mention of the stretch-out. The union leader had heard the noise of worker discontent but not fully understood its substance. Gorman's speech at the Conference of Code Authorities was a weak opening salvo, but it was a start.[3]

If Gorman's speech at the Conference of Code Authorities revealed that he had not fully heard the concerns of the union's southern membership, subsequent events made clear that the vice president possessed a keen interest in finding out what they were. At the same time that the Conference on Code Authorities was held, UTW field organizers and Executive Council members met in Washington. This was an extended opportunity for southern and national UTW leaders to exchange information. For the first time, leaders of the International explicitly recognized that the national office needed to create an internal structure to channel the massive discontent from below. The shift from the UTW's traditional approach was explicit. "If we discussed only the plans of the International Office and the operations of the Recovery Administration, we would not rise to the real challenge of this meeting," a summary of the conference in *The Textile Worker* read. "That real challenge is this: What shall we do more completely to organize the textile workers? What practical steps shall we take?"[4]

At last southern field organizers had their opening. National UTW leaders heard a chorus of criticism about the enforcement of the Code in the southern states. The Code Authority and the Bruere Board took too long to handle complaints. The Bruere Board was not dealing with the stretch-out issue, as was its mandate. Wages were as low as $5 a week in Alabama, despite the Code. The Code Authority was an arm of the manufacturers.

But even among the southern leadership, dissatisfaction with the Bruere Board had not escalated into full-blown opposition. This was in early March, and the worst of the Bruere Board decisions were yet to come. Instead, field organizers called for future complaints to be handled only by the Bruere Board, bypassing the Code Authority altogether.[5]

The March meeting was a turning point in the history of the union. Vice President Gorman was authorized to set up what he called a "Research Department" in Washington—separate from the union headquarters in New York—to pull together statistics on the nature and extent of complaints against the Code. He instructed union locals to send their complaints first to the Research Department, which would then forward them to the Cotton Textile Code Authority. This way the International Office could learn the nature of workers' complaints and act as an advocate for its membership. Not incidentally, this process would enable the UTW to monitor the actions of the Code Authority, whose secrecy concerning its statistics made it all but impossible to determine exactly what it was doing.

Gorman's Research Department filled an enormous vacuum in the UTW's national structure. Not only could it educate the national leadership about issues at the local level, it could also give Gorman the information he needed to effectively supervise the activities of field organizers. It was the beginning of an integrated national union.

Gorman's Research Department was also the union's de facto organizing department. Gorman proposed that the Research Department staff prepare leaflets, for example, describing "the first steps for new local unions," or what workers should do if their employers argued against the union, or how to run a local union meeting. "In all this our purposes are plain," concluded Gorman. "They are, *first*, to promote organization, and *second*, to maintain helpful contacts with new locals."[6]

The UTW also hired new organizers for the South. They included Paul Christopher and another textile worker from Shelby, Council M. Fox; J. Ralph Gay, a local UTW president from the Sibley Textile Mill, in Augusta, Georgia, and later president of the Georgia Federation of Textile Workers; and G. J. Kendall, a railroad machinist who had been coordinating the work of a host of "volunteer organizers" in the Charlotte area and who helped form the Western Carolinas Textile Federation based in Charlotte and Gaston County.[7] This new field staff joined the already overworked John Peel in South Carolina and Albert Cox who had been covering Alabama and southern Georgia. Cox attempted to organize Alabama alone until the late spring, when the UTW finally sent John Dean, the veteran organizer and native North Carolinian, down from New York to help him.[8]

These paid organizers were a bare-bones staff for an enormous field of work. Their efforts were supplemented by a host of what the veteran union leader Eula McGill called "volunteer organizers," factory workers who devoted "almost all of their waking hours to helping to organize mill workers."[9] These included McGill herself; Alice Berry, a union member who had been fired from the Selma Manufacturing Company in Birmingham; John Howard Payne, a weaver from the Chadwick Hoskins Mill in Charlotte; Lloyd Davis, a weaver and loom fixer from Columbus, Georgia; and Homer Welch, an intrepid young mill worker from the Callaway Mills in Hogansville, in the Chattahoochee Valley of western Georgia.[10] Others, like Ike Robinton from Alabama, were craft unionists who helped organize cotton mill workers on behalf of the State Federation of Labor or simply on their own.[11] Mollie Dowd of the Women's Trade Union League joined in the organizing in Alabama with the fervor and dedication of the best of the millhands.

This new influx of staff energy intensified the pace of organizing among the cotton millhands of the South. Mecklenberg and Gaston counties alone, home of Charlotte and Gastonia, respectively, boasted forty new locals from January through April. South Carolina claimed an additional twenty thousand workers.[12] In Alabama, organizing brought the number of textile union locals up to twenty-five by the summer of 1934.[13]

Tensions within the Southern Branch of the UTW

The creation of a research/organizing department and the hiring of new organizers was a major advance for the UTW, but it did not fully overcome the tension between local organization and national unionism. UTW leaders and southern workers not only differed in their attitudes toward their relationship with the federal government; they also clashed in their approach to organizing.

The worst scenarios occured when national unionism was "brought" to a mill with no previous tradition of collective protest. Here UTW organizers often left the impression that the national office was performing a service for the workers in exchange for membership dues. Even volunteer organizers like John Howard Payne organized potential members by suggesting that the UTW was a service organization. "Now, we're not going to tell you that you're going to get a big wage increase, or hours cut so much, or something corrected about how you're working, or something like that," he would say to workers, "but we're working toward getting all your complaints corrected."[14] When such implicit promises were not fulfilled, southern workers became disenchanted, writing to UTW national headquarters that it was "no use" to be a member of the union. UTW Treasurer James Starr expressed what must have been a common feeling at the national office when he replied to such a complaint from Hickory, North Carolina: "I certainly do not like to read letters such as the one you wrote me. . . . surely you do not expect that after only a month or two of organization you can get results that other organizations have been working for for years. . . . It is too bad your members are so impatient."[15]

Another persistent problem was the UTW's policy of moving organizers around and supplementing its regular staff with "commission organizers," field staff who were paid half the initiation fee of every new member they signed up. Once having signed up the workers, commission organizers inevitably left for territory where workers were not organized, leaving the new union without a leader or cohesion.[16] Even more serious, the blunt exchange of money for union membership nourished southern workers' suspicion that the UTW was only a scam to get workers' money.[17]

Organizing results in Georgia revealed how ill-suited some of these tactics were in the South and how dependent the UTW was on how well workers on the ground had tilled the soil of unionism in the pre–New Deal years. The intimidating antiunion posture of Georgia manufacturers gave rise to and reinforced a cautious and defensive craft union movement. Fearful of the recriminations that would come back to organized labor if textile workers mobilized, the Georgia Federation of Labor resisted textile union organizing in general and the UTW in particular. As early as 1929, Federation leaders had demanded that the State Federation of Labor retain absolute control over any organizing of textile workers done in their state. UTW Vice President Gorman had vehemently protested this suggestion, but in the end agreed that any organizing campaign would be jointly sponsored by both parties. In what must have been a privately maddening capitulation to the Georgia Federation, the UTW agreed to contribute fifty cents of each new membership fee in Georgia to the Georgia Federation of Labor's organizing fund.[18]

Partly as a result of this earlier agreement, the UTW did not place a full-time staffperson in Georgia, but instead employed commission organizers, some of whom, apparently, did not make a satisfactory accounting of funds collected. C. W. Bolick was briefly sent to Columbus, but for unknown reasons he was transferred out of the state sometime in May. However unfair to him, Bolick's departure had the worst possible repercussions. "People in Columbus are very much upset over your failure to return," wrote one local leader to Bolick. "Mill managements are telling people that you ran out on them and they are about to believe it."[19] Faced with an attack from the Georgia Federation on their scruples, the UTW capitulated further, turning over *all* authority to select organizers to the AFL representative and former Vice President of the Georgia Federation George Googe.[20]

The turf struggle came to a climax when Georgia textile workers met for the first time on a statewide level in July 1934. The workers immediately asked that organizing no longer take place through the State Federation of Labor, but through the UTW International, and that organizers be bona fide textile workers and not from any other craft.[21] But the damage had already been done. With the consistent exception of Columbus, on the Alabama state line, and Augusta, on the South Carolina state line, few strong union locals emerged out of Georgia. Hampered by the interference of a defensive and possessive craft union organization, and faced with the most intractable opposition from mill owners, Georgia textile unionists barely managed to create an organizational home for themselves. In the other three southern textile states, discontent had snowballed beginning with North Carolina's campaign to remove State Board Chair Theodore Johnson on April 10. The movement had accelerated and spread down to South Carolina and across the mountains to Alabama. Yet in Trion, Georgia, the union could not find a meeting place because the mill owned all the property. As late as July 1934, the Chickamauga local was insisting, "We must get together in our organization."[22]

The absence of deeply rooted union structures in Georgia reaped a cruel harvest, one that can best be illustrated by glancing briefly into the future, to the final days before the general strike was to begin in September. Veteran UTW staffmember Joe Jacobs describes how workers in Georgia hurried to become last-minute union members in order to be eligible for strike benefits:

I have seen time after time, where they had two crates. One laying flat, one standing up, on top of it, and the guy is sitting on one, standing up on the end—regular old fruit crates—with a receipt book. [The workers were] paying one dollar to join the union. They *had* that dollar because they just had walked off of work, and he was signing receipt after receipt after receipt, thousands of them. . . . But what happened in that strike has plagued us ever since, because everybody knows—my aunt, my uncle, my brother, my father, my mother—they lost their jobs and the union didn't help them. Paid one whole dollar! Some of them maybe never paid another dime. . . . And I don't care how much you talk to them. They could still see that line, with everybody with that one dollar and they paid it.[23]

One may usefully contrast the situation in Georgia with organizing results at the Dwight Mills in Gadsden, Alabama, where the UTW was built on earlier collective solidarity. Here workers were able to build a strong union presence amidst conditions of employer hostility equal to that in Georgia. While the presence of three industries—rubber, steel, and textiles—in Gadsden had created the potential for a strong working-class solidarity, Dwight mill owners had persuaded owners of the other companies to keep their workers' wages at or below those of the mill workers. Precisely because of the volatility of the situation, management's control was repressive in the extreme.[24] Representatives of organized labor who had repeatedly attempted to sign up workers in Gadsden despaired of the effort, vowing that they would "not be a party to taking these people into deep water and leave them to drown[;] when they are discharged at one mill they can't get a job at any other which shows that they are blacklisted."[25] Such half-finished efforts created understandable suspicion of organized labor among Gadsden mill workers. Laura Beard, a retired Dwight worker, remembers: "They started signin' up in '32. We was green. We gave him [the organizer] one dollar and he picked up and left us."[26]

To finesse this problem, local Gadsden leaders Walter and Margaret Pearson and Burns Cox organized their own independent union, the Dixie Federation of Labor. Walter Pearson urged the "men and women of the Gadsden district" to be wary of organizers who are "using high pressure methods to get your money." "Keep your money," he urged. "Hold on to it. We are meeting quietly every week and enrolling members with the greatest possible care and as rapidly as possible. Don't be swept off your feet. Take time to study this. It won't hurt you to wait a while. Hold steady."[27] Cox remembers that when they first got started, "we'd only have eight or nine people, and then we'd tell these eight or nine—we'd go over town on the river up here, or get out in the woods . . . where we don't want nobody touching us, and these people would come back and spread it to their people."[28] Only the greatest secrecy could protect union organizing in Gadsden.

Dwight workers' cautious approach was swept away in July 1933 by their conviction that it was the intention of the new recovery legislation for workers to join the UTW to act as Roosevelt's watchdog in the local mills. Not long after July 17, they abandoned the Dixie Federation for the UTW. Yet the early solidarity created by Pearson was reflected in the *way* they joined the UTW: workers chipped in to one large pool to pay membership dues to the UTW as a group. Support for the UTW was strong: "Once we come out in the open," remembers Cox, "our people come to these meetings. . . . We had as much as 100 to 125 people coming to these meetings."[29] While the response of employers was predictable—over fifty workers were fired for union membership—the Dwight union never gave up. To the contrary, a year later it led the Alabama walkout that began the General Textile Strike. Where organizing was rooted in this kind of local solidarity, the union was effectively built.

Turning against the Stretch-out

Despite tensions between the national union's organizing practices and the needs of local unions, the UTW had by April 1934 made great progress toward understanding the grievances of southern workers. Yet the leadership had yet to take a stand on the issue most critical to the successful integration of the southern membership into the UTW: the stretch-out. In hearings and meetings in Washington, Gorman continued to focus instead on the question of skilled workers' wages. Yet, as shall be seen, Gorman's willingness to confront the NRA served as a wedge, polarizing the atmosphere in such a way as to bring the UTW and its southern members closer together. Indeed, it can be seen as the beginning of the UTW's own path to the general strike.

The issue of skilled workers' wages married a traditional AFL concern—the AFL had historically feared minimum wage legislation on the grounds that it would drag down skilled workers' pay—with a real grievance of skilled textile workers. Gorman's Research Department was flush with reports from locals throughout the country that skilled workers' wages were being reduced. Gorman adopted the slogan, "the minimum has become the maximum," meaning that the $12 per week minimum wage was becoming the wage for workers who had previously earned more. On March 19 Gorman warned NRA officials that the UTW was prepared to fight for the preservation of wages for workers in "the higher brackets."[30] Days later, at hearings over Senator Wagner's proposal to create a new labor board to replace the eviscerated NLB, Gorman charged that skilled hands were "up against the wall." If Wagner's bill was not passed, Gorman threatened to call a general strike in the textile industry.[31]

Industry leaders vigorously denied Gorman's charges, leading Gorman to demand a hearing before the head of the NRA, Hugh Johnson. Once again Gorman asked every local in the country to help him by sending in a report on wages and working conditions in their mill. The fervor of the response gave an additional boost to Gorman's increasing sense of power.[32] By April, the UTW Emergency Committee was asking Hugh Johnson for another opportunity to discuss the questions of hours and skilled workers' wages.[33]

Combined with the controversy in Shelby and other areas, the UTW attack on Code administration of wages and hours generated a sense of crisis among cotton textile manufacturers. Thomas Marchant, the president of the American Cotton Manufacturers' Association (ACMA), began to complain about the "repeated stirring up of political uncertainties" generated by those who wished to alter the NRA's administration of the Code. At its April meeting, the ACMA passed a resolution asking that the Code not be changed in any way until sufficient time had passed for it to prove itself.[34]

These twin challenges to the NRA forced Bruere to emerge from his position behind the scenes into an open statement of his sympathies. Speaking before the April ACMA meeting, Bruere reassured anxious industry leaders that despite having received over two thousand complaints, his board had been deliberately slow to make any precedent-setting decisions because he did not want to start any "disturbing currents running through the industry."[35] The statement marked a decisive break from Bruere's role as a mediator. However calming his remark was for industry leaders, it infuriated southern unionists, who lost any remaining sense of obligation to maintain cooperation with the Board. "Nero fiddled while Rome burned, so it is said," declared a disgusted Peel, who then proceeded to castigate Bruere for permitting mill managements to "whip the workers into line."[36]

Gorman's attack on the NRA enforcement of skilled workers' wages coincided with the burst of anger in North and South Carolina over the Bruere Board's intransigence (see chapter 6). But now, instead of chiding workers for their lack of cooperation, both McMahon and Gorman had reason to pay new attention to the fomenting discontent from below. Engaging in their own personal disputes with the NRA, the UTW leaders found workers' restlessness an asset. National union leaders began to listen, perhaps for the first time, to what southern unionists were actually saying. At the convention of the South Carolina State Federation of Textile Workers on April 23, UTW President McMahon acknowledged, at long last, southern workers' opposition to the stretch-out. "The load of the textile workers in the south is too great," he announced to the crowd, "so much so that it is destroying the physical as well as mental health of the workers. . . . The humanitarian principles spoken of by the manufacturers when the hearings were being held in Washington prior to the signing of the Code by President Roosevelt are a thing of the past."[37]

The southern discontent even provoked South Carolina's own Senator Byrnes to take action. The originator of the stretch-out committee that became the Bruere Board, Byrnes formally asked Hugh Johnson to explain what had happened to his committee. It was an inquiry that Johnson could not ignore. Byrnes's request prompted Bruere, once again, to play his hand. In his response, Bruere made clear what the workers had suspected all along: that he did not take seriously their claims to being stretched out. It was unrealistic to expect, Bruere replied to Byrnes, that "as a result of the establishment of our Board there would be no further extension of the so-called stretch-out. When you consider that every introduction of improved machinery or technical methods is likely to be interpreted as stretch-out you will appreciate the optimism of your hope. The protest of the workers in the textile industry against the so-called stretch-out is as old as the introduction of the power loom."[38]

Bruere's emergence as an ally of the employers helped clarify the true nature of the conflict, making it easier for the UTW to fully embrace its role as a representative of its unhappy membership. McMahon now became more confrontational in his dealings with NRA Administrator Hugh Johnson. The Bruere Board had originally been formed "to consider questions of 'stretch-out and machine load,'" he complained, but instead it had become "an agency for settlement of strikes and impending strikes." The "big problem," the stretch-out, had "not been tackled."[39]

The UTW and its southern membership had for the first time achieved something approaching a common understanding of philosophy and strategy. But it was not clear that the UTW had gotten its organizational house in order in time, for by April some mill owners were systematically weeding out union members by laying off workers. Membership in the UTW local in Bessemer City, North Carolina, for example, declined from two hundred members down to seven by June 1934.[40] Much of the attrition could be attributed to apparently selective and discriminatory layoffs. In East Tallassee, Alabama, wrote one worker to UTW headquarters, management began to lay off workers, "till way over 200 lost their jobs, but remember most of them were members of the union, and all the active ones have never been rehired. We are actually scared here to mention the Code, also the union."[41] For organizational reasons, if for no other, it was necessary for the union to act. Yet action was risky, for both workers and leaders had a lot to lose.

The June Strike Threat

The moment of truth arrived in late May 1934, when the Code Authority voted to curtail production hours by 25 percent for the next twelve weeks, beginning June 1. This would effectively reduce weekly minimum wages from $12 to $9. The Code Authority had announced a similar curtailment the previous December, but at that time, it will be recalled, McMahon had been powerless to halt it. Now the situation was different. The UTW threatened a general strike on June 1.

The strike threat provided the occasion for everyone in the organization to put forth their grievances in the strongest terms. McMahon, of course, was disgusted that labor had not been consulted in the curtailment decision. Gorman pointed out that the curtailment was a direct result of the stretch-out—the fact that production per worker had been increased so much that goods were overstocked. Why should the workers suffer by having their wages reduced? "We are punished," he wrote, referring to the curtailment, "because we produced too much."[42] For Peel, the strike grew not from the curtailment issue but out of the failure of the Bruere Board to deal with an accumulation of grievances: "Labor deplores the necessity of a strike," he wrote, "but we have no other means of redress, now that Dr. Bruere, Chairman of the CTNIRB, made a definitive statement to the ACMA that of over 2,000 cases before the Board, no decision has been rendered because of the disturbing influence that such decisions might have on industry. If this is the attitude of the board set up to handle the complaints, then there is nothing left for the workers to do but strike when the manufacturers fail to make adjustments."[43]

To stave off an open confrontation over his board, Bruere arranged a meeting with southern union organizers and grassroots leaders. The meeting provided southern workers with an opportunity to explode with anger. "Just what can we expect at the hand of your Board?" said UTW member Furtick. "If we have a mill organized 100% and the management won't recognize us and won't meet the committee, and we pull a strike, you can't come in and force them to do anything." Furtick concluded with a statement that summed up the sentiment of all whom he represented, that they might "just as well not have a state board or a national board."

But if Bruere's meeting crystallized southern workers' discontent, it also siphoned off rank and file concerns and absorbed grassroots energy, leaving McMahon to face the industry alone. McMahon was not without resources, however: the UTW president had taken it upon himself to warn congressional representatives about the negative implications of the proposed curtailment program. In an attempt to head off further congressional criticism, Johnson intervened personally, persuading the head of the Code Authority, George Sloan, to meet McMahon. Yet manufacturers' hostility to the UTW was so strong that Sloan agreed to meet with McMahon only if it was understood that he was speaking for himself, not the industry, and only under the condition that McMahon and Sloan sit in separate rooms while Johnson shuttled between them. This was the closest the UTW leader had come to industry-wide collective bargaining.[44]

Amazingly, just as the UTW had reached its peak of influence, the organization let it slip away. Bruere's ploy of divide and conquer—meeting separately with union organizers, while Hugh Johnson organized the meeting between McMahon and Sloan—was decisive. Shorn of a visible reminder of the demands of his rank and file, McMahon fell back on his traditional demand: labor representation on the Code Authority. The UTW president almost assuredly perceived labor representation in the halls of power as a more comprehensive, far-reaching reform than any agreement on substantive issues such as wages or working conditions.

Seeing an easy victory, Sloan agreed to grant McMahon's wish, except that the UTW would now have representation not on the Code Authority, but on the Bruere Board! The Bruere Board would be expanded from three to five. The fourth member would be a representative of the UTW, and the fifth another representative of industry, to keep the labor-industry balance. In return for this concession to labor, the industry would be granted the authority to order a temporary curtailment of production. McMahon called the strike off.

What had happened? McMahon had gained labor's coveted "access" just at the moment when the union's own organizers had made clear in a separate meeting that the body to which it was gaining access was corrupt from top to bottom. Meanwhile, the industry had given no guarantee that wages would remain at their current levels and certainly had made no promises with regard to the stretch-out. Needless to say, industry did not recognize the UTW as a collective bargaining agent.

L. R. Gilbert, the National Board secretary and past President of the Southern Textile Association, could not contain his delight at the settlement. He saw the expansion of the Bruere Board as a means to co-opt the UTW leadership, strengthening the legitimacy of the Board while simultaneously limiting the union's ability to maneuver. "To be perfectly frank," he said to Bruere, "whether McMahon knows it or not, he is on the spot, he is in a hole." "If we get a United Textile Worker on this Board," Gilbert observed to Theodore Johnson, "they can't pull crazy strikes all over the country." To George Googe, Gilbert reinforced his opinion that it would now be up to McMahon "to keep his industry quiet."[45]

Industry representative Geer was equally delighted. To him, such a settlement did not only maintain the status quo, but opened the door for intensified repression of unions in the southern mills. The southern textile industry could now begin the business of consciously wiping out the union altogether. As Geer commented to Breure: "It is going to be the end of his [McMahon's] domination. He is going to get the worst licking he ever had."[46]

8

NO TURNING BACK

I'm glad in a way that the general strike was called off, but in a number of ways I am terribly disappointed. I hope it's only a postponement, because I think that's what we need more than anything else, and the same thing has been told me innumerable times by the workers.
—Paul Christopher, June 4, 1934

McMahon's May 31 decision not to stage a general strike threw the fragile southern union into chaos. As will be seen, southern workers responded by taking matters into their own hands, staging walkouts in all four southern textile states in June and July. Their actions sent a decisive if unspoken message to UTW leaders: if McMahon and Gorman were to perform the function of leadership, they had to follow the wishes of their membership. To stave off a complete disintegration of the southern union, UTW leaders scrambled to create a forum for the membership to act within the structure of the UTW. Most decisively, the UTW moved the date of their biannual convention from September to August to accommodate the growing demand for a general strike authorization. The UTW leaders thus averted one crisis: the union regained its position as the vehicle for southern workers' collective action. But whether the UTW had the power to stop the increasing employer repression of its fragile organization in the South was another matter. McMahon's retreat in June functioned as a signal to southern mill owners that the union was ripe for complete destruction. Nor was the UTW's claim to leadership secure, as the summer's walkouts established southern workers' claim to shaping the character of the general strike to come.

Repression and Resistance: North Carolina

The June settlement increased the possibility that the union could be destroyed at the national level. If the Bruere Board could enlist the cooperation of the UTW in its decisions, the rights of the textile workers could be taken away with the union's consent. Bruere himself used the occasion of the June settlement to present a new aggressive posture, warning Googe that he was "not going to be intimidated any more" by striking workers.[1] But the union's unwillingness to expose the hypocrisy of the Bruere Board also emboldened employers to destroy the union at the local level, through the use of force if necessary. At the Victor Monaghan Mills in South Carolina, for example, managers *"Boldly* announced they would punish the Textile Workers Unions to Death Before they would start their plants till September."[2] Even in Augusta, Georgia, where unions had initially been recognized, the mills "now refuse to handle complaints" or meet with workers.[3]

Southern textile workers thus found themselves fighting a battle on two organically related fronts. Increasingly they refused to work through the state boards, instead contacting those outside the Bruere Board to help them. In North Carolina, of course, workers had already been boycotting the State Board since before the June settlement. As early as April, workers at the Waverly Mills in Laurinburg had struck over a new round of speedups and new deductions in workers' pay for services in the mill villages that reduced their paycheck to almost nothing. Defying bureaucratic protocol, the strikers appealed directly to the Labor Department.[4] This tactic distinctly annoyed Bruere, who commented that the North Carolina workers were foolish to take such a "high hat" position by refusing to go through State Board Chair Theodore Johnson.[5] The workers' tactics also prompted National Board Secretary L. R. Gilbert to plead with other NRA agencies to absolutely refuse to respond to labor complaints in the cotton textile industry. "If all original complaint letters from every source throughout the country could be sent directly to this office," Gilbert wrote, "without any attempt being made to reply or to investigate the charges made, the splendid cooperation of the Cotton Textile Institute would continue with the belief that it [the CTI] still had the confidence of the administration and the public." The function of the Bruere Board had never been made more explicit.[6]

Belatedly the UTW leadership understood a change in tactics to be both necessary and unavoidable. At its June 19 meeting, the UTW's Executive Council finally voted to instruct workers who were assigned additional workloads to no longer await the outcome of Bruere Board investigations, but to stop working immediately.[7] Gorman, later challenged to make his position clear, indicated that direct action was now "the only effective method" of contending with the stretch-out. "We have arrived at the point where it is foolhardy to expect any concessions from the employers, unless the organization is able to demonstrate its strength."[8]

But the strength of the Laurinburg strikers alone was hardly a match for the mounting employer repression. Southern UTW leader Paul Christopher appealed to union locals far and wide for money and food. "They are on the verge of starvation," he wrote in an appeal for relief, "some of them eating only fat meat and bread for their every meal, and those meals are irregular and less than three times daily. There are 24 cases of colitis, one baby having died last week as a direct result of the disease. And yet, they are maintaining their fight for union justice."[9] Tension increased as strikers were fired upon by snipers; eight strikers were wounded and sent to the hospital. Henceforth the picketers carried guns. It was an ominous escalation of tactics.[10]

Still hoping for government cooperation, McMahon appealed to Bruere to intervene. But Bruere refused to intervene as long as workers did not go first through the State Board. Finally, on July 11, McMahon wired Bruere that if the Laurinburg case was not settled he would be forced to authorize a statewide strike in North Carolina.[11] Bruere did nothing.

Almost as if a signal had been sent off, manufacturers across North Carolina responded. On July 13, managers of the Spofford Mills in Wilmington, on the coast, locked workers out of their jobs. At the Highland Cordage Mills in Hickory, near the mountains, union members were laid off and replaced by workers from the countryside. In Lumberton, near the South Carolina border, workers were fired "merely because they attended a labor meeting," or because "they were seen talking with an organizer."[12] This kind of blatant discrimination had been commonplace in Georgia and Alabama, but for North Carolina textile workers, this represented a new level of intimidation. The crackdown on the union was now in earnest.

Resistance and Repression: South Carolina

An almost identical hardening of industry's position took place in South Carolina, except that in South Carolina mill owners were able to enlist the active involvement of their state government. The "Laurinburg" of South Carolina was Piedmont, just south of Greenville. Here, a crisis had been brewing since late winter when the president of the Piedmont local, Neal Bass, and his daughter, had been fired from the mill on a pretext.[13] Then, in mid-April, the mill had increased the workload of the doffers in the spinning room. Appeals to the State Board produced no response. On May 28, five doffers whose work had been extended walked off their jobs, followed by the rest of the workers in the mill. As was the case with the Laurinburg workers, the confrontation at Piedmont threatened to become violent as nonunion workers attacked union workers with picker sticks, long sticks used in the weaving process.[14] By July 11, three thousand South Carolina workers in at least ten different mills had walked out in support of the Piedmont workers, and the Piedmont strike had become the rallying cry for workers across South Carolina.[15]

Piedmont local President Bass wrote Frances Perkins, begging her to intervene. "You are the only power that can free us," he wrote, "from section seventeen subsection three of textile code and textile board's inaction."[16] Once again, however, the government refused to take action, leaving South Carolina manufacturers free to take matters into their own hands.[17] Along with National Board member Benjamin Geer, himself a South Carolina mill owner, Piedmont's owner S. M. Beattie decided to make an example of his workers. It was time, Geer wrote to Bruere, to "clear up the Piedmont situation," since Geer was "of the opinion that the Piedmont case has been taken up almost in all the mills in this vicinity." Piedmont's mill management secretly orchestrated a delegation of loyal workers "to Columbia to see the Governor," who promised them "all the protection they needed" to return to work. Although Geer was aware of these developments, he did not make them public since, as he wrote to Bruere, "I felt that it was better that this phase should not be mentioned."[18] By July 13, Geer told Bruere that a "settlement" would happen the next day.[19] At the last minute, Bruere asked Geer to attempt to delay the use of state troops.[20] But this was too little too late. On July 14, thirty state constables arrived at the Piedmont mill armed with blackjacks, rifles, and pistols.[21]

The UTW immediately threatened a sympathetic strike if the troops were not removed.[22] Peel charged that the troops were being used as strikebreakers; the Piedmont local union asked sarcastically who had paid for the troops, the state or the mill.[23] Meanwhile, South Carolina union locals pledged cooperation with "the movement of the statewide textile strike."[24] But the threats were for naught. The next day, Geer announced that an "agreement" had been reached with the workers to reopen the plant.

General Strike in Alabama

Developments escalated even faster in Alabama, where the state Cotton Manufacturers Association had announced a July 10 meeting "to clear the textile industry of the enemies that threaten its very existence."[25] To firm up local union organization, the UTW sent veteran organizer John Dean and Shelby unionist Council M. Fox to the scene. Throughout the first week of July, individual Alabama locals met and took votes about their willingness to participate in a statewide general strike.

Once again, however, events happened faster than the union could plan. At the Dwight Mills in Gadsden, workers had been plagued by persistent acts of discrimination by the mill management. Workers had sent complaints to the State Board, but the Board merely sent copies of every complaint letter back to the Dwight management. Five union activists lost their jobs. In response, the entire Dwight workforce walked out on July 12. Two days later, workers also struck at the Saratoga Victory Mills in Guntersville, twenty miles away.[26]

UTW organizer John Dean hastily called a meeting of all Alabama locals for July 15. It was, reported the Associated Press, "the first time in the history of the industry of the state" that the Alabama millhands had gathered together "to discuss their problems and working conditions."[27] After seven hours of discussion, forty out of forty-two locals announced their decision to join the striking Gadsden workers on July 17. In Alabama, however, no statewide militia came in to quash the strike. The general strike in Alabama was on.[28]

The UTW Regains Leadership

The UTW leadership responded to the Alabama walkout by scrambling to regain leadership of its own union. Still hoping that the strategy of government cooperation would bear fruit, Gorman had promised Bruere that he would counsel North and South Carolina workers not to stage a general strike in response to the actions by the Alabama workers. Gorman kept his word. But at emergency meetings of the southern state textile councils following the announcement of the Alabama strike, Gorman convinced workers in other states that this was simply a postponement until a national UTW convention could be called.[29] As an indication of its good intentions, and to accommodate the escalating pace of events, the UTW national leadership also moved the union's scheduled September convention to August.[30] The entire UTW membership was to meet in New York from August 13–16 to decide on the necessity of a general strike to begin not earlier than midnight, Saturday, September 1.

The summer statewide meetings proved to be crucial forums for the UTW to reestablish its legitimacy as leader of the southern workers. Remaining to be hashed out were differences of opinion over the crucial question of demands. Throughout the summer, the stretch-out had vied with the curtailment of production as the union's central grievance. Despite the fact that both McMahon and Gorman had understood the centrality of the stretch-out issue, when it came to a general strike, McMahon's beef with the industry was its decision to curtail hours without maintaining wages. McMahon's perspective was shared by AFL southern representative George Googe, who argued with Alabama delegates about this issue during the seven-hour meeting in Birmingham, July 15, to decide on the Alabama general strike. Delegates finally agreed to place first on their list of demands McMahon's original insistence that workers be paid at least $12 despite the reduction of the workweek to thirty hours. In return, however, the delegates made their own concerns clear in demands two through six—"eliminate stretch-out, reinstate workers fired by stretch-out, re-employ persons fired by the union, recognize the union, no further speed-up of machines."[31]

The Alabama "compromise" however, did not go far enough to satisfy the organizationally stronger South Carolina Federation of Textile Workers. They demanded the elimination of the stretch-out, the reduction of machine speeds, recognition of the union, and reinstatement of all workers discharged for union membership. Wages and hours were not even mentioned.[32] By the time the convention occurred, the voices of the southern unionists were at the forefront of the union. For a brief moment, at least, there would be no mistaking what they had to say.

Uprising in Columbus, Georgia

Before the convention could take place, however, the South witnessed one final climactic explosion of conflict. The setting was Columbus, Georgia, the one part of the state where workers had a history of strong organization extending back at least as far as the 1890s. The center of the hurricane was the Eagle and Phenix Mills where, despite union organization, conditions were among the worst in the country. "The manufacturers here have violated every code of principle, honor, and fairmindedness . . . by allowing the virtue of young women to be demanded by Superintendents and overseers," wrote UTW organizer Albert Cox. "Windows are closed tightly even in the hottest of summer and women and children faint from suffocation. Oh! There are so many other things."[33] The Eagle and Phenix management was so contemptuous of Bruere's dispute-resolution process that in late May the superintendent simply fired the members of their employees' committee. Eight thousand workers attended a meeting of workers to determine what to do, and on May 28 they walked off their jobs.

Eagle and Phenix employees' anger had been fueled even further by an act of provocation by general manager Frank J. Bradley that made clear the extent of his contempt for Section 7(a). On June 21, in an unexpected act of conciliation, Bradley wrote to the union negotiating committee agreeing to enter into discussions about the workload, especially complaints of stretch-out by loom fixers and carders. Bradley's letter also promised that the mill would not discriminate against striking workers. Joyful millhands attempted to return to their jobs the next day, only to find that new workers were being hired in their places. When a delegation went to Bradley to discuss the meaning of these events he fired them and admitted that the letter was a joke.[34] Workers threatened another strike. Local union leaders wrote to Roosevelt himself warning that the situation would be "uncontrollable" unless "immediate federal assistance" was forthcoming.[35]

Inaction by Bruere and the NRA once again permitted the controversy to escalate. A dispute that had begun a year earlier over the wages of slasher tenders—skilled workers who prepared the looms for weaving—had stalled inside the Bruere Board bureaucracy. Although the Georgia State Board had finally handed down an unusual pro-worker decision regarding the slasher tenders in May 1934, the Eagle and Phenix Mill management scuttled it by appealing to the National Board. The management then failed to show up for a scheduled June 14 hearing, leading the National Board to delay the case until its August 1 meeting. By this time, the Georgia Board had resigned, partly because of other controversies, and partly because they were disgusted with the National Board's delays and unwillingness to support them in the slasher tenders' case. Unable to count on the deflection of protest by the State Board, the National Board groped for a strategy. Geer favored the creation of a special local board in Columbus. Bruere suggested that George Googe be called in to look at the situation. In fact, neither action was taken. The Bruere Board did permit conciliators from the Labor Department to be sent to the scene, but only under the condition that they had no authority to act.

The last straw occurred when the slasher tenders' August 1 hearing was also postponed. On August 8, workers voted to strike on August 16 unless the Bruere Board took up their case. "We do not expect a letter of acknowledgement," the employees committee told Gilbert, "but we expect action not later than August 16, 1934. The people of this plant are very restless and unless something is done and by August 16, 1934, there will be a walkout at Eagle and Phenix mills."[36] Unrest spread to other mills in the city.[37]

Tension finally erupted into violence on August 10. W. N. "Reuben" Sanders, a worker from another mill, was killed when a strikebreaker drove a car past the picket line of the Columbus-based Georgia Webbing and Tape

Company, where a strike had been in progress for over a month. Whether the killing was intentional was never determined, but workers were convinced that it was.[38] Eight thousand people viewed Sanders's body as it lay in state at the Central Textile Hall in the heart of the city on Sunday, August 12. The next day workers staged a funeral procession to the cemetery consisting of 617 automobiles and 450 men on foot.[39]

Federal labor conciliator C. L. Richardson worried that this open display of defiance was a direct challenge to the authority of the city's manufacturing interests. Indeed, the management of Georgia Webbing and Tape was getting pressure from the city fathers to open the next day, "as if nothing had happened and as a lesson to labor unions."[40] Tensions escalated further on Tuesday, August 14, two days after Sanders's funeral, when Eagle and Phenix mill officials discharged G. A. Bland, a member of the employees' committee, over an incident that had taken place Monday, August 13. Even though Monday had been Bland's day off, the overseer had been harassing Bland for doing union business. Bland was fired when he punched his overseer in the face. Once again the threat of violence hung in the air. Even local union leader E. B. Newberry admitted that it was "impossible for me to hold these workers in line."[41]

But anger and defiance became mixed with fear. Not for the last time, workers looked to the federal government in a desperate plea for help. "For the sake of humanity," wrote a group of Eagle and Phenix workers to Roosevelt himself, "won't you have an investigation made of the pay and working conditions of human beings in the Eagle and Phenix mills of Columbus Georgia."[42] McMahon himself wrote to Bruere asking why the Bruere Board was taking no action. Bruere disingenuously replied to McMahon that the unrest at Eagle and Phenix was "largely due to the absence of orders resulting from the present state of the market and in part from cancellation of orders due to the recent strike."[43]

Finally the Columbus central labor union and the UTW local both wrote to the Labor Department begging them to assume jurisdiction in this case. Labor conciliator Richardson was again sent to the scene. But Richardson's report only confirmed the complete breakdown of communication between workers, management, and the government. Despite hours of negotiation, he was unable "to gain the impression that the management has any notion of living up to Article 7a of the National Industrial Recovery Act." As for the employees, Richardson found them "almost desperate, claiming they had written to several sources attempting to get help in what they allege to be illegal and unbearable conditions."[44]

Having exhausted every recourse, four thousand Eagle and Phenix workers met on August 15 to set the exact time of the strike. The next day, twenty-two hundred workers from the Eagle and Phenix Mills stayed away from their jobs. By August 22, only 100–150 people were working in the mill.[45] Newberry feared for the safety of the strikers: "Public sentiment is running high over the death of last week. Police departments are preparing for trouble with both reinforcements and warfare material."[46] It was true. "Squads" of city police were reported standing at street corners in groups of eight to ten.[47]

No Turning Back

The action at Columbus dramatized the desperate state of the southern branch of the union, as word of events down south was brought to New York by the more than two hundred southern delegates who joined with delegates from the northern-based silk, wool, and hosiery industries for the UTW's biennial convention from August 13–August 16. At this gathering, members of northern-based UTW locals had their first face-to-face encounter with southern cotton mill workers.[48] Although northern UTW union locals had experienced the same deterioration of working conditions that southern cotton textile workers had, discrimination against local union members never achieved the systematic intensity that it had in southern mills.[49]

Southern delegates brought both an urgent plea and an example of courage to the audience. Appearing before the delegates badly beaten, union leader William Adcock of Huntsville proclaimed that he "would be glad to give my life to get better conditions for the southern textile workers."[50] Sol Stetin, a member of the New Jersey dyers' union at the time, remembered vividly the relative poverty of the southern unionists. "Seven or eight delegates from the South" would be packed in one hotel room, "with food all over the place, canned food, because they had no money, and they had to share their resources, and many of us made collections for the people that came from the South."[51]

The August UTW convention climaxed a new stage of the textile workers' conflict. Southern workers had built a momentum of such force that, as McMahon was to say after the convention, only the President of the United States would be able to stop a general strike. Over fifty general strike resolutions came before the delegates. When it came time for a vote, there was no doubt of the outcome. President McMahon called the strike a "dire necessity." In fact, the decision to stage a general strike had already, de facto, been made. As one delegate shouted out from the convention floor, 75 percent of cotton textile workers were "practically on strike now."[52] Support was so overwhelming that the strike vote was almost unanimous: 490 to 10.[53]

In terms of grievances, the UTW convention was a notable victory for southern workers. UTW President McMahon called the stretch-out "the main cause of the strike," and indicted the Bruere Board for its failure to act on workers' grievances. "Out of several hundred cases on the stretchout we have placed before the Board we haven't received one adjustment," Mc-Mahon said only days after the convention had ended. "On discrimination we can't get adjustments. People are fired and that's the end. Nothing has been done to combat the stretch-out evil. It is worse under the code than it was before."[54]

For his part, Gorman never hesitated to make clear at every possible opportunity that it was his membership that was forcing him to take such a defiant stand. Grimly he announced that the union had no alternative but to conduct the strike until a settlement that was satisfactory to the workers was reached.[55] The membership would permit no other course of action. "We are at a crossroads," Gorman had written in *The Textile Worker* that summer, "there is no turning back."[56]

9

ANATOMY OF A STRIKE

"The International had no money. Gorman, Fox, they didn't have anything in the worst way. They didn't have a staff. They didn't have people. And we were looking—anybody who could get up on a platform and talk, he became either an organizer or a leader." This is how the general strike was remembered by Joe Jacobs, who at the time was a young labor lawyer who helped bring relief to striking textile workers in Atlanta.[1] The prospect of coordinating a walkout in hundreds of mills scattered up and down the East Coast would have daunted the most well-equipped union. But this was a strike for which the UTW had not even prepared. With less than a million dollars in its treasury, the UTW's Strike Committee determined that the workers could hold out for two, possibly three weeks.[2] In a statement that raised the ire of southern employers, AFL southern representative George Googe claimed that the new federal policy of providing relief to unemployed striking workers would give the union the resources it needed to win. But few took this claim seriously, particularly in light of the existing opposition by local southern elites to dispensing federal aid to "unworthy" people.[3] Southern textile employers' local political influence almost guaranteed that when it came to feeding unemployed strikers, the union would be on its own.[4]

Gorman put up a brave front in the face of dire warnings that the strike was foolhardy. With the fierce commitment of the southern delegates firmly in his mind, the UTW vice president downplayed the importance of money and staff. "Remember," he said, "it is not money that wins strikes of this sort. The strike will be won by the spirit of the men and women who have invested their lives in this industry."[5] Nor did Gorman insist that the federal government support them, despite Googe's words to the contrary. In the tradition of classic AFL unionism, the UTW saw itself as abandoning union-government cooperation and staking its future on a simple test of economic strength between union and employer. As the garment union leader David Dubinsky had preached at the August UTW convention, textile workers could no longer rely on codes or the NRA: "It's ultimately up to the force of labor to attain its own ends."[6] Here was the traditional AFL posture of voluntarism, or self-reliance.

Southern millhands did not see the strike in this way. For them, union-ism came not out of the AFL tradition of voluntarism but rather out of the missionary spirit engendered by the NIRA and the New Deal. From the beginning of the New Deal in July 1933, the southern members of the UTW had seen themselves as righteous agents of New Deal justice. If federal government agents were no longer able, or willing, to enforce workers' vision of the New Deal, then workers would assume the burden of enforcing it themselves. Whatever else the strike was, it was also an attempt to make the NIRA a "living thing" in the textile mills of the South.

Southern unionists never doubted that—whatever the sins of NIRA bureaucrats—their version of justice was also Roosevelt's. Sporting American flags to legitimate their struggle, strikers took to the streets as the president's agents: "as long as the Stars and Stripes are over the White House we have a friend that will protect us."[7]

Nor did the general strike engender the same kind of trepidation for southern workers as it did for UTW leaders. For southern workers, the prospect of a general strike actually put them back on more familiar ground. Rather than engaging in formal appeals, filling out forms, attending hearings, and following protocol, southern millhands were returning to their traditional means of settling disputes with their employers: direct action. Through their time-honored tradition of swift justice, southern millhands hoped to enforce the Code better than a myriad of boards, agencies, or investigators had been able to do in over a year.

But southern unionists' moral fervor extended even beyond their commitment to the New Deal. Roy Lawrence, president of the North Carolina Federation of Labor, expressed the belief that striking workers were agents of a more universal justice. "The first strike on record was the strike in which Moses led the children of Israel out of Egypt. They too, struck against intolerable conditions, and it took them forty years to win that strike."[8] Echoing the words Paul Fuller applied to the Horse Creek Valley strike the previous October, union leader H. D. Lisk from Concord prayed to God to help the workers in their "battle for human justice." Lisk spoke at a mass meeting in Charlotte, North Carolina, on Sunday, September 2, a meeting the *New York Times* correspondent Joseph Shaplen described as indistinguishable from a religious gathering. "God is with us," declared Lisk, "and no power on earth can stand up against those who battle for the right."[9] The journalist W. R. Gaylord compared the striking Alabama workers to the early Christians, who, despite being persecuted by the Romans for their beliefs, "kept the faith," believing in "the coming of a New Day for the workers."[10] This powerful collective faith, combined with the southern union's organizational discipline and workers' community solidarity, gave the southern textile strike its enormous force.

Dimensions of the Strike in the South

How the ideological postures of southern workers and UTW leaders affected the strike's reception in Washington is a critical issue warranting close examination (see chapter 10). First, however, it is necessary to determine the strike's actual dimensions on the ground. The UTW's minimal staff and resources meant that, whatever front Gorman put on before the public, the major part of the strike coordination would have to take place with little help from the top. The character of the strike would be determined by the behavior of indigenous southern unionists. Yet southern workers were entering this climactic battle with their union organization as yet unfinished. Five years of union building, erected on a foundation of generations of community mutual aid and direct action, had created only partial solidarity.

To appreciate the task before southern unionists, it is useful to imagine three different measures of organizational strength in the textile South. In such towns as Charlotte, Columbia, Spartanburg, Dalton, and Huntsville, union support approached 100 percent, and employers had not engaged in relentless antiunion retaliation. At the other extreme were mills where unions had never taken root, and where employer control was so great that no amount of strike power could penetrate it. In between was a gray area, mills where some but not all workers had joined a local chapter of the UTW, and where the union's legitimacy had been contested throughout the year. Tactically, the general strike represented the commitment of southern unionists in solid union locals to shore up the strength of the union in the more vulnerable mills.

Another factor shaping the character of the strike was the vast geographical spread of the southern industry. In an era before wide use of telephones, union coordination was a particular challenge. As shall be seen, the peak of strike support did not occur until perhaps the middle of the second week. The walkout's power extended slowly from the core areas of union strength, its full dimension emerging over time.

Statistics can more graphically define this reality. During the first few days of the strike, about 25,000 out of a workforce of 60,000 walked out in Georgia; 29,000 out of 65,000 in South Carolina; and 71,000 out of 110,000 in North Carolina. To these numbers should be added about 20,000 who had walked out in Alabama in July, out of a workforce of 35–38,000 mill-hands. Roughly half of the southern textile workforce had left their jobs by the end of the first week of September.

By the end of the second week, as many as 44,000 out of 60,000 workers were off their jobs in Georgia. In South Carolina the numbers slowly built from 29,000 to 36,000 by the second week and finally to 38,000 by the third week of the strike. In North Carolina the number of workers on strike dropped from 71,000 to 62,000 by the end of the second week and remained near that level until the walkout ended. Altogether the number of workers participating in the walkout in the four southern textile states totaled 134,000 by September 5, 163,000 by the end of the first week, and 167,000 by the end of the second week. Including the approximately 7,000 workers who joined the strike in Tennessee, the number of workers on strike in the South topped 170,000, or just under two-thirds of the South's 272,000 textile workers.[11]

These raw numbers, however, reveal little about the patterns the strike took throughout the South. To determine how the southern union attempted to extend its power beyond the core of union strength, it is necessary to examine the dynamics in each southern textile state.

Claiming Territory in Alabama

The strike in Alabama, which had begun six weeks before the September 1 general strike date, provides an illuminating preview of the dynamics the strike would take throughout the South. The strength of the strike in northern Alabama is a powerful testament to the organizational accomplishments of unionized mills. In towns like Huntsville, Florence, Gadsden, Birmingham, Anniston, and Walker County, the union completely closed down the mills. In these towns, previous union organizing made worker solidarity strong enough that they endured even the kidnapping of union organizer John Dean without returning to their jobs.[12]

Outside of the "strike zone," however, was a different story. At Donald Comer's Avondale Mills, located in a ring of towns below Birmingham, manufacturers claimed rigid and absolute control. At the Avondale Mill in

Pell City, for example, twelve hundred workers were kept on the job by guards stationed around the mill, as one employee put it, "to keep any strangers from coming on the companys property," and by "signs that they have at our drinking fountains in the mill against the unions."[13] At some mills, guards were stationed as far as fifteen miles outside of town. The Alexander City Mills were guarded by the millhands themselves, who would "leave their regular job, go on duty as guard and make an extra shift as one of the guards." Anyone who talked "in favor of labor unions," according to a sympathetic local doctor, was laid off.[14]

Nor did the union have much of a chance on the Alabama side of the Chattahoochee Valley, along the eastern border of the state opposite Columbus, Georgia. At the onset of the Alabama strike, the mill in Opelika, Alabama, had staged a "Yes We Have No Union Parade," with 250 mill employees and fifty cars. The area had been surrounded with private deputies to prevent outsiders from causing trouble.[15] In Troup and Chambers Counties, home of West Point Manufacturing Company, "every way you looked you saw a guard or a spy." According to one observer, "they had bales of cotton piled up along the road and they would stop cars and search the people." One car "did not stop quick enough and they shot his tires off."[16]

The nationwide general strike in September offered textile strikers the opportunity to inject new energy into the Alabama battleground. On September 6, twenty-five carloads of unarmed Columbus strikers crossed the state border to Opelika in the hopes of getting the workers there to join the strike. But they quickly retreated when they were met by one hundred guards armed with shotguns, revolvers, clubs, and tear gas. Opelika workers never did join the 1934 strike.[17] Union and nonunion strongholds remained virtually unchanged in Alabama through the duration of the national walkout. Each side controlled clearly defined geographical territory that was tenaciously held for the duration of the conflict. As it turned out, this would be the case in the other southern textile states as well.

Claiming Territory in the Rest of the South

Textile unionists in the rest of the South would get an opportunity to symbolically demonstrate their strength on Labor Day, September 3. This holiday was the first practical day of the nationwide walkout, since the official strike date—midnight, September 1—was a Saturday. Would workers work on Labor Day, a holiday traditionally not recognized by southern employers?

The answer became apparent by early morning, as textile employers across much of the South closed their mills even before picket lines appeared.

In Gastonia, all but eight mills closed, while thousands of workers in Gastonia marched in the first Labor Day parade in the city's history. In nearby Belmont, a meeting between local union leaders and executives of mills had produced an agreement by a majority of the mills not to open on Labor Day.[18] The Crown Cotton Mill in Dalton, Georgia, closed while textile workers joined craft workers in a parade of fifteen hundred, stretching over eight city blocks.[19] Even Georgia mills "for the most part" observed the Labor Day holiday, albeit with uneven levels of enthusiasm. In Atlanta and Macon plants sat idle while workers paraded, while at Newnan, three hundred had to surround the Arnall Mill to shut it down when it tried to open.[20]

If Labor Day was a portent of the future power of the strike, the next day, September 4, that power was revealed. In Charlotte, Gastonia, and Durham, North Carolina, in Spartanburg and Columbia, South Carolina, in Augusta and Columbus, Georgia, and countless other mill towns where UTW locals had been organized, workers by the tens of thousands stayed

News accounts reported ten thousand people marching down Gastonia's main streets on Monday, September 3, 1934, in the city's first ever Labor Day Parade. (UPI/Corbis-Bettmann)

home, joining the approximately twenty thousand workers already on strike in Alabama.

Here was the core of the strike's strength. So strong was local union organization that workers in these textile communities had no need to appeal to the government for relief. Instead, workers received financial backing from local merchants. Strike leader John H. Payne from the Chadwick Hoskins Mill in Charlotte set up a commissary store where members of his union could get food during the strike. They had no trouble filling the store with potatoes, bread, beans, and vegetables from sympathetic grocers around the city. In Durham, North Carolina, merchants freely aided the strikers.[21] In Belmont, North Carolina, signs in shop windows read "Textile Union We Are Behind You 100%."[22] Belmont union members easily closed several mills simply by drawing up a petition signed by three thousand workers asking the mills to close.[23] In Columbia, South Carolina, the union was so strong it was hardly even necessary to picket. The *Columbia State* openly favored

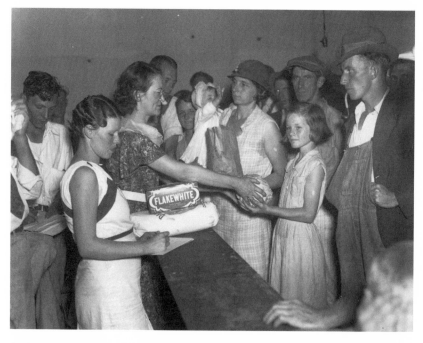

Strikers at the Knit Products Corporation in Belmont, North Carolina, receive food and other necessities at the headquarters of UTW Local 2159. These families received food for the duration of the strike. (UPI/Corbis-Bettmann)

Although men held the formal positions on the union strike committee, women played crucial roles in local organizing. Here, women strikers guard the gate at the Exposition Cotton Mill in Atlanta, Georgia, where the entire workforce of fifteen hundred joined the strike. (UPI/Corbis-Bettmann)

an increase in textile workers' wages and encouraged merchants to support the strike, noting that "business and workers are in the same boat." All Columbia mills closed by the fourth day of the strike.[24] In Gadsden, according to one participant, "We had people out in the country, they come in here with chickens, potatoes, and stuff like that. They helped us a lot. We didn't go hungry."[25] In Huntsville, Alabama, retail merchants petitioned Washington "to have differences of the textile strike now in progress here arbitrated and endeavor to effect settlement at once."[26] In all of these cases, the support for the mill workers from the merchants did not materialize out of the strike but had been built up over years. The support was as much a product as a source of union strength.

Where the union was strong, the strike was so calm that journalists yearned for something to happen. "The presence of only pickets who appear to be on a picnicking jaunt . . . has been a keen disappointment to the visiting newsreel men," reported one. "Time after time they have dashed hither and yon over the Carolinas . . . and nothing has happened anywhere."[27] At Crown Mills in Dalton, Georgia, mill workers experienced the strike as a picnic. Remembered one participant: "We had a ball."[28]

Contested Territory: The Flying Squadrons

Had unionized workers simply defended existing strongholds, however, the strike would have had little of the drama that eventually ensued. In order for the strike to be successful, workers understood that they needed to extend its reach beyond their areas of strength. Beginning September 4, therefore, in plants with little previous union organization, mill superintendents and workers were met by caravans of hundreds and occasionally thousands of textile workers who traveled the South's highways to spread the news of the strike and to close down the mills. Called "flying squadrons," this collection of men and women became the signature of the textile strike in the South.

From a tactical point of view, flying squadrons afforded the union a necessarily swift means of communication for a geographically far-flung workforce. They also implemented the union's strategic decision to force the closing of all mills, whether they were Code violators or not. "We've not come to make trouble, but you've got to close and stay closed," said the leader of one group of pickets who surrounded the Dunean Mills in Greenville, South Carolina.

But the flying squadrons also provoked a powerful response from mill owners, who flooded the offices of the southern governors with letters and telegrams describing the strikers as "ruthless marauders" who went from mill to mill "crushing doors, pulling switches, blocking gates, intimidating and closing plants," creating a "reign of terror" in the South.[29] B. B. Gossett called the strike situation "perhaps the gravest emergency which has confronted our people since Reconstruction Days."[30]

Union leaders took great pains to explain that the flying squadrons were engaged in peaceful picketing that lay completely within their constitutional rights. They pointed out, accurately, that the squadrons inflicted no harm to person or property. "We have been charged with all manner of coercion, intimidation, and violence," wrote John Howard Payne of Charlotte, "because zealous workers have formed groups and through peaceful picketing have closed some plants they have been called roving bands of bandits and numerous other things, but there is no grounds of proof of these charges."[31] The Gastonia attorney J. L. Hamme wrote to Governor Ehringhaus on behalf of fifty other people: "I have had some personal experience with this strike, have been on the scene of some of it and have yet to see anything like a show of violence."[32]

Considerable evidence supports the contention that the flying squadrons were not violent. "Movietone" newsreel footage of the closing of the Parkdale Mill in Gastonia shows a crowd of union supporters waiting quietly in the mill yard while a delegate negotiates with the mill manager a time to close the mill. Upon emerging from the building, the union leader speaks to the crowd about the mill superintendent: "This man is a responsible talking man. He's a fine man. He don't want to do nothing wrong. He is willing to shut down and the people turn off their motors and the people come out. And whenever we find people willing to do that, let's let it go at that." Workers cheered, and the mill was closed.[33]

But the characterization of the squadrons as "peaceful picketing" misses entirely their character as extralegal enforcers of justice. Swiftly, militantly, the squadrons were not only picketing but forcing the closing of the mills. At King's Mountain, a mill official witnessed the arrival of a caravan of autos and trucks carrying "at least two hundred or more people . . . yelling so loud I could scarcely hear my voice. . . . Their faces were white from apparent anger." When the mill official asked who was the leader of the group, "they yelled back they had no leaders. . . . They were like crazy men." The owner had wanted the mill to close at the end of the shift but the crowd insisted that it be done immediately. The owner asked for five minutes and it was granted to him.[34]

In Spindale, North Carolina, a crowd described as consisting of thousands of workers "invaded" the town "in trucks of all descriptions, moving vans, transfer trucks, automobiles and anything to ride on." Although they damaged no property, the crowd was "boisterous and loud in their shouts to the working people of Spindale to stop work, using very bad language, a large variety of vulgar, cursing terms to drive their point of argument to the spot. Women and men alike used very forcible cursing before our women and children." After closing Spencer Mills the flying squadron moved to Stonecutter Mills, "around which there is a strong metal fence; as they were refused entrance they said they would tear it down, that they had the measurements of the gates and had sufficient ropes and chairs with a wrecker derrick for automobiles to pull the gate and fence down and began backing the derrick near the fence."[35] As it turned out, the derrick was not necessary, for the owner agreed to shut the mill down. At this point, reported the *Charlotte Observer*, "the strikers rushed through the gates and became uncontrollable." Still, the paper admitted that "no damage was done."[36]

The squadrons provoked so much alarm that UTW leaders pleaded with workers to "put on the brakes," or "we're going to have the troops down on us."[37] But southern workers were reluctant to rein in their enthusiasm; despite their willing use of the UTW as their vehicle of protest, their goals were larger and more far-reaching than UTW leaders envisioned. The South

A "flying squadron" led to the closing of the Apalache Mill near Greer, South Carolina, on September 5, 1934. (UPI/Corbis-Bettmann)

was witnessing textile workers celebrating, often joyously, their claim on the New South's public space. Women also figured prominently in the flying squadrons, shouting as well as parading around the mills. Taking to the streets in their newly available automobiles, textile workers not only challenged the economic power of the mills, but the southern social order as well.

In the end, no one could deny that the squadrons were extremely effective in extending the reach of the strike beyond the centers of union strength. Many mills closed down at the first appearance of the squadrons.[38] Even when the mill refused to close, the squadrons' visits were persuasive. When the presence of a crowd of five to seven hundred strikers failed to close the Gem Yarn Mill, squadron leader John Howard Payne received permission to go into the plant and ask workers why they wouldn't come out. Although Payne achieved no immediate results, the next morning so few reported for duty that the mill was unable to begin operation.[39] Strikers even closed the Loray Mill, scene of the Communist-led strike in 1929. Hundreds of workers from Gastonia and nearby Shelby and Charlotte surrounded the plant and prevented workers from entering. By the end of the week, all 104 mills in Gaston County had closed, blanketing the area with an eerie silence. It was a triumphant symbol of the organizational strength of the textile workers union.[40]

A similar dynamic occurred in the other textile states. In South Carolina, workers formed a giant rambling parade that began in Spartanburg and travelled through tiny mill villages toward Greenville, picking up support until it totalled two thousand persons.[41] In Georgia, according to former union official Joe Jacobs, "We'd get a group together, get somebody with an American flag—we always had a flag—march down the road, we'd start marching around the mill, singing all the two-three union songs. We'd go round and round and round. A few of them would come out after a while, a few more, and a few more. And then you'd begin to hear the motors in the mill going off. And eventually they went off. And when they did, everybody clapped."[42]

The strike in the North shared many of the characteristics of the strike in the South. The walkout gathered momentum slowly, building as it became clear to the more timid that it was a serious effort. In many areas the mills closed peacefully. The country witnessed the strike's most violent encounters between workers and troops in Rhode Island, where full-scale rioting prompted the governor not only to call out the National Guard but to demand federal intervention. By the middle of the third week, however, the strike's front lines, both north and south, remained intact. A survey by the Associated Press counted 421,000 workers idle nationwide, which actually represented a slight increase over the previous week.[43]

Employer Strongholds

If workers in "union territory" shut down their workplaces completely, inside manufacturer-controlled territory was a very different story. Almost without exception, workers at nonstriking mills were kept at work by armed guards. Many accounts of the general strike have focused on the role played by the National Guard in stemming the tide of the walkout. Despite the crucial role of the National Guard, however, its size—amounting to seventeen hundred in South Carolina and twenty-three hundred in North Carolina—was actually quite limited.[44] The use of "sheriff's deputies" and private guards was a far more serious employer tool. The total count—fifteen thousand in the Carolinas—is staggering. One mill in Greensboro, North Carolina, reportedly had so many guards that "unofficially there was a guard for every shift position."[45]

Police protection made it possible for fearful workers or workers loyal to their supervisors to cross picket lines.[46] In Kannapolis, North Carolina, center of the Cannon empire, twelve hundred pickets were forced to turn back by a force of two military companies supplemented by ninety-nine "sheriff's deputies" with shotguns stationed at every entrance to the mill.[47] In Laurinburg, North Carolina, sheriff's deputies and private guards pushed pickets so far away from the Waverly Mill that strikebreakers were easily brought in to run it. In a devastating blow to morale, the Waverly Mill ran "full force" during the national strike.[48] Horse Creek Valley mills remained open and about half-staffed, while across the river, police protection made it possible for a partial single shift at three of the Augusta mills.[49] At the Pepperell Mill in Lindale, Georgia, just outside of Rome in the northwest corner of the state, the superintendent kept the mills running by deputizing members of the mill baseball team, adding two hundred guards to the regular security force, and arming them with clubs manufactured in the mill's own carpentry shop.[50]

Fragile outposts of unionism or nonunionism in "enemy" territory sometimes survived the organized strength of the opposite side. One such union outpost was the Dunean Mill in Greenville. So powerful was the militia presence in Greenville that out of thirteen thousand workers, only fifteen hundred stayed out during the strike.[51] When 75 percent of the workers at the Dunean Mill defied the odds and struck the first day of the September strike, the state sent 425 National Guardsmen equipped with helmets, fire

Picketers at the Cannon Mill in Concord, North Carolina, jeer at two nonstriking workers as they arrive at the mill for work on September 8. The Cannon Mills were protected by two companies of the National Guard as well as ninety-nine "sheriff's deputies." (UPI/Corbis-Bettmann)

hoses, tear gas, submachine guns, and orders to "shoot to kill" if necessary. "This is the hard-boiled company of the state," said the Guard captain to the workers.[52]

Yet in this case the troops were not powerful enough to get the workers to return to work. When a flying squadron arrived to reinforce the Dunean strikers, the management decided not to force the issue, but to close the mill to avoid bloodshed.[53] For the duration of the strike, the Dunean Mill remained the scene of daily tension as National Guardsmen formed a line on the mill side of the road to keep pickets from advancing, while pickets formed a line on the opposite side of the road to keep scabs from going in the mill. Picketer Ollie Hopkins remembered that the militia "began to push us gradually further away from the mill," until all they could do was "stand by and watch the thugs scare the more timid workers into the mills."[54] Still, the Dunean Mill never did get a full complement of workers.

The union standoff at the Dunean Mill mirrored, with the sides reversed, the situation at the Loray Mill in Gastonia. Gaston County was a union stronghold: despite a "formidable array" of soldiers and deputies in Gaston County, strikers "held their lines without difficulty."[55] The Loray Mill, however, was the exception. While pickets had closed the Loray Mill on the first day of the strike, the shutdown did not endure. The mill opened a week later, after the management persuaded the governor to send the National Guard to the mill. In the interest of preventing violence to themselves, the pickets retreated.[56] But they remained on duty during the entire strike period. Tension between guardsmen and strikers heightened as the pickets taunted the militia—largely young, frightened, and occasionally trigger-happy boys—calling them "Boy Scouts" and "Tin Soldiers." Provoked, the guards responded by advancing with their bayonets. Peace was restored only when a mediator intervened.[57] The tension caused by enemy footholds in such clearly defined "territories" suggests how polarized the two sides had become.

In other regions, however, efforts to avoid violence were not as successful. The conflict in Georgia was especially volatile. In Macon, UTW organizer J. Ralph Gay was arrested and put in jail under $75,000 bail; in Porterdale, strikers trying to prevent a train from entering a plant were "driven off the tracks with a fire hose" and arrested; in Cedartown, eight were arrested on charges of rioting.[58] The first death since Sanders was killed in Columbus in August occurred in Trion, Georgia, on Wednesday, September 5. A mill guard and a foundry worker were killed and more than twenty others were wounded in a battle that erupted between the Trion Cotton Mill's forty-six company guards and a flying squadron of strike sympathiz-

At the Trenton Mill in Gastonia, North Carolina, National Guardsmen drive back strikers attempting to picket the plant and prevent its reopening. By September 12, four out of sixty mills in Gastonia were reopened by the National Guard, including the Loray Mill, site of the 1929 Communist-led strike. (UPI/Corbis-Bettmann)

ers from nearby Rome. That same day a mill guard killed two pickets in Augusta, Georgia.[59]

The worst bloodshed of the conflict occurred in South Carolina. Mill guards stationed inside the Chiquola Mill at Honea Path killed seven union members out of a crowd of hundreds in the mill yard and injured over seventy-five others as they fled. (The Honea Path killings will be discussed in detail in the next chapter.) The only death in North Carolina occurred in Belmont on September 18. National Guardsmen had been ordered to disperse a crowd gathering across the street from the Knit Products Mill. As one guardsman advanced, he got into a scuffle with a worker, Ernest Riley, and inadvertently stabbed him with his bayonet.[60] Added to Sanders's death in Columbus and the killing of two additional strikers in the North, these events brought the total number of deaths as a result of the conflict to fifteen. For some textile workers, the strike resembled a war.

The State Militia

Given the overwhelming use of private guards and sheriff's deputies during the walkout, the role of the National Guard can be overstressed. However the calling of the guard does reveal the degree to which southern political leaders complied with manufacturer demands. In North Carolina, Governor Ehringhaus made an initial effort to show an even hand, waiting three days before finally calling out the militia to prevent "intimidation" and "coercion" by roving groups of strikers.[61] State troops in North Carolina were sent only to those gray areas of territory, where the union had tried but had been unable to close the mills altogether, or where employers had been unable to secure "sufficient capable deputites" from the local population. Troops went to Marion, scene of the 1930 defeat of the union and murder of six workers, to Kannapolis and Concord, home of the Cannon mill chain (and not since World War I a home to unions), and to Greensboro, where for nine years the Cone Mills had successfully resisted several attempts by workers to unionize. Guardsmen also helped mills stay open in Henderson, North Carolina, scene of a failed strike in 1927.[62] Troops also went to Spindale, creating a climate Paul Christopher described as equivalent to martial law. "One can't even get in the Post Office without first being searched and identified," he wrote.[63] In all these places the union had been weakened by an earlier defeat; the presence of the National Guard forced the opening of such mills.[64]

By contrast, South Carolina's Governor Ibra Blackwood did not even wait for a pretext to use the state militia. Three days before the national strike even began, state troops were escorting workers into Seneca's Lonsdale Mill, which strikers had kept closed since mid-July. Local union leaders pointed out in vain that there had been no violence and that state officials had ignored the local sheriff, who had been handling the situation and had not requested help.[65] But Blackwood insisted that there was "immediate peril" and that a "grave situation" existed. By the second day of the nationwide strike, Blackwood had called out eight companies of the National Guard to Greenville, the center of antiunionism in the state. He claimed that the state was suffering a "ruthless and insolent invasion" by groups "bent on illegal and destructive enterprises," a statement that appeared to ignore the fact that the flying squadrons in South Carolina originated in Spartanburg with unarmed, native South Carolinians.[66]

Remarkably, the Georgia militia was nowhere to be seen, at least at first. Despite a flood of requests from mill owners, Georgia's Governor Eugene

Talmadge refused to send troops, forcing centers of union opposition, such as the Bibb Mills and the Goodyear Plant at Cedartown, to close. By the end of the first week, over half of Georgia's sixty thousand mill workers were not at their jobs. By the end of the second week the number had increased to forty thousand. Despite the lack of a strong UTW presence in Georgia, the workers appeared to have achieved for themselves a remarkably strong position.

Talmadge's refusal to send in troops appears highly unusual given the speed with which the governors of North and South Carolina deployed the militia in their states. In fact, however, the explanation is fairly straightforward. Talmadge was running for re-election on Wednesday, September 12, and he wanted the support of the state's textile workers. Responding to numerous mill owners' requests, Talmadge replied that "no giant corporation or big interest will ever dictate to me what to do while I am the Governor."[67] Because of his stand, many textile workers supported the governor in his bid

Strikers picket the Sargeant Mill in Newnan, Georgia, on September 5, 1934, during the first week of the walkout. Strikers are holding picker sticks, which are used in the weaving process. The situation remained peaceful until September 17, when Governor Talmadge declared martial law. Among the first to be arrested were workers from Newnan travelling to nearby mills. (UPI/Corbis-Bettmann)

for re-election. Some even helped campaign for him.[68] When the election came, Talmadge won by a landslide vote.

On the Friday before the election, however, the governor had met with leaders of the most important Georgia textile firms and accepted a $20,000 campaign contribution in return for a promise that he would call out the National Guard after the election was over. Over the weekend, secret preparations were made to deploy troops the following week. Following the election, Talmadge declared a state of martial law and announced that the National Guard would be sent to the strike zone. Over the next several days, four thousand troops were dispatched in what one student of the subject has called "the largest peacetime mobilization in the state's history."[69] In the most celebrated troop action, the National Guard arrested sixteen women and 112 men near Newnan, Georgia, along the western border of the state in the Chattahoochee Valley. They were taken to Fort McPherson near Atlanta and placed in an outdoor camp with a barbed wire fence that was later used to house German prisoners of war during World War II. The prison site has since achieved legendary status in textile lore as a "concentration camp" for the textile workers.

The declaration of martial law in Georgia was a serious blow to the integrity of the strike. At first, the damage was far less severe than observers were led to expect. The next day only eleven of Georgia's mills reopened. But because all groups of textile workers seen travelling from mill to mill were now subject to arrest, the communications network between strikers in Georgia mill towns began to break down. Bewildered, some strikers in outlying Georgia mills voted to return to their jobs even though no one had indicated that the strike was over.[70] Augusta UTW organizer J. Ralph Gay was arrested and placed in jail with an astronomical $75,000 bail. Strike leaders told the press that the organization in Georgia had been "badly shaken."[71] By September 19, twenty-four mills altogether had reopened in Georgia, and between five thousand and seventy-five hundred more workers in the state had returned to work. This brought the number of Georgia workers who returned to their jobs close to ten thousand.[72] By September 20, a majority of Georgia workers were still away from their jobs, but organizers were afraid. The union, they said, was "virtually unable to offer any organized resistance" to the "anti-strike drive."[73]

Outside of Georgia, however, the strike lines did not weaken. No troops were called out in Alabama; in that state, mills that had closed in July remained closed. In North and South Carolina, troops forced the reopening of only a handful of mills; only about four thousand workers returned to work. H. F. La Cons, of Columbia, South Carolina, told the press that the strike would continue "until we win or starve to death."[74] It remained to be seen whether the firmer hold of textile unionists in the other southern states could offset the power of the antiunion forces in Georgia.

A Divided Employer Response

No account of the strength of the strike would be complete without some attempt to gauge the response of the industry itself. Under normal circumstances, no southern textile manufacturer would have considered recognizing a union in his mill. But these were extraordinary times. Despite the fierce rejection of the southern strike force in nonunion strongholds, the amazing spectacle of over 170,000 southern workers off their jobs gave manufacturers pause.

The industry had always been divided along sectional lines over the value of a union for creating industry-wide stability. Self-styled "enlightened" mill owners from New England, who already had a relationship with the UTW, had a lot to gain from the rising southern standards that would result from a successful strike. "All enlightened mill owners know that you are fighting for a reasonable and just cause," the prominent northern mill owner Robert McCandlers reportedly told striking workers.[75] The *New Republic* spoke of "this large group of Northern manufacturers who cannot altogether regret the strike, and who may in fact indirectly have abetted it."[76] In fact, the strike so obviously worked to the competitive advantage of New England mills that some southern manufacturers believed that New England mill owners had "fostered and engineered" the strike."[77]

But sentiment against so-called code chislers extended to some southern manufacturers as well. This was particularly true of what Turner Battle, the assistant to Secretary of Labor Perkins, called "the reputable manufacturers of the South," who had paid higher wages to their workforces only to find their competitors undercutting them, or who had operated with regular workloads only to find their competitors stretching out their workers, increasing productivity, and cutting into their market. Although such southern manufacturers had "opposed the organization of their mills in the past," Battle commented, they "would now like to see the industry 100% organized in preference to reverting to the unfair competition of two years ago, much of which still continues."[78] The frantic calls for the National Guard in the southern states came from a powerful and militant segment of southern manufacturers, but not all. "Some of the finest men that I know are among the textile manufacturers of this County," the Gastonia attorney J. L. Hamme wrote to North Carolina Governor Ehringhaus; on the other hand, his re-

gion also included "some of the most unprincipled scoundrels. . . . I can almost tell you just whom has written you or wired you for troops."[79] Privately,
North Carolina mill owner O. Max Gardner called the strike a "catastro-
phe" and concluded that its resolution could be "extremely embarrassing to
the industry." "I am terribly afraid," he wrote to his superintendent O. M.
Mull, "that we now have a condition confronting the South that will set us
back as long as you and I live, and longer."[80] Cognizant of the number of
times in recent memory that repression had brought negative publicity to
the industry, Gardner simply closed his plant for the duration of the strike.
Southern mill owners were thus scarcely united in a decision to kill the union
once and for all.

Had the resolution of the strike, therefore, taken place on the ground
in proportion to the levels of pressure and resistance in the South, one can
imagine a partial, if fragmented, victory, probably not significantly different in kind from the concessions made to striking workers in South Carolina in 1929. But 1934 was different. Thanks to economic hard times and
the persistent reality of the stretch-out, workers had recognized that their
fates were linked to the ability of the government to regulate the industry.
Thus workers at strong and weak mills had thrown their lots together in favor
of a strong NIRA. Whatever pressure strikers had created on the ground,
they were looking to Washington D.C., home of the New Deal, for the resolution of their strike.

But the CTI, as the power behind the Code Authority, also resided in
Washington, D.C. The arch enemy of the textile strikers exerted power from
inside the home of the workers' most inspirational friend. The New Deal
was at war with itself.

10

WHICH SIDE ARE YOU ON?

The New Deal had always been more than a set of policies and procedures, duly enacted by legislators in Washington. It was also the words spoken by President Roosevelt when he went over the heads of legislators and local politicians and, by means of his radio broadcasts, spoke directly to the people. The radio and workers' letters had formed a call and response, giving voice to a flood of aspirations from working people previously barred from expression through traditional politics. Across the country thousands of workers had joined unions because they believed that their version of justice was the same as Roosevelt's. Through their own involvement, citizens had in fact brought to life the ideas of justice they had first heard as New Deal rhetoric. These ideas now had a force of their own in the land.

But what was that vision? Americans had heard it over and over again in speeches and press releases: to "put people back to work." To anyone who cared to investigate, the general textile strike was occurring because textile mills were not fulfilling this basic goal. This was particularly obvious to southern citizens who were themselves not textile workers but who lived in textile districts. "The mills here have not taken on more people as the NRA intended," wrote a Statesville, North Carolina, woman, who also described how the mills had overworked some and laid off others.[1] The president-elect of the American Legion Auxiliary in Martin County, North Carolina, wrote: "There are entirely too many people out of employment and on relief rolls who are entitled to an opportunity to earn an honest livelihood for any thoughtful unselfish person to lean entirely to the side of the manufacturers in this textile strike."[2] J. L. Hamme, an attorney from Gastonia, wrote:

"There is no doubt but that the strikers of this community are acting in the only possible manner in which the benefits of the NRA may be realized."[3] Mr. and Mrs. J. Q. Thornton, sellers of grain and feedstuffs for animals, stressed that they were "in no way" connected to the textile industry, but felt that it was "doubly not right for these large Industries to force their men into time and a half or double time production in order to work and make the minimum wage and there might not have been near the trouble there has been if the mills had not practised this stretch-out system."[4] For such observers, the Code violations were not only sapping textile workers' own strength, but that of the NIRA itself.

But in 1934 the southern mills were a long way, physically and psychologically, from Washington. Those men and women who believed so fervently in the NIRA—the strikers and their supporters in the South—failed to realize that the goal of putting people back to work was not, in a strictly legal sense, a goal of the NIRA. The letters and the radio broadcasts existed on a plane entirely divorced from the legal center of power. In Washington, negotiations over the shape of NIRA took place behind the scenes, with southern politicians representing elite classes, and with the UTW and well-meaning reformers purporting to speak on textile workers' behalf. Issues were not employment or the burdens of work, but stability and profits for industry, purchasing power for merchants, financiers, and economists, and institutionalized power for unions. The Cotton Textile Code had created a federal bureaucracy that, although it cloaked itself in the rhetoric of the New Deal, was pursuing policies directly contrary to that rhetoric. Nothing in the Cotton Textile Code promised workers a job, nor did it even promise an end to the stretch-out. This was the larger hypocrisy of the early New Deal, of which the Bruere Board was only the most visible manifestation. In this crucial aspect, the NIRA's rhetorical and legal reality were completely different. A program that the president had claimed would put people back to work was actually killing them on the job or laying them off.

It took a year of struggle, and the amassing of thousands of workers in the textile industry, to expose this hypocrisy. In the general textile strike the channels of public participation—letters, strikes, radio speeches—finally confronted the channels of bureaucracy and legislation out of which the NIRA had been born. No wonder the *New York Times* called the textile strike "the gravest strike threat that has confronted the Roosevelt administration in the last year."[5]

To win their strike, therefore, southern textile workers had to create the political pressure necessary to give the government in Washington the backbone to reform itself—to cut out of the New Deal those forces sapping its strength—and to implement workers' vision of a true New Deal. The winning of this strike did not depend only on workers' demonstration of solidarity on the ground. It was enough, perhaps, that grassroots actions had finally gotten textile workers' dissatisfaction out into the open. The issue was how the walkout would be interpreted in Washington. The '34 strike would test whether a wide spectrum of individuals and groups in power in Washington were committed to the vision of the New Deal that the American citizens themselves had tried to bring to life.

It is a tribute to the integrity of UTW leaders that, to the end, they stayed true to the demands of the southern membership to end the stretch-out. But the UTW could not combat the misunderstandings and deliberate misinterpretations that others put on textile strikers' objectives. Even before the strike began its meaning became distorted, as inside the New Deal administration, politicians, administrators, and labor leaders with their own interests or agendas responded to the strike's threat. Without honest brokers, southern textile workers suffered from a terrible failure of communication. In short order the fundamental message of the general textile strike was lost. The door was open for the most vigorous opponent of the strikers' objectives, the Cotton Textile Institute, to redefine the strike in terms that fully obscured the morality or justice of its cause. The result is a cruel irony: while southern workers were certain that their actions constituted a most ardent defense of Roosevelt's programs, members of the industry insisted the opposite, that this strike was, "more than any other in our history . . . a strike against the government itself."[6]

Uncertain Allies

Throughout the ranks of organized labor, the threat of the textile strike instilled a deep unease, as it promised to gravely undermine the cozy relationship between labor leaders and the government that existed inside the Roosevelt administration. AFL President William Green provided only lip service in support of the walkout, promising financial support but delaying his efforts until it was too late.[7] Nor were southern AFL leaders strong supporters. Reflecting the traditional antagonism between southern craft unions and textile labor, Alabama State Federation Secretary W. O. Hare put his organization squarely against the strike until forced by the strikers themselves to retract his statement. The *Birmingham Labor Advocate* also opposed the Alabama strike. "Who started this textile strike, and why?" it asked. "It is the government's, not the workers' responsibility to enforce the NRA."[8]

Inside the New Deal, administrators worried that the strike would disrupt income for the workers and a steady flow of profits for business so essential to the success of the NRA. What would happen to plans for increased purchasing power if the economy was disturbed by a labor dispute of such magnitude? Turner Battle, the assistant to Secretary of Labor Perkins and a prominent southerner, reported fears in the South that if the textile strike succeeded there would be "strikes in many more industries" and that this would "seriously retard the steady increase in payrolls that has been evidenced since March, 1933."[9] Could the textile workers' complaint truly be so serious as to upset the entire recovery program? Secretary of Labor Perkins simply avoided mentioning the strike altogether in her Labor Day speech on September 3, speaking instead about the need for the "cooperation of labor" in policies and programs that were "in the interest of all people."[10]

For President Roosevelt, the impending strike had different but equally disconcerting implications. It was politically damaging for a president who was widely considered to be a friend of the working people not to come to the aid of a demonstration of these proportions in support of his programs. But inside Washington, Roosevelt's political power rested not on the support of southern workers, but on the support of of its elites, who were represented by southern congressmen on over half of the congressional committee chairmanships. Besides, Roosevelt simply could not take seriously the hypothesis that southern mill owners were as heartless as the strikers were portraying them to be. Secretary of Labor Perkins had made certain that the president was familiar with the benevolent practices of southern mill owners like Donald Comer. In addition, southern mill owners were among Roosevelt's acquaintances in Warm Springs, Georgia, where he often spent his holidays. On occasion, Roosevelt reportedly relaxed at "the magnificent country home of Cason Callaway," owner of Callaway Mills in LaGrange, Georgia.[11] One is left with the impression that the president did not believe these men to be capable of the kind of cruelty that workers spoke of when they talked about the stretch-out and discrimination. No doubt the president believed such practices existed, but in his mind they could not have been as widespread as the union was claiming. Some suggested that the strike was being fomented by Socialists and, since the leader of the Socialist Party, Norman Thomas, had spoken to the UTW convention in August, Roosevelt was of a mind to believe it.[12]

Therefore, when North Carolina Congressman Josiah Bailey asked Roosevelt not "to thrust the Federal Governnment" into what he called "our situation," Roosevelt obliged as much as he could.[13] No federal troops were sent to the textile battlegrounds, nor would the president require collective bargaining or even support an arbitrated settlement.

Roosevelt was aware that in the North, however, businesses willing to work with unions were at the heart of his New Deal political coalition. He therefore appointed liberal John Winant, a former New Hampshire governor who in his early days had fought vigorously for the forty-eight-hour week in the New England mills, to chair a committee to study the issues raised by the strike and recommend a course of action.

The UTW on the Defensive

From the very beginning, Code Authority Chair George Sloan understood that it was crucial how the strike was to be viewed. He even hired the NRA's top public relations spokesperson to work for him, assuming that, as always, if the industry could only conceal reality and reinterpret what was going on, they could win. With an uncanny eye for the union's weak spot, Sloan attacked the textile strike as a strike against the government itself.[14] The UTW position was an attempt at "law-making by strike," he challenged; the situation was "intolerable."[15]

Sloan had intended his statement to apply to the union's demand that manufacturers pay forty hours' wages even though the work week had been curtailed to thirty hours. Since this change could be legally accomplished only through action by the Code Authority, Sloan was right: the textile strike was a strike against the government. But the walkout was a strike against the government in a much broader sense, an implication that Sloan did not intend. Workers were staging a last-ditch attempt to stave off the destruction of their union, a destruction abetted by the government itself, that is, by the Code Authority and the Bruere Board. This was the secret that the strike threatened to expose and that Sloan was determined to conceal: that forces inside the government were undermining everything that, from the workers' point of view, the New Deal was trying to achieve.

Sloan's accusation created a perfect opportunity for Gorman to reveal the strikers' larger vision and to challenge the New Deal government to measure up to that vision. But the UTW leader did not do this. To the contrary, no accusation could have been more painful to an ambitious labor leader in the early New Deal than the accusation that the strike was a strike against the government. Baited by the charge, Gorman staged a tactical retreat, calling Sloan's statement a "deliberate attempt to mislead and confuse the issue."[16] Defensively and somewhat disingenuously, Gorman downplayed the union's dispute with the government: "I emphasize to you that we are striking against the management of the industry. . . . Surely the government does not own the mills. They are privately owned, mostly by corporations."[17]

Gorman was forced to confront the UTW's dispute with the NIRA bureaucracy, however, when he rejected an offer of mediation extended by Robert Bruere. In his letter of refusal Gorman insisted that the UTW had no intention of having anything further to do with Bruere. "We should be unfaithful to the thousands of our members who have suffered through the delays and indecision of the board if we were to submit our present crisis to the same board." Still, Gorman tried to sidestep the issue of the UTW's experience with the Bruere Board. "This is not the occasion to detail our disappointment with the operation of the system of industrial relations boards originally set up under the Cotton Textile Code," Gorman wrote. "Suffice it to say that though the national board was set up particularly 'to make proper provision with regard to the stretch-out,' in an entire year it has not begun to control this greatest of our problems. How could we have confidence under such circumstances?"[18]

Even such mild rebuke had instant repercussions, revealing why the UTW was leery of directly confronting the Roosevelt administration with its complicity in the previous years' events. As New Dealers saw it, Gorman was criticizing the National Labor Board! "Of course that could not be true," replied Gorman.[19] Gorman replied to the criticism in a tone of weariness that suggested defeat before he had even begun. "I suppose we have submitted more than 2,000 cases to Chairman Bruere, with results so small as to be just about negligible," he wrote. "We are plenty tired of that, and our membership throughout the cotton textile region is determined there shall be no more of it. I wonder whether the Bruere Board procedure is generally understood. I know of nothing like it."[20]

This was, indeed, the point. The Bruere Board procedure had not been generally understood. Thanks to the sophisticated leadership of Bruere, its existence was hardly known to people outside the textile industry. Its apparent similarity in function to the National Labor Board caused even greater confusion, for the chairman of the National Labor Board, Senator Robert Wagner, was among labor's greatest champions. If the textile workers were challenging the integrity of the NLB, what hope was there for institutional reform for working people inside the Roosevelt administration?

From the point of view of the UTW leadership, the enormity of the challenge of the general strike was now clear. How to justify to people unfamiliar with the tumultuous events of the past year the workers' apparent lack of gratitude for all that the NRA had done? How to penetrate the edifice of goodwill created by the Cotton Textile Code Authority's yearlong public relations campaign? If the public did not understand the means by which textile workers' grievances had been silenced for the past year, the strikers had no credibility. But the UTW leadership avoided any statement of grievance that directly criticized the government. Inevitably, the full nature of the textile workers' grievances was simply not clear. Gorman found himself responding to suggestions that the textile strike was "a bolt out of the blue."[21]

Losing Control of the Agenda

Labor leaders and NRA administrators with their own agendas took advantage of the apparent confusion over what the textile workers wanted, redefining the strike in a manner that once again diffused the strikers' message. AFL President Green boldly announced the chief slogan of the strike to be: "The company union must go."[22] Such a demand had never even been articulated by the union. Green also bluntly reinterpreted the UTW's actual demands to suggest cooperation rather than confrontation with the government. According to Green, the UTW was striking to *win* labor representation on NRA bodies. "That is in line with the consistent position we have held," Green said the day after the strike vote.[23] Strategically speaking, Green was at the stage McMahon was at before the June strike. The hosiery leader Emil Rieve similarly feared a frontal attack on the integrity of the NIRA, preferring an insider's approach to gaining power. "Rather than withdraw from the NRA," he had said at the UTW convention, "we need to secure control, for experience has shown that control can produce results."[24]

NRA administrators twisted the union's objectives even further. According to Breure, NRA Labor Advisor Sidney Hillman had suggested that "this talk about stretch-out" was "nonsense." Bruere claimed that, for Hillman, the chief issue in the textile industry was the need for a reduction in hours.[25] AFL southern representative George Googe added his cynical explanation of the strike, perhaps revealing more about his own motivations than he did about those of McMahon and Gorman. The strike, he said, was "purely a political maneuver on the part of McMahon and Gorman whose positions of leadership were threatened because of their failure to maintain membership."[26]

Lost in this reshaping of the strike's goals was southern workers' basic dissatisfaction with the federal government's enforcement of the law. Indeed, in the coverage of the UTW convention in the *New York Times*, the North Carolinians' boycott of Board Chair Theodore Johnson appeared as a separate article, apparently unrelated to the larger reasons for the general strike.[27] Such facile reinterpretations of the workers' demands suggest how much counterpressure ordinary union members had to put their leaders simply to ensure that they stayed true to their concerns.

And yet, in the face of overwhelming pressure to "cooperate" with the NRA, Gorman had finally put the UTW on record in opposition to the Code Authority's front line of defense against labor insurgency: the Bruere Board. Textile workers' actual success in holding the lines of the strike ensured that Gorman would keep his promise. But this was the limit of the UTW's militancy. The Bruere Board would be sacrificed, excised like a diseased part of an otherwise healthy body. Larger issues regarding the true nature of the New Deal experiment would remain unexamined. Labor leaders would retain their standing as honorable partners in the NRA. As far as the UTW's relationship with the government was concerned, the broad outlines of what a resolution of the general strike might look like had been determined before the strike had officially begun.

Honea Path

The tenuous support for the strike in Washington was not only due to deliberate misinformation. Years of myths about southern textile workers had worked their mischief, especially on observers far from the southern piedmont (although these viewpoints were certainly still alive and well among constituencies in the South). It was hard to overcome the belief that southern mill workers were weak. Weren't they sickly, barefoot women and children, victims of a backward "poor white" culture? How could such a people wage a successful strike? Equally damaging impressions—that southern mill workers were disorderly and potentially violent, incapable of a disciplined labor protest—often took hold when observers saw angry southern mill workers on the picket line. There was also the myth that southern workers were simply incapable of waging such a protest on their own; "outsiders" must have provoked it.

How these myths reaped their inevitable harvest can be seen in the public reaction to the murder of six workers at the Chiquola Mill in Honea Path, South Carolina, on September 6. So controversial were these murders that it is important to determine exactly what happened.[28]

A tiny mill village located southeast of Anderson, South Carolina, Honea Path was largely isolated from the growing tide of unionism in the South prompted by the NIRA. Workers' resentment came out of a frustration less with the stretch-out than with the control exercised by the mill over people's personal lives. Emphasizing that control with a certain starkness, the superintendent of the mill, Dan Beacham, was also the town's mayor.

The lack of a galvanizing issue around which to rally workers severely weakened the union at Chiquola Mill. Estimates vary, but perhaps half of the workers in the plant were UTW members. Workers who opposed the UTW feared that unionism would undermine whatever favored positions they had acquired through loyalty to the mill management. The mill was ripe for the kind of divisive tactics pioneered in South Carolina by mill owners at Piedmont and later in Seneca—except that in Honea Path there was no need for the National Guard. Instead, the company simply hired and armed from fifty to seventy-five deputies to guard the mill.

Tension began building in the pre-dawn hours of September 6. The newly deputized policemen had been given instructions not to "knuckle down" to the strikers. By dawn, a handful of armed officers had already stationed themselves inside the mill. Meanwhile, strikers from the neighboring mill villages of Belton and Ware Shoals had travelled to Honea Path the night before in the hopes of seeing the mill closed down the next morning. Many of the strikers stayed up all night, excited by the events taking place around them. By six A.M. the yard was filled with fifty to seventy-five union members hoping to prevent that day's workforce from entering the mill. Nonunion workers also began to gather, not knowing whether they would work that day or not. As tension built, the chief of police separated the two crowds, union and nonunion, and told each side to stay where they were.

A resident who was a young boy at the time remembered what happened next: "So a few minutes later we see a fellow [inside the mill] going down through the mill weave room throwing out brand new picker sticks for the people that didn't belong to the union." (Picker sticks were long sticks used in the process of setting up the looms for weaving.) The picker sticks were being handed out the windows to nonunion members, but some union members got ahold of them. In fact, a fistfight took place over the picker sticks. One of the union members who got ahold of a picker stick was a man named Shaw.

The observer continued his story: "I was right at the mill door. Well, directly here comes Mr. Cummings, fellow, an old man. He says, 'Ain't no damn son of a bitch gonna keep me out of that mill.' Well the fellow Shaw hit him right back of the head with a picker stick and knocked him right at my feet. Knocked him flat. His eyes just about that big, and I thought he'd killed him. I backed off from him, and then Mr. Rob Calvert, he started from the office out there and Lee met him." Mr. Calvert was an officer of the mill. Lee was Lee Crawford, a leader of the union. "Well he shot Lee in the stomach. That was the first shot that was fired. Well, I was standing just about fifteen steps from him when he shot him. Well he didn't kill Lee. He was gettin' up. Gettin' up on his all fours. A policeman by the name of Big

Charles Smith was there. He come to him and kicked him with his foot, just kicked him, just give him a great big kick and emptied his gun in him, just emptied his gun in him. Well his sister, a Davis woman, she run in there to pick him up, and her old man, Ira Davis, run in there to help her and a deputized policeman he shot him, layin on the ground, just killed him. . . . Then all kind of firing, firing out of the mill, you couldn't tell who was firing out of the mill."

Other observers added to the catalog of violence. "It was just a roar," one nonunion sympathizer remembered. "You couldn't distinguish a shot, just a roar. And it lasted a minute, minute and a half." The gunfire came from inside the mill and was aimed at the union workers in the yard. "And they all run, just scattered, like birds. Throwing their sticks down . . . . I think I would be safe in saying nobody knows a record of the wounded, but there was upwards of fifty. A lot of them was shot in the back as they were running."

For one witness, the memories were almost tangible: "It was sickening." The witness ran into a bathroom and vomited, so nauseated was he by "the smell of gunpowder," "the stillness," and "the smell of death." When the smoke cleared, four union members had been killed. Three more were seriously wounded and died soon after, making a total of seven killed. The event traumatized the community so badly that it was not publicly discussed for sixty years.

Both supporters and opponents of the strike instantly used the killings to make their point. Ten thousand attended the funeral of the six people killed on September 6. (The seventh did not die until after the funeral had been held.) Local strike leaders telegrammed Secretary of Labor Frances Perkins the truth: "No shots fired by pickets," wrote one, "but 7 already killed by deputised thugs."[29]

But an entirely different portrait came from antiunion spokespersons who suggested that the murders had been caused by the presence of workers from neighboring towns injecting themselves into the local situation and inflaming sentiments. Ignoring completely the presence of the armed guards stationed inside the mill, the *Greenville News* reported that the killings occurred during "rioting among employees who wished to enter the mill and picketing strikers who sought to detain them."[30] Newspaper headlines continued to blame "outsiders" for causing "trouble" in the mills.[31]

There is evidence that at least part of the truth was known by federal authorities. Commenting on the general strike for the first time on September 7, Secretary of Labor Perkins made clear at least that the seven union members had been shot by deputized workers. But rather than describe the killings as a deliberate act by the owners of the Chiquola Mill, Perkins called the whole affair an "unfortunate situation," caused by local governments deputizing "non-striking workers unaccustomed to police duty," who then shot because they were "frightened."[32]

With the truth once again clouded, the kind of galvanizing outrage that such an act should have produced simply did not occur. In World War I and in 1929, the harshness of the mill owners' repressive tactics had generated a new sympathy for the textile workers. This did not happen in 1934. Instead, news of the killings seemed to validate what so many in the labor-government hierarchy thought they knew: that the strike was a foolhardy enterprise getting increasingly out of control, and destined only to produce bloodshed and tragedy.

Gorman immediately took action to "prevent further slaughter" of textile workers. Claiming that he feared "a reign of murder," the UTW vice president suggested arbitration under the auspices of the new Winant Board if the industry would agree to close all the mills during the arbitration period.[33] The South Carolina union leadership similarly begged the governor to order all mills in the state closed to prevent further bloodshed.[34] But neither state nor federal governments heeded these calls.[35] Meanwhile, Sloan rejected Gorman's arbitration offer out-of-hand, and Gorman, after extending the offer a full twenty-four hours, withdrew it. For the first time, Gorman suggested that his confidence in the union's mission was being shaken. "We did not want it," he said, referring to the strike. "We did all that we could to avoid it. [But] management would not yield."[36] Faced with such a lack of public reaction, and overwhelmed by the tragedy, Peel called off the flying squadrons in South Carolina.[37]

Losing Resolve

In truth, the strike lines remained firm after Honea Path. By Monday, September 10, only three mills in South Carolina had reopened. And those that reopened did so with only skeletal staffs.[38] Local union leaders felt vindicated. "The mill owners have contended that it was force and intimidation on our part which moved the great masses of Carolina workers to quit the mills and that if only the mills were given the protection of militia bayonets, the workers in large masses would return to their jobs," proclaimed strike leader Council M. Fox. "Nothing of the kind has happened."[39] By September 13, the *New York Times* correspondent Joseph Shaplen admitted that the numbers of workers on strike showed "little fluctuation."[40] By the beginning of the third week, he observed that in the Carolinas, the much publicized "counter-offensive" by the mills had "made little progress in persuading desertion from the strike ranks."[41]

How UTW national leaders interpreted the strike at this crucial point is difficult to say, since union records for this period are scarce. It does appear, however, that the union's information about its own strike often came from constituencies less than sympathetic to the cause. Images of violence and union weakness may have powerfully weakened Gorman's resolve, and the UTW rarely had its spirits replenished by good news. Continually fed information from craft union leaders deploring the textile strike, and without the resources to determine for themselves what was going on in the South, UTW leaders fell prey to a flawed assessment of the strike's strength. In Alabama, Mollie Dowd, a member of the Women's Trade Union and a volunteer organizer, complained bitterly that "Gorman and McMahon seem to have forgotten Alabama altogether, except McMahon writes and bawls us out for the crazy letters our enemies write in about us." Dowd was undoubtedly referring to the leaders of the Alabama State Federation of Labor, who were "working against us day and night, having letters sent into Gorman and McMahon that we cannot be found, that the organizers are off drunk somewhere and not tending to their business." Dowd, who along with John Dean and Albert Cox helped coordinate the Alabama strike, was furious that "we go twenty-four hours a day and still have this other to contend with. It seems to us that with as many as we have had out in Alabama for three months and not even a fist fight the whole time, shows some leadership, and certainly that someone has stayed on the job."[42]

Even if UTW leaders themselves had discounted "this other" information from hostile observers, it might not have made a difference, since others inside the New Deal government were also subjected to interpretations of the strike that underplayed its strength. Without a clear *public* understanding of strikers' position in the South, UTW leaders were increasingly unable to maneuver.

The declaration of martial law in Georgia, the arrest of strike leaders there, and the prohibition of mass picketing in the state constituted the most serious blow to Gorman's negotiating position (see chapter 9). Yet even before martial law in Georgia had been declared, Gorman was already in conference with members of the Winant Board, the committee appointed by President Roosevelt to investigate the strike. Since the CTI had insisted that no one was authorized to negotiate for thousands of individual mill owners, what remained to be negotiated, from Gorman's perspective, was whatever action the government itself could take.

The Settlement

By September 17, only one day after Governor Talmadge had declared martial law in Georgia, the Winant Board had a document ready to present to Secretary of Labor Frances Perkins for review. Although the contents of the report were kept from the public until September 21, Gorman had been intimately involved in its formation. The completion of the report represented Gorman's silent concurrence that its contents represented the basis for a settlement. It seemed a preordained conclusion that the UTW was going to back it.[43]

Gorman had reason to feel some confidence in the Winant Board. The Board had attempted to demonstrate its independence from the Code Authority (and the union) by sending thirty investigators from the Department of Labor into the field to gather information for the report. In its long closed-door sessions, the Board had listened carefully as Gorman outlined the contents of a report that would be acceptable to the union. The Bruere Board had to be abolished. It was essential that the Winant Board acknowledge the need to regulate the stretch-out. Happily, these were two actions that the government could take by itself: neither required approval by the industry.

When the report was released, southern workers learned for the first time under what circumstances the strike was to end. The Board recommended that the president ask the workers to call off the strike and that the manufacturers take back the workers without discrimination. The Bruere Board would be abolished, and the workers' grievances, which the report listed in some detail, would be considered by a newly created "Textile Labor Relations Board" (TLRB). This new board was to be different from the Bruere Board because it would not report to the Code Authority but directly to the NLB's replacement, the National Labor Relations Board. In addition, no further extension of the machine load would take place until a special stretch-out committee submitted a report on the possibility of regulating the workloads in the textile mills. The authors of the Winant report were optimistic about the possibility of workload regulation, but in the short time available to the Winant Board, it could not do the necessary calculations to determine workloads in every possible circumstance. Thus Winant recommended a separate board.

The next day, President Roosevelt indicated his acceptance of the Winant Board report by asking workers to return on the terms that the report had outlined. The industry kept a cautious silence, awaiting the union's next move. All eyes were on the UTW. Would its leaders be willing to counsel its members to return to their jobs on the basis of government promises alone? If industry did not also agree to the Winant report, did the workers stand a chance of having the government promises carried out? At stake was the fundamental issue over which the strike had been called in the first place: the power of the government to enforce its own laws, to stand behind its word in the face of a recalcitrant industry.

The International was reportedly flooded with telegrams from local unions opposing any settlement on these terms. The NRA had utterly failed to carry out its responsibility to enforce the Code over the previous year; what guarantees did the workers have that these new promises would not meet the same fate? At a minimum, the industry had to agree publicly to accept the terms of the report before workers returned to their jobs. But all Sloan was willing to say was that the industry would give "sincere consideration" to the proposals in the report.[44]

The following day, the UTW Executive Council unanimously approved a resolution to end the strike on the terms outlined by the Winant Board. Gorman later claimed that the union had agreed to end the strike based on "personal assurances" from the president that the manufacturers would not discriminate against the strikers. The president could make such assurances because he was personally acquainted with some of the leading southern manufacturers.[45]

It was undoubtedly refreshing to read the Winant Board report's acknowledgment that the widespread discontent among the cotton textile workforce had some foundation. As a basis for a settlement, however, the report repeated the terms of every decision made by every board in every labor dispute in the cotton textile industry since the NIRA began. Strikers were to return to their jobs with the understanding that they would be taken back to work and that their concerns would be considered in due course. The industry agreed to nothing. "For all the oratory and enthusiasm," wrote *Newsweek*, it appeared that the country's textile workers were going back to work "with little more than a pious hope." The magazine's reporter could see no difference between the conditions over which the workers had walked out and the ones to which they were returning.[46]

The UTW leadership saw it differently. They had gotten rid of the hated Bruere Board. The new Textile Labor Relations Board would be truly independent of the Cotton Textile Code Authority. "The union has won an overwhelming victory," wrote the strike committee in its report on September 22. "We have now gained every substantial thing that we can gain in this strike." *The Textile Worker* was even more starry-eyed in its interpretation of the settlement. "The stretch-out is ended," it declared. "There will be adjustments of wages and hours. The union will grow stronger. The textile workers at last are free."[47]

11

AFTERMATH

Like a collapsing dam, the end of the strike unleashed a flood of manufacturer retaliation. Hundreds of mills quietly but firmly refused to take back strikers. Some simply closed their plants completely, explaining that they could not begin operating until their workers had the "right attitude." "There must be perfect coordination in a cotton mill," explained one owner, "and if the operatives are not mentally set for perfect coordination, it is believed far better not to attempt to open until they are of such a mind." The *Daily News Record*, a leading paper in the textile industry, reported that mill managers were "frank to say that it is absurd to have people working for them who are not satisfied, who speak against the management and create dissatisfaction."[1] One superintendent told strikers that they would have to "humble down to him" before he would treat them right again.[2] "You cannot imagine how it is here," Mollie Dowd wrote to a friend. "Mills [are] still manned with machine guns and guards and refuse to allow the strikers to even come near enough to apply for their jobs back. Manufacturers still have us run out of town wherever possible and the whole city government is behind them in saying they will have no union organization in the town of any kind."[3]

In Griffin, Georgia, the military was reportedly preventing former strikers from returning to work.[4] Paul Christopher reported that at King's Mountain, near Shelby, North Carolina, "things are pretty blue," for the management was attempting to evict union members from company houses.[5] Workers at the Avondale Mills in Birmingham charged that plant foremen made systematic visits to the homes of workers and demanded that they turn their membership books over to the superintendent. If they failed to do so, the foreman would "find cause" to dismiss them.[6] By October 23, according to the UTW, 113 northern and 226 southern mills had refused to rehire strikers.[7] The *New York Times* estimated that seventy-two thousand strikers were locked out of their jobs and suggested that the conflict was developing into "a finish fight, in which the life of the union in the South appeared to be at stake."[8]

The union discrimination was too much for millhands at Roanoke Rapids, North Carolina. Paul Christopher reported a meeting of upwards of two thousand workers, "howling for another strike."[9] Apparently they were not alone. According to the *New York Times*, Gorman was getting "terrific pressure" from workers across the South to resume the strike.[10] The UTW did authorize new strikes at twenty-eight mills where workers threatened to "declare outlaw strikes if the UTW refused to give their approval."[11]

Other workers were less defiant. Where the union had always been contested, the end of the strike led to bitter divisions. While some union members renounced their membership and went back into the mills, unrepentant strikers were visited by "loyal" workers who told them they would either have to leave town or abandon their union activities.[12] From the point of view of loyal union members, these men and women had "turned against" them. The feelings of antagonism were powerful. "We have been, and are being treated, worse than beasts," Mrs. H. M. Huskaup from Lonsdale, South Carolina, reported. Nonunion or former union workers were now "talking and treating the union people so we can't hardly bear it. . . . We can't walk through one of the 'scab's' yards because we are union members. . . . They won't go to church with us, they claim the union is not fit to associate with. . . . our children can't go to Sunday School or school either without being jeered at. . . . I pray each day and night for help."[13] "These people cannot have their friends visit them in their own home," Mollie Dowd wrote to a friend. "You seem to think we won something. I just cannot see it. Things here are in a much worse condition than they were three months ago."[14]

The Settlement Evaporates

It was by dealing with the fallout from the strike settlement that the UTW leadership learned the bitter lesson of the union's defeat. Over the next several months, UTW leaders helplessly watched working conditions and union strength erode so severely that by the end of 1935, the union was as weak as it had been before Roosevelt was elected.

One of the vehicles for paralyzing the union was the very board that UTW leaders had so enthusiastically heralded to be the textile workers' liberator: the Textile Labor Relations Board. The *Textile Worker* spoke glow-ingly of the TLRB as "the quiet but resistless power of the nation" that would "surround these mill towns with a sense of power hitherto unknown to them."[15] To be sure, the TLRB had considerably greater integrity than the Bruere Board. Unlike the Bruere Board, for example, the TLRB took a firm position on the need for employers to rehire striking workers. B. M. Squires, the chair of the TLRB, called the return of strikers to their former positions "a fundamental issue which must be met."[16]

But the TLRB was hardly the all-powerful government agency the union proclaimed it to be. In appointing its members, Roosevelt had simply added a new assignment to the three members already appointed to the Steel La-bor Relations Board the previous spring. Unfamiliar with the internal dy-namics of the textile industry, Board Chair Squires was "at a loss to under-stand why there should be such a tremendous number of complaints charging discrimination and unwarranted evictions" following the end of the strike.[17] Playing two roles, as members of the textile and the steel labor boards, TLRB members were also hopelessly overworked and understaffed. So desperate was the TLRB for field investigators that it turned—amazingly—back to the Cotton Textile Code Authority for staff help. The Code Authority in turn "loaned" the TLRB some investigators to conduct the Board's "impartial" investigations.

The result bordered on farce. Louis Galambos, a leading historian of the Cotton Textile Code Authority, summarizes how the Code Authority slowly but surely regained control over the "independent" TLRB. "If the problem had not been so serious," writes Galambos, "the government's performance in this interlude would provide fine material for a bureaucratic comedy. Each time the situation was studied, the investigatory process had slipped back into the CTI's hands."[18]

The TLRB did rectify some of the most blatant abuses. The Board made certain, for example, that no Code Authority investigators took part in dis-crimination cases. Field investigation reports demonstrated a refreshing willingness to concede that the workers might have had a case. But for a worker to be reinstated required a hearing before the TLRB to determine if the worker might not have been legitimately dismissed. Often the issue turned on whether or not the employer could persuade the TLRB that the worker had been responsible for acts of violence during the strike. Given the realities of mill owners' power, the hearings took the form of inquisi-tions for the workers despite the fact that it was the workers who were ac-cusing the management of wrongdoing. Tight-lipped workers were ques-tioned closely by counsel for the employers, and sometimes by their own supervisors, about exactly what they did during the strike, on a particular day, at a particular hour. Workers were often asked to name fellow workers who might have been involved in particular strike activities, thus potentially "incriminating" others who would then also be dismissed. In at least one instance, this "hearing" was held in the superintendent's own office. Terrified, many previous strikers renounced their union affiliations. Even more disheartening, the hearing often seemed not to have been worth the trouble. The TLRB would often decide in favor of reinstatement only to learn several weeks later that the mill had never taken the worker back on the job.

Southern mills had apparently taken the advice of the *Textile Bulletin*, "to entirely ignore the so-called 'impartial investigators' of the National Textile Labor Relations Board . . . . Neither the 'impartial investigators' nor the 'conciliators,'" the *Bulletin* promised, "have any authority or power which has been confirmed by the courts. The only penalty for the application of boots to seat of pants is through a local indictment and possibly a small fine."[19] The UTW cited at least 117 southern cotton mills that never complied with TLRB decisions.[20]

Georgia manufacturers were particularly defiant. "Mill owners openly boast that they control the state government," wrote the *Raleigh Union Herald*, "and that Talmadge will respond to any request made upon him. Mill owners openly boast of defiance of the Federal Boards and agenices inquiring into the wrongs of the mill workers."[21] A field investigator for the TLRB confirmed that there was a "combination of mill owners in Georgia to oppose to the limit the principles of collective bargaining, and they are not likely to stand for anything which appears to be even remotely connected with it."[22] In Greenville, South Carolina, employers issued a statement denouncing collective bargaining.[23]

Meanwhile, the Code Authority used its control over statistical reports to completely camouflage the violations of the southern mills. If the strike had given textile workers any hope of influencing public perceptions, that hope was now completely gone. Instead, the headlines of a *New York Times* article announced the results of the Code Authority's December 17 study of itself:

FINDS FEW VIOLATE
THE COTTON CODE

Authority in Report for 16
Months Asserts Nearly All
Complaints Are Adjusted.

---

23 EXCEPTIONS LISTED

Nearly Half of Charges Dismissed as Work of Cranks or
of Misinformed Employees.

The report found 80 percent of employee complaints against cotton manufacturers to be baseless. In the 20 percent of cases where Code violations
were found, the report noted, "such employers have gladly and promptly
corrected them." Even these violations should not be taken too seriously,
the report added, since they largely occurred in the first few months of the
Code "as a result of a misunderstanding or misinterpretation by mill managements of their obligations under the new code."[24] The public relations
hand of the Code Authority could not have been more boldly or more deftly
played.

The hand of the Code Authority appeared to be everywhere, even in the
report of the Bureau of Labor Statistics on wages in the textile industry. Here
the union was certain it would win a victory, particularly with regard to differentials for skilled workers. But the report determined that there had been
an "overwhelming compliance" with the wage provisions of the Code.[25] The
amendment to the Code providing for the study and possible adjustment of
workloads was drafted by Code Authority Chairman Sloan himself.[26]
Galambos summarizes these developments: "Quietly and skillfully Sloan and
[his assistant] Dorr guided the Institute back into the tone of the defensive
positions that had been lost in the settlement; seldom was the influence of
the association leaders more obvious."[27]

Gradually it became clear to the UTW that responding wholeheartedly
to the Winant Report was a mistake. "If we were not strong believers in peace
and co-operation," Gorman said in December, "we should be forced to say
that there exists in the industry today ample cause for another national
strike."[28] By February 1935, Gorman was testifying that the union leadership was "beginning to wonder if we did the right thing in urging our members to end our strike last September."[29]

The crowning blow was the government inquiry into the stretch-out,
conducted by a committee called the Textile Work Assignment Board (WAB),
appointed by the president at the end of the general strike. This board was
to be composed of three individuals: one "impartial" chairman, one representative of the employers, and one representative of the union. No gov-

ernment work could have been more important for textile workers, for, despite the moratorium on extensions of workloads proposed by the Winant Report, only three months after the end of the strike workers in 122 mills in the four southern textile states had submitted complaints relative to work assignments and workloads.[30]

Amazingly, the union permitted Geoff Brown—the "efficiency" expert that the union had sent to the southern mills during the aborted UTW organizing campaign in 1930—to represent the UTW on the Board.[31] The WAB took its time deciding about the extent of the stretch-out. Observing the government's inaction, mill after mill in the South stepped up its pace of work.

Finally workers could wait no longer. On March 1, approximately two thousand workers in six Callaway mills in western Georgia walked off their jobs to protest the implementation of the "Bedaux" system, a particularly harsh form of scientific management. The Callaway management had attempted to implement this time and motion study during the summer of 1934, but had backed off as momentum for the general strike increased. Now, in March 1935, the management apparently felt confident that it could succeed. The move threatened to eliminate as many as one thousand jobs.

UTW leaders threw the union's whole resources behind the Calloway Mills strike. Gorman called the dispute "the most serious situation since the September strike," and a "test case" for the implementation of the stretch-out across the South. The Georgia union leader S. A. Hollihan told reporters that if mill owners were allowed "to continue the practices installed here this week the NRA Code for the textile industry is just as good as dead."[32]

For nearly eight weeks the union held out while appealing to the TLRB for a decision. But they could not last forever: the strikers included only about two-thirds of the workforce, and Governor Talmadge had again called in the state militia. When the mill began evicting strikers near the end of April, desperate workers petitioned the federal government to do something.[33] Finally, on May 11, the TLRB handed down its decision on the controversy. But the ruling could not have been worse for the strikers; the new work system was completely legitimized.[34]

Gorman understood only all too well what had happened. "I feel that this decision forms the climax of a long line of decisions," he said after the ruling was issued. There was no longer any meaning to the word "compliance": "Defiance, not compliance, has been the watchword." The TLRB had given the mill "a clean bill of health to go and sin some more. Not only that, the Board has run up the signal to all southern mills to go to it and smash standards all the way."[35] By the end of the spring of 1935, Gorman was denouncing the TLRB as a "strikebreaking agency" along the same lines that workers had denounced the Bruere Board the year before.[36]

The decision to permit the Bedaux system to be installed in the Callaway Mills simply set the stage for the public release of the findings of the Work Assignment Board two days later. Reversing completely the recommendation of the Winant Board, the May 13 report determined first, that it would be unwise to establish standards for workloads and second, that it would be a burden for the manufacturer to petition for permission to increase the workload before making any changes. Few employees actually suffered from excessive workloads, the report concluded; to the contrary, some workers did not have enough work to do! The statistical maneuverings are worth noting. The WAB recorded complaints against the stretch-out from 249 out of some twelve hundred cotton mills in the country. It investigated thirty-six of these complaints and found excessive workloads in eleven. On the basis of this work, the WAB reported that "it can be assumed" that only 6.5 percent of the cotton mills in the country were stretching out their workers.[37]

This time it was Peel who took on the Board: "If the manufacturers had been given the right to write the report they could not have made it more favorable to themelves. It is an open invitation to every employer, whether there is organization of the employees in his plant or not, makes no difference, for them to increase the machine load. It is incomprehensible, unjust and unfair to the employees in the Cotton division of the Industry." Peel charged that the Board's investigators were either former mill superintendents or engineers who had installed the new machinery, and that the workers who had been selected to be interviewed had been selected by the management. Peel also attacked the report's presumption that the stretch-out was simply the installation of more efficient machinery, listing the names of thirteen mills in South Carolina where workloads had been increased despite the fact that no new machinery had been installed. Peel concluded that the report's insistence that few workers suffered from overwork insulted the intelligence of hundreds of cotton textile workers who were claiming that they suffered precisely that. Peel asked rhetorically what possible reason the Textile Work Assignment Board could have for continuing to exist, since by its own report very few textile workers were stretched out. "It is ludicrous, yea, borders on absurdity, that a Board be set up with so little to occupy its time and efforts."[38]

Any hope that textile unionists had was now dashed. By the end of May 1935, President Green of the AFL reported that wage cuts were taking place "in every direction."[39] When the NRA was declared unconstitutional in June, workers were overwhelmed by desolation. One Callaway worker wrote: "We couldn't be in a worse fix than we are now."[40]

Internal Union Collapse

To speak of what happened to southern textile unions after June 1935 once again requires an examination on two planes: on the local level, where the ingredients of insurgency continued to exist, although in altered form; and on the national level, where, having thrown its lot in with the government, the UTW no longer had the perspective or the credibility to engage the southern millhands. UTW leaders watched, heartsick and dismayed, as the union's southern organization simply fell apart before their eyes.

Evidence of the crumbling UTW southern organization could be found everywhere. Local unions were decimated by manufacturers' discrimination against their leaders; they were demoralized by the unrelenting series of broken promises from government and union officials.[41] Former members of the union local in Caroleen, North Carolina, sent their charter back to UTW headquarters when the local president moved away and there was "not anyone left" in the union.[42] By 1936, Durham and Pittsboro were the only places in the state with any notable textile union activity.[43] Even a dedicated organizer like Christopher was paralyzed. "Sure I'm trying to tell workers that the only way to stop it [the stretch-out] is to organize," he wrote to Peel that April, "but it doesn't seem to have an effect. I haven't signed up a single member."[44]

In Georgia almost no strong locals remained by 1936, not even in Columbus.[45] Despite four thousand UTW members in Columbus in October 1935, workers were not active. "In '35 we tried to get people together," remembers former Columbus union leader Lloyd Davis, "and we could get my mill, and we would go down to the union hall, but we couldn't get nobody to take the lead. So it just finally died out, although we had a lot of union people there, a lot of union people."[46] In South Carolina, the union strongholds of Spartanburg and Rock Hill lost most of their membership, although outposts of union strength remained in the nearby villages of Gaffney, Inman, and Union.[47] By April 1937, membership in the southern branch of the UTW had declined from its peak of approximately upwards of eighty thousand in the summer of 1934 to an estimated 5,472 members.[48]

By the time of the 1936 UTW convention, the entire organization was adrift. Not only was the membership in most of its locals decimated, but within what organization remained one could find only "dissention [sic], mutual suspicion, and distrust . . . internal bickering . . . petty jealousy." Francis Gorman was blunt in his assessment of the lack of interest among the membership in the union: "Reports have come to me that certain sections of our membership have become so disgusted and so disinterested that they would not even send delegates to this convention."[49] Christopher, always the diplomat, hoped that some action would be taken to clear the air. "I wonder if we will ever get to have that organizers meeting for the Southern representatives?" he asked in May 1935. "I believe the International could make a premium from such a meeting . . . we could straighten out some of the wires that I am afraid are crossed."[50] Like frustrated doctors examining a sick patient, everyone had a diagnosis for "what is the matter with this International and our methods of organizing, building up and holding members."[51]

But the strike's defeat had a double edge. Even though union locals died, many workers continued to be "union." "Union" was not a function of a membership card or of payment of dues, or even of attending meetings; it was a state of heart and mind. Even when Lloyd Davis's local died, they still had "a lot of union people" there. Louis Holloway from Gadsden remembered how the local at Dwight Manufacturing Company collapsed. "Well, everybody, you see, they dropped that union, they left that union, on account of they thought they got bit, you know that they said they got bit, that they [the union had] run off and left . . . . They were still union in heart. They still wanted the union because they were being pressured so hard, like I told you, by the bosses, about, you do this, or you do that, or I'll get your job, 'til they wanted a union."[52]

Sometimes worker resentment burst out in uncoordinated energy, no longer under the auspices of the UTW. The cotton textile industry witnessed ninety-four strikes and lockouts in the last four months of 1934 and the first seven months of 1935.[53] In fact, more textile strikes took place in 1935 than in any year since 1921, and these strikes increased in frequency every year thereafter until 1938.[54]

Only in Alabama—where mills practiced much less discrimination after the '34 strike—did the UTW maintain organizational strength. Even though the Alabama textile workforce was only about 15 percent of the total southern textile workforce, union members in Alabama in 1936 made up an astonishing 68 percent of the total membership in the four southern textile states. Alabama had 3,744 union members, more than the other three southern textile states put together.[55] The two foci were Huntsville, where the union had flourished with the support of local merchants since 1930, and Walker County, where the ongoing presence of both coal miners' and farmers' unions continued to provide fertile cultural ground for organizing textile workers. So strong were worker organizations in both the Huntsville mills and at the Jasper Mills in Walker County that former strikers there experienced no discrimination whatsoever.

In retrospect it is possible to identify several reasons for the persistence of a formal union movement in Alabama. First, a relatively favorable political climate for labor in the state meant that textile employers had not been able to secure the use of the National Guard to break the strike. Second, Alabama workers had the initiative to call a general strike alone despite enormous pressure from others to wait until workers were gathered together at a national convention. They had remained on strike as a unit for six weeks before the rest of the country joined them. Indeed, Alabama workers had forced the national strike to take place. Textile unionists in Alabama had demonstrated initiative independent of the national union, and that initiative sustained their locals through the years when the national union could provide no direction.[56]

Assessment

From the perspective of the overall organization no one was in a better position to assess the failure of the union's work than Francis Gorman. The UTW vice president had his first opportunity to speak before the membership since the end of the '34 strike at the UTW Biennial Convention in 1936. After two long years of pondering what had happened, Gorman had apparently decided that there was much the union could do to face the problems confronting them. His musings provide a revealing epitaph to the tragedy of 1934.

"Many of us did not understand fully the role of Government in a struggle between labor and industry," Gorman wrote in a draft of his speech. "Many of us did not understand what we do now: that the Government protects the strong, not the weak, and that it operates under pressure and yields to that group which is strong enough to assert itself over the other. If nobody learned anything but this from the strike it was worth the lesson."[57] Gorman called the months from October 1934 to June of 1935 "the long, disillusioning months following the end of the strike."[58] The TLRB was "a bitter disappointment."[59] "We know now," he wrote ruefully, "that we are naive to depend on the forces of Government to protect us."[60] The UTW vice president also acknowledged the tremendous toll that the stretch-out had taken on his membership in terms he would never have used a year before. The stretch-out today, he wrote, "is making harried, broken old men and women of the textile workers before they even reach the age of 35."[61]

Gorman had two suggestions for avoiding such problems in the future. First, labor should organize an independent political party. Indeed, in the two years since the strike's defeat, Gorman and other local New England textile union leaders had already become among the independent labor movement's most vigorous proponents.[62]

Gorman's second suggestion was internal union reform. Launching an attack on "careerism and bureaucracy," Gorman proposed an increase in "rank and file democracy and collective leadership."[63] It was only too obvious to Gorman that the union had become strong in 1933–34 precisely because local unions had the freedom of action to develop local strategies. "The members of the local unions must be made to feel that they are the controlling factor in this union. They must be encouraged to take the initiative in making policies of the organization. This cannot be done unless the local union membership is allowed the widest latitude possible, within the limits of our constitution, to direct and guide their own affairs under leadership of their own choosing."[64] Gorman was addressing a central problem with the UTW structure: the problem of leadership accountability to its membership.

One year after the 1934 strike ended, UTW Vice President Francis Gorman (left) advocates the formation of a National Labor Party in a radio interview at the AFL Convention in Atlantic City. Gorman is being interviewed by Chester M. Wright, publicist for the union. (Harris & Ewing Photographers, Washington, D.C.; George Meany Memorial Archives)

With the weight of the 1934 settlement still on his shoulders, Gorman argued for a change in the way the union made decisions. Power was too concentrated in 1934. "No one person," he argued, "should be vested with that much power or responsibility. Our organization must be administered by a group of people, chosen from our own ranks by the delegates . . . and directly and at all times responsible to the membership for its actions. This necessitates certain organic changes in our Constitution."[65] Among Gorman's changes was the proposal that "the calling off of a general strike and the terms of settlement thereof" should be "subject to a ⅔ vote of approval by the membership."[66]

Gorman also suggested that the union set up a committee to look into the possibility of agreements between manufacturer and union that were not national in scope.[67] This issue had become a serious bone of contention within the union following the 1934 national strike. Many workers agreed with Lloyd Davis, the Columbus union member, that the settlement should have been a national agreement, even when it might have been possible to secure individual local agreements. "I felt, and others like me felt, that as far as our company was concerned, all we had to do was say, 'look, we want to sign a contract.' But we wanted an International contract, we didn't just want a piece of paper, we wanted the International . . . . We wanted to get a contract that the Eagle and Phenix, the Bibb, the Old Swift, Thomas Mill, you name it, all of them belong to the same International union."[68] A national agreement also jibed with a long-term goal of the union: to achieve nationwide wage standards that would prevent southern mills from undercutting their northern competitors.

In retrospect, however, some felt that it was the national nature of the strike settlement that doomed the union to its ignominious defeat. The national settlement tied all unions to the same common denominator instead of enabling stronger locals to exact a better settlement. Some felt that once it became clear that the industry would not negotiate directly with the union, agreements should have been worked out on a mill-by-mill basis. Jack Rubenstein, a member of the Dyers and Finishers' Federation during the '34 strike, wrote in 1935 that there was "no doubt" in his mind that "had this been done, had not the workers been sent stampeding into the mills, that agreements could have been worked out for an orderly retreat in some cases even with concessions in the mills where we were firmly organized. To say the least we would have avoided the spectacle of mill gates being slammed in the face of many of our most loyal union members."[69]

Interestingly, Paul Christopher had nearly secured an agreement from the Minette Mill of Grover, North Carolina, for a closed shop agreement during the national strike. In asking the national strike committee to approve it, Christopher called the Minette Mill agreement "the first closed shop agreement we have gotten in this state, or in the South, so far as I know, since the Code became effective."[70] The only problem was that the mill management was not willing to agree to one demand—the demand for forty hours' pay for thirty hours' worked—unless a change in the Code was won to that effect. If, however, that demand was also won, the mill had agreed to pay the wage difference retroactively.

But the national leadership would not approve the contract. Gorman had called it "dangerous" for the union "to sanction any individual contract just now when all our endeavors are centered in an effort to line up an industrial agreement."[71] The debate over individual or national agreements continued into 1935. Christopher continued to be a proponent of greater local flexibility. But McMahon in particular remained firm. Writing to Christopher in February 1935, he said, "I cannot visualize victory through the striking of individual mills. North and South, East and Middle West, where there has been an attempt made to do this, we have met with failure. Adjustments have been made, in some cases, only to be immediately broken when the workers return."[72]

But Christopher was not convinced. In 1936 he looked back on the '34 strike effort and identified the thirty-hour clause as the "stumbling block" to achieving closed shop contracts "embodying the terms for which the strike was called," not only in the Minette Mill but in several others as well. In its myopic focus on a single national agreement embodying wage and hour standards, the UTW national leadership took away the room for maneuver so critical to victory in the South.[73]

The difference of opinion over national versus individual campaigns was symptomatic of the different visions of power suggested by the southern strategy and by the northern leadership. McMahon's was the strategy of a declining union attempting to protect what it had. Christopher's was the strategy of a new union attempting to gain a foothold. McMahon's perspective reflected the relative unity of voice among New England mill owners; Christopher's reflected the deep divisions and the fierce individualism among mill owners in the South. The marriage between the southern and northern union had been fragile indeed.

Politics

Gorman was not the only leader of the southern textile strike to call for workers to become involved in politics. In both South and North Carolina

UTW leaders became convinced that until politicians were more responsive to workers' interests, unionism could not flourish. In what must have been a highly satisfying act, textile workers in East Laurinburg "marched as a unit to the polls" in the spring of 1935 and elected as town commissioner the president of their local, Robert L. Thompson.[74] Textile workers in Cordova, Alabama, also elected a labor slate to local offices.[75] Such fragments of evidence lead one to wonder how much political activity took place in mill towns of the South after 1935.

Local politics was one thing; to win at a state level, however, was quite another. Textile labor could not mobilize a majority at the state level alone: they needed sympathetic allies. In the South, however, such alliances were too fragile to overcome the traditional power of the southern Democratic party.

In North Carolina, Paul Christopher threw himself into mobilizing labor's support for the 1936 campaign for the Democratic gubernatorial nomination of Dr. Ralph McDonald, a teacher from Winston-Salem. McDonald's pro-labor stance did not emerge organically out of the tumult of the '34 strike; his core supporters were professionals and teachers centered around the University of North Carolina. That McDonald was textile labor's candidate was clear, however, from the identity of his chief opponent in the race, Clyde Hoey. Hoey was the attorney who had prosecuted the leaders of the 1929 Gastonia strike after the killing of the police chief (see chapter 2). This "silver tongued orator" was vehemently antiunion. He was also the brother-in-law of O. Max Gardner, the mill owner and former governor.

Hoey was able to squeak out a first-place victory over McDonald in a three-way primary only after his campaign workers "found" two thousand absentee votes in the state's western counties.[76] In preparing for the runoff primary, which would pit Hoey in a head-to-head race against McDonald, Hoey had to face the serious possibility that McDonald, supported by a coalition of industrial workers and liberals, would win. At this critical juncture, his brother-in-law Gardner returned to North Carolina from his law practice in Washington to save Hoey's candidacy. Within a short time, Gardner had repainted Hoey as a liberal, strongly committed to Roosevelt's policies. While labor interests stayed loyal to McDonald, other North Carolina liberals defected to Hoey, now a respectable candidate of the traditional North Carolina political machine. Hoey won easily.[77]

In South Carolina, textile workers initially had greater political success. In 1934, coinciding with the end of the general textile strike, they elected Olin Johnston, a former mill worker, as governor of the state. Johnston's political career had been built by the textile union insurgency. After a brief stint in the mills, Johnston had become a lawyer and, in 1932, used his new credentials to defend the cases of workers in a South Carolina mill who had been evicted from their homes during a strike. Johnston's election catapulted to power a leader of an organized and ideologically mature textile labor constituency. He defeated not only the "progressive" opponent, Wyndham Manning, who lost in the first primary, but also his nemesis, Cole Blease, a man who for years had secured the white working-class vote in South Carolina with his racist appeals and his statements of contempt for upper-class snobbery.[78] A key to Johnston's victory was textile union organizing.[79]

Johnston's election in 1934 and McDonald's candidacy in 1936 represented the high tide of southern textile labor political strength. The growing strength of the northern Democratic party after 1936 closed rather than opened the doors for political change in the South, at least in the short run. The reason is simple. From 1933 to 1936, southern business elites were stealth conservatives, preaching superficial loyalty to Roosevelt but remaining privately opposed to his pro-worker policies. They were able to maintain this posture in part because they could count on the political influence of southern congressmen to stave off any policies opposed to their interests behind the scenes.

After 1936, however, southern Democrats no longer commanded the same power in Washington as they had before 1936. A new Democratic party had been built around them, so to speak, responsive to specific political constituencies of the North. This New Deal administration had a concrete reform program that it hoped to spread, even to the South. By 1938, business elites had emerged into open opposition to Roosevelt. Textile interests in particular formed a core of opposition to Roosevelt by joining the Liberty League in the late thirties and supporting Wendell Willkie in 1940.[80]

How this "new" New Deal affected southern politics can be gleaned by what happened to Olin Johnston in 1938. One hundred percent loyal to Roosevelt and the New Deal, Johnston by 1938 became associated in the public eye not with the New Deal that the state's southern textile workers had tried to make a "living thing" through their organizing in 1933–34, but with the New Deal that reflected a constellation of northern interests and northern constituencies. Johnston's opponent, Cotton Ed Smith, seized on the mobilization of the northern black vote that the 1936 election had generated for Roosevelt and preached with alarm that Johnston's re-election would undermine the viability of white supremacy in the South. Of course, in this assessment Johnston's opponents were right, for in the long run the Democratic party did become the vehicle for southern blacks to secure civil and political rights.

In the short run, however, this fear of black participation in the Democratic party created the opportunity for a resurgence of conservative politics. Whatever fears southern mill workers might have had about black southerners, the textile labor vote for Johnston remained solid. But others who had previously supported the former mill worker now abandoned him for Smith. By 1938, in short, the New Deal was an "outside" force, without sufficient "homegrown" visibility to prevent it from being used by its opponents to bring to the surface deep-seated racial prejudices and sectional hostilities.[81]

The CIO and Southern Textiles

Had southern textile labor been able to generate a more powerful political voice, events after 1934 might have been different. Instead, southern mill workers found themselves once again dependent on a New Deal government and a union that purported to speak for them, but did not.

Gorman's belief that workers had trusted too much in the government was not broadly shared in Washington. To the contrary, most national observers believed the strike's failure demonstrated the folly of workers abandoning the leadership of the New Deal and taking matters into their own hands. So anxious were government officials to limit the disruptive effects of such walkouts in the future that, in early October 1934, President Roosevelt had called for a strike truce.[82] Weary labor leaders nodded their heads in agreement. In Alabama, Mollie Dowd advised a group of striking workers to "just keep on building your fine unions, but don't tear them down by striking." Noel Beddow, state NRA Compliance Director and later director of the Steel Workers Organizing Committee in Alabama, also told cotton mill workers that "for their own benefit they must forget their power to strike for the moment and turn to thoughts of selling themselves to the public as worthwhile organizations."[83]

The suggestion that workers needed to "sell themselves to the public" implied that workers only needed respectability to gain victory, that millhands ought to secure their goals by cultivating the favor of powers greater than them, rather than relying on their own strength. It was, of course, a reformulation of the advice to unions the previous year to "cooperate" with the government.

Textile workers had heard this advice before. They had been told not to strike but to trust in the Bruere Board. Then they were told not to strike but to trust in the TLRB. Each time they were not simply disappointed, but betrayed. Would anyone else have the effrontery to ask southern textile workers to trust the government to solve their problems, if only they did not strike?

Two years later the UTW, now reshaped by the CIO, the new industrial union, as the Textile Workers' Organizing Committee (TWOC), asked southern textile workers to do precisely that. Armed with a permanent, constitutional Wagner Act and flush from CIO victories in major industries in the North, the TWOC proudly brandished flyers explaining to workers that "Now it can be done!"—*now* the government was behind them. Campaign literature contained cartoons with TWOC leaders driving a car up a long hill on the right side of the road, with recalcitrant manufacturers careening down the hill on the wrong side. The caption asked rhetorically, "Who is on the wrong side of the road?" A silent plea was implicit: surely the backing of the U.S. government would convince both workers and manufacturers that they should work with the new union.[84]

But as TWOC organizers entered southern mill villages, they discovered that the Wagner Act did not have the force they had assumed it would. If anything, textile manufacturers had become more hostile to unions than they were in 1934. Evidence of manufacturers' stiffened resistence to unions

From the *TWOC Parade*, published in Atlanta by the CIO. (*Survey Graphic*, March 1938, p. 149)

could be seen simply by driving past mill after mill across the South. Whereas before 1934 very few mills in the South had fences around them, by 1938 nearly all did.[85] Certainly in Anderson County, South Carolina, life continued as if the Wagner Act had never been passed. Company-hired thugs attempted to run two TWOC organizers out of town. Union leaders recalled that when they appealed to the county sheriff for protection, he replied "that the Wagner Act did not affect Anderson."[86] The textile union probably had a better chance of gaining industry compliance with government laws in 1934 than it did in this new era of contempt.

The story of the CIO southern textile organizing drive from 1937 to 1941 reveals the same friction between national union leaders and southern workers that the UTW encountered in the South in the early 1930s. True, TWOC leaders had a more sophisticated understanding of the obstacles facing them. The director of the TWOC, Sidney Hillman, who was also a founder of the CIO, understood that unionism in the South could not succeed unless workers also broke the political stranglehold of southern bourbons.

Yet, as was the case with the UTW, the TWOC did not organize around the stretch-out. Instead, it stressed the familiar goals of "stabilization and fair competition in the industry; living wage; value of purchasing power; the elementary political rights; and the need for organization and collective bargaining."[87] Union leaders were at pains to reassure employers that the union did not oppose technological change, but favored "good machinery" in an "adequate system." Far from opposing the stretch-out, the union "demanded only that all changes in working conditions be accomplished in full consultation with the union," and that "all savings in production be shared with workers in a manner agreed upon by the union."[88] Fearful of labor militancy, TWOC leaders urged a moratorium on strikes in favor of a "constructive program" of "education, organization, union contract, and responsible collective bargaining."[89] As was the case with the UTW, the driving force behind the TWOC was not the actual grievances of southern workers, but the effect of low-wage southern competitors on the economic health of the New England mills.[90]

In spite of the odds, many southern workers joined the TWOC. But the union's organizing philosophy "caused trouble" among southern unionists since, in the words of Paul Richards, it led the union to stifle the energies of "groups of workers angry about arbitrary management procedures and exhausted by speed-up."[91] Veteran organizers like Paul Christopher were particularly leery of the strategy. Writing to a fellow southern organizer, Christopher confided, "It's hard to try and discipline workers to pursue the policy we have outlined when the company is taking every advantage of our peaceable attitude to impose additional injustices and hardships on our members."[92] By the end of 1938, friction between the TWOC and southern union members was so great that CIO leaders found they could no longer work with the old UTW organizers who had been kept on staff in the South. The union slowly weeded out the old organizers and replaced them with younger ones from the mills. Gorman called it a "systematic purge."[93]

Diehard southern unionists, however, stayed with the TWOC, now re-formed as the Textile Workers Union of America–CIO (TWUA). But by 1941 the TWUA had secured contracts from only a few southern mills, and organizers were violently rebuffed by both hostile employers and fearful workers. Struggling to find a winning strategy, TWUA leaders and southern unionists once again found themselves in open disagreement over how to handle stretch-out complaints. In January 1941 over five hundred delegates from all over the South arrived in Atlanta to hear the the TWUA leadership explain its organizing philosophy. Paul Richards, historian of the TWUA in the South, describes how the national officers "spoke against the small, scattered strike actions which had been the main response to the stretch-out." While union leaders reassured the delegates "that they thoroughly understood how serious the stretch-out problem was for all textile workers, they warned them that effective control of the problem could not be won through strike action. Stretch-out and time-study men were here to stay."[94]

There was no way such talk could placate southern unionists. At the annual TWUA convention in October 1941, nine months later, astonished southerners watched as national union leaders put forth a convention resolution that claimed that the union was succeeding in controlling the stretch-out in the southern mills. Among those present was William Adcock, Huntsville leader during the '34 strike, renowned for his stubbornness and "hotheadedness," and a key spokesperson for the southern membership.[95] The Huntsville leader objected to the convention resolution, saying that it seemed to him that the stretch-out was "being ignored too much to satisfy a large number of textile workers of the south." He could not understand why "we do not try to do something concerning the stretch-out." As Richards summarizes, Adcock "criticized the union's practice of telling the workers to organize first before they struck over issues, because many times this meant telling workers on strike to go back to work and settle for conditions worse than those over which the strike occurred." Adcock said, "We want this question of the stretch-out—something done about that. We admit that we cannot stop progress, but some of us cannot see this point from the view that other workers see it, from some of the officers of our International union."[96]

Impatient International union leaders responded to Adcock that they, too, were concerned about the stretch-out, but that the southern worker was hardly in a position to make demands of the leadership, since the northern-based union was paying for much of what was turning out to be a very costly southern drive, and since the southern worker was still responsible for dragging down wages nationally, maintaining a differential of over seven cents an hour.[97] On this rather unsatisfactory note, matters rested. While the stretch-out never disappeared altogether from TWUA campaign literature, neither did it ever become a serious focus of organizational energy.

The triumph of the stretch-out is an enduring legacy of the 1934 general textile strike. Other than the installation of air conditioning, the most important difference between working conditions in the mills of today and the mills of the twenties and thirties is that in contemporary plants, "they have to work harder."[98] Manufacturers' rationalization of the workplace made it increasingly difficult for workers to integrate work and home life, a development that southern textile workers speak about with a profound sense of loss. James Cortez, a retired textile worker, speaks simply but eloquently about the loss of the kind of community that nourished the workers' spirits and families: "Used to be . . . they would play ball in the afternoon. And everybody that wanted to go to the ball game, they'd stop their work off at five o'clock, so that they could go to the ball game. But nowadays they won't stop the mill whenever you die."[99]

World War II saw a new advance in southern textile union organization, as conditions similar to the First World War—a desperate need for labor, and government regulation of labor management disputes—created the conditions for real collective bargaining in the southern mills. By the end of the war, over eighty thousand workers were under union contract with the TWUA-CIO, a number roughly equivalent to the number of southern workers who had joined the UTW in 1933–34. For five years after the war's end, these unionized workers maintained a precarious but precious foothold in the South. The arduous efforts of textile workers' unions over the previous generation had finally borne fruit.

Yet once again the regional priorities of the southern textile workers and the national union could not be reconciled. Like their predecessors, unionized southern workers continued to cherish their union's ability to control non-wage issues, such as arbitrary management and abusive treatment, as much as wage issues. Yet southern wage increases, dramatic as they were, did not prevent the continued migration of plants and jobs out of New England to the low-wage South. TWUA leader Emil Rieve's call for a showdown over the wage issue in southern mills finally wrecked the delicate coming-to-terms unionized southern mills had reached in the postwar era. The disastrous 1951 general strike eliminated the largest base of textile unionism the South had ever seen.[100]

CONCLUSION

There was in southern politics a level of conflict and insur-
gency . . . that had little in common with the New Deal and
that often found itself as much opposed to national liberalism
as to local conservatism. . . . [In the South] the most successful
insurgents of the 1930s . . . were advocates of a vision of
reform far different from that of the New Deal.
—Alan Brinkley, *Liberalism and Its Discontents*

Given the magnitude of the strike's failure, it is easy to understand why the event was purposely forgotten, not only by those who participated, but by the union that led it and the members of the New Deal
administration whose decisions affected its outcome. The pain and embarrassment of the conflict for all parties leads one to ask why the story should
now be told.

First, the '34 strike forces us to reconsider certain long-held explanations
about the failure of unions to thrive in the South, at least from the 1930s
onward. For example, the indigenous southern organizing that led to the
strike makes clear that southern textile workers did not suffer from any cultural defect that made them less committed to unionism than their northern counterparts. A year after the strike, Paul Christopher called the textile
workers' union "the most militant organization of workers in the entire
nation today."[1] Indeed, what is remarkable is how long many millhands clung
to the union spirit long after the material possibility of unionism in southern textiles had receded.[2]

Scholars must also be cautious about concluding that southern workers
failed to form strong unions because southern mill owners were significantly
more hostile to unionism than owners of northern industries. Southern textile employers were fiercely opposed to unionism; yet unionism succeeded
in equally hostile company towns in the North.[3] As one scholar notes, "The
South had its Charles DeBardelaben [owner of coal mines in Alabama], the

North its Henry Ford . . . . the pronouncements of the National Association of Manufacturers were no less hostile to labor than were those of the
Southern States Industrial Council."[4]

If there is a regional explanation for the failure of the '34 strike, it rests
in the different position of southern workers in regional and national politics. The powerful combination of internal and outside pressures that made
it possible for northern industrial unions to win in the automobile, steel, and
coal industries in the 1930s was simply not present in the South. The deep
sectional roots of the Democratic party in the 1930s muted the opportunity
for working people in the South to claim the Democratic party as their vehicle for empowerment in the same way that northern workers did. There
is a great irony connected to the failure of southern labor insurgency to bear
political fruit. Roosevelt built his Democratic majority in Congress by graft-
ing together his elite southern Democratic base and his new northern working-class base. This Democratic party majority, in turn, played a key role in
ensuring the success of organized labor in northern mass production industries. Roosevelt's failure to aid southern workers was, in this sense, a silent
price labor paid for the success of the New Deal and the rise of labor union
strength in the North.[5]

The 1934 strike thus powerfully illustrates the schizophrenic impact of
the New Deal on the South. While the rhetoric of the New Deal mobilized
the South's poor to challenge local established authority in unprecedented
numbers, the New Deal's political structure worked in the opposite direction, reinforcing the power of the South's economic elites. To challenge the
foundation of that power required the exercise of considerable political
muscle. But southern textile workers were never strong enough to revolu-
tionize southern politics; they were only strong enough to try to take advantage of a shift in the rhetoric offered to them by the larger society, in this
case the rhetoric of economic security offered by the NIRA.

———

The strike story is worth telling for a second reason: it brings to light the
ideas that were expressed through it, ideas that were muffled by workers'
defeat and subsequent silence. Southern textile worker organizing gave voice
to the sentiment that "modernization" could have a terribly destructive effect on workers' lives, particularly in situations when work, family, and community were so closely linked. Had southern cotton mill workers not organized, this message would not have been delivered.

That New Deal reformers did not clearly hear this message was a product of both their ideological narrowness and textile workers' own political

weakness. New Deal reformers were blind to the evils of the stretch-out in part because of the unquestioned devotion by some of them to the principles of scientific management. Embraced across the political spectrum by individuals as diverse as mill manufacturers and socialist labor leaders, scientific management expressed the belief that the "value-free" perspective of the scientific or technical expert would make workplace management more "objective," more rational. Scientific study by an "expert" would make work less subject to the arbitrary whims of temperamental overseers at the same time that it eliminated "archaic" customary work practices. In so venerating the technician, those who subscribed to scientific management removed decisions regarding the proper or just use of technology and the organization of work from community accountability.[6]

Textile workers were not entirely powerless before this cultural imperative. The organization of southern millhands between 1929 and 1932 did succeed in creating some accountability to local community standards on the part of mill owners. Yet southern mill workers could not achieve a similar power at the national level. Here the problem was not ideological, it was political. The NIRA elevated labor-management conflicts in southern textiles to a national stage so swiftly in 1933 that workers were forced, as an understandable expedient, to work within already existing national organizations, such as the UTW, or with individuals with influence at the federal level, such as Frances Perkins, or Senator Byrnes, or even Hugh Johnson, to get their ideas across. Forced to depend on the power of these intermediaries, textile workers inevitably risked having their own positions distorted, either through ignorance or, as it turned out, deliberately, to serve the agenda of others.

The intermediary that textile workers should have been most able to rely on, the UTW, simply could not break from its historic alliance with liberal textile employers in the North. Even though southern workers successfully forced their perspective onto UTW leaders such as Gorman and McMahon, this historical bias hampered the ability of these leaders to act as an honest broker for the southern workers during the strike negotiations. Nor were labor leaders in the AFL forced to contend with textile workers on their own terms. Instead, the massive uprising of textile workers in 1934 bacame a blank slate onto which labor leaders wrote whatever agenda suited their purposes.

The 1934 strike also sheds light on the NIRA, a much-maligned program of the New Deal. The NIRA offered a powerful ideological framework for southern textile workers not simply because of its endorsement of union organizing, but because it represented a genuine, if severely compromised, attempt to come to grips with the destructive effects of cutthroat competition in the textile industry. Given the poor marks the NIRA has received in historical accounts, it is easy to overlook its potential for mobilizing broad-based working-class support for government regulation of the economy.

To be sure, the way that the NIRA was implemented in the southern mills revealed its internal flaws. Most importantly, the government was never really in a position to exert the kind of oversight the NIRA required. Lacking the necessary bureaucratic apparatus to regulate production in every industry, the federal government had little choice but to permit industry trade associations to regulate themselves. In retrospect the government's goals were extraordinarily ambitious, leading to the conclusion of one historian that the NIRA was "overpromised."[7]

But the vision of a regulated industry embraced by southern textile workers was defeated not simply because of a weak federal bureaucracy. It was also lost because the idea of limits on production that were at the heart of the NIRA ran counter to notions of a dynamic, expanding economy. As the NIRA came under increasing attack, New Dealers turned to the option that finally prevailed: increasing demand to meet productive capacity by raising wages and injecting government funds into the money supply. Not only was the economics of abundance a more hopeful and appealing prospect, but the political coalition that made demand-side economics possible was more durable. Merchants joined with reformers interested in increasing the welfare of workers and labor unions whose campaigns to organize workers fit perfectly with liberals' desire to extract higher wages from manufacturers. This political coalition also served the needs of capital-intensive industries seeking expansion, both domestically and overseas.[8] The journalist Walter Lippman reflected this shift in thinking when he commented in 1935 that the country's experience with the NIRA had "demonstrated . . . that reflation, not planning, not regimentation . . . is the remedy."[9]

The increasing coherence of this "second New Deal" coalition had an impact on the New Deal government's willingness to consider regulating workloads. As early as the fall of 1934, so-called consumer interests within the NRA, described as "businesscrats" by Louis Galambos, were promoting government policies that would encourage efficiency in industry, thus assuring the lowest possible prices for purchasers. Like advocates of Keynsian economics from which this viewpoint was derived, these government functionaries were not inherently antiunion. They were aware that an environment that encouraged low prices would induce manufacturers to cut labor costs, and so they supported protecting the rights of labor unions as a countervailing force. But consumer interests did not concern themselves with manufacturer's cost-cutting measures that might extract a toll from workers in ways other than in the amount of their paychecks. Rather, such analyses frowned upon government intervention into the production process as interfering with the natural tendency toward increasing efficiency in manufacturing.[10]

The defeat of the textile strike and the rise of the influence of these consumer-policy makers ensured that the policies that emerged to replace the NIRA would give a freer hand to businesses in the organization of their work. In June 1935, for example, the National Industrial Relations Board, the group assigned to replace Hugh Johnson, moved decisively to have future government regulation of labor focus only on wages, hours, child labor, and Section 7(a)—that is, the right of workers to organize and bargain collectively. Workloads were no longer mentioned. Only days later, the NIRA was declared unconstitutional.[11]

At that very moment, textile workers went in the opposite direction. Far from wanting to pare down government regulation to include only wages and hours, workers felt that the NIRA didn't go far enough. For them, the problem was not the concept behind the NIRA, but the way the law had been administered. In the immediate aftermath of the collapse of the NIRA, the UTW proposed textile-industry regulation overseen not by a trade association, but by an independent body. The National Textile Bill (or Ellenbogen bill) provided for a National Textile Commission composed of seven persons appointed by the president to determine wages, hours, wage differentials, vacation pay, employment of minors, night work, work assignments, volume of inventories, and hours of plant operation. Mills would be required to submit reports to the commission and permit access to their books.[12] But the political mix that made such government regulation a viable option in 1933 no longer existed after 1935. The Ellenbogen bill, never passed, was the last time that the New Deal government seriously considered regulation of workloads in any industry. Not until the union health and safety movement of the late 1960s would there be another nationwide focus by workers on regulation of the workplace.[13]

In the end, the most enduring legacy of the southern textile strike is the way that the New Deal helped uplift and transform the consciousness of southern workers. The New Deal offered workers an identity, so long denied them, as first-class American citizens. Through the union organizations spawned by the NIRA, southern workers found the strength and solidarity necessary to give voice to their grievances. Southern leader John Peel commented on this phenomenon at one of the long hot meetings of the southern workers in the summer of 1934, and one of Peel's listeners recorded his words: "The NRA had helped give the textile workers more freedom of thought, he said, and also guaranteed them the right to assemble and freely discuss their problems, without fear of intimidation from the employers."[14]

Of course the vehicle for workers' increasing self-activism, the NIRA, was also the vehicle for containing their insurgency, and indeed for imposing on them the very work discipline they were fighting against. For some, this truth was too painful to recognize. Even as most workers denounced the NIRA and the Bruere Board, they held out hope that Roosevelt, once alerted to the nature of his administration's injustice, would rectify the problem. Only this faith in Roosevelt can explain why striking workers obediently returned to their jobs at his request, even though they had no assurances from industry that they would be rehired.

For other textile unionists, however, the hypocrisy of the New Deal proved decisive. This was especially true for leaders of the southern movement, whose ordeal over the previous year had taken them into the heart of the beast that was the NIRA bureaucracy. They emerged from the yearlong process disillusioned, perhaps, but also imbued with a stark clarity about the true nature of power, unencumbered by any cultural myths. Refusing any more to submit to a humiliating appeals process, they resolved to build their movement "by main force," based on workers' power alone.

To stand up to both enemies and allies in this way—however strategically implausible—was psychologically liberating. In their flying squadrons, their caravans of cars, their parades, and in their speeches, textile workers freely expressed themselves in 1934. Indeed, their visibility was the most remarkable aspect of the strike. No matter how others had misrepresented them for generations, they were now speaking and acting for themselves.

In the long run, such expressions of personal and cultural liberation can have powerful and profound consequences for the building of a sense of dignity among a people. "As a demonstration of the strength of the workers," said Paul Christopher in 1938, "the textile strike of 1934 has never been surpassed."[15] Even contemporary observers noted that something special was being demonstrated by the sheer determination of the southern unionists, particularly the strikers in Alabama. Writing in November 1934, W. R. Gaylord commented, "That ten-weeks strike in the mill hells of Alabama is rich with material for the writing of an epic poem. It may be that out of its throes will come a poet who lived it through, who will sing its song for the nation to hear."[16]

Gaylord was describing a critical part of any successful long-term struggle: the process of turning the sacrifice and dedication of a people, whether they have won or lost, into a cultural strength, girding them for the long haul. The tragedy may not be that textile workers struck, or even that they lost, but that for sixty years no poet emerged to sing the textile workers' song. The Uprising of '34 was hidden for decades, not only from the public, but from textile workers themselves. A source of embarrassment to the institutions that were complicit in the strike's failure, it was conveniently excluded from both New Deal and textile union histories. Because the strength of the '34 strike was overlooked, historians failed, until recently, to appreciate the latent power of textile labor. The failure to recognize this latent power has in turn led to a limited understanding of what might have been possible to achieve, even in an extremely repressive environment like the South.

APPENDIX A

UTWA Southern Locals in 1934

ALABAMA		1878	Alabama City
997-A	Blue Mountain	1879	Gadsden
997-B	Anniston	1887	Clanton
997-C	Oxford	1892	Opelika
997-D	Anniston	1898	East Tallassee
997-E	Oxford	1915	Sycamore
1745	Piedmont	1918	Huntsville
1766	Birmingham	1925	Roanoke
1781	Siluria	1978	Huntsville
1787	Selma	2004	Guntersville
1788	Florence	2051	Winfield
1789	Birmingham	2066	Huntsville
1807	Boylston	2086	Huntsville
1814	Montgomery	2093	Albertville
1815	Jacksonville	2261	Huntsville
1823	Florence	2262	Huntsville
1824	Florence	2271	Fayette
1825	Prichard	2273	Haleyville
1847	Cordova	2280	Gadsden
1850	Uniontown	2281	Russellville
1856	Prattville	2283	Stevenson
1864	Jasper	2378	Anniston
1865	Alexander City	2379	Lanett
1872	Crichton	2410	Anniston

GEORGIA

1124	Columbus
1605	Columbus
1693	Augusta
1764	Macon
1816	Hogansville
1826	Rome
1830	Rome
1831	Rome
1833	Chickamauga
1843	Scottdale
1849	Rome
1852	Rome
1871	Douglasville
1880	Newnan
1886	Chattahoochee
1893	Dalton
1899	LaGrange
1907	Trion
1922	Union Point
1938	Egan Park
1939	Shannon
1940	Cedartown
1984	Grantville
2028	Greensboro
2036	Social Circle
2039	Augusta (c)
2050	Augusta
2068	Summerville
2072	La Fayette
2073	Villa Rica
2109	Eatonton
2122	Covington
2142	Porterdale
2152	Rockmart
2174	Porterdale
2181	Clarksdale
2198	Monroe
2199	Atlanta
2212	Monroe
2213	Aragon
2239	Atco

2246	Manchester
2250	Cedartown
2256	Columbus
2289	Macon (c)
2294	Villa Rica
2307	Atlanta
2313	Commerce
2318	Atlanta
2319	Carrollton
2320	Lindale
2352	Barnesville
2353	Forsyth
2355	Roswell
2360	Milstead
2365	Remerton
2368	Griffin
2414	Columbus
2417	Columbus
2436	Columbus

NORTH CAROLINA

1221	Mooresville
1269	Salisbury
1271	McAdenville
1273	China Grove
1285	Cooleemee
1312	Flint-Groves
1732	Salisbury
1769	Salisbury
1770	Winston-Salem
1777	Burlington
1812	Winston-Salem
1854	Statesville
1857	Lenoir
1875	Lincolnton
1894	High Shoals
1900	Charlotte
1901	Shelby
1902	Concord
1904	Fayetteville
1910	Lumberton
1927	Selma

1931	Pittsboro	2162	Tarboro
1944	Kings Mountain	2184	Wilmington
1947	Gastonia	2187	Franklinville
1995	Spindale	2221	Tarboro
1999	Goldsboro	2230	Roanoke Rapids
2000	Bessemer City	2241	Stony Point
2002	Charlotte	2243	West Erwin
2003	Granite Falls	2245	Weldon
2018	East Belmont	2263	Salisbury
2019	North Belmont	2265	Kannapolis
2024	Brookford	2274	Gastonia
2027	Forest City	2277	Sanford
2049	Rocky Mount	2278	Erwin (c)
2054	Marion	2284	Hillsboro
2052	Forest City	2285	Charlotte
2067	Hickory	2290	Grover
2074	Avondale	2291	Valdese
2075	Caroleen	2292	Charlotte
2078	Paw Creek	2293	Charlotte
2079	Fayetteville	2302	Lexington
2081	Henrietta	2303	Huntersville
2082	Cramerton	2305	Rockingham
2084	Laurinburg	2308	Durham (c)
2088	Hope Mills	2316	Greensboro
2092	Saint Pauls	2334	Hillsborough (c)
2095	Cumberland Mills	2335	Henderson
2102	Stanley	2343	Thomasville
2108	Cliffside	2347	Dallas
2113	Enka	2357	Reidsville
2115	Gastonia	2372	Haw River
2117	Ashboro	2374	Neuse
2120	Stanley	2376	Wadesboro
2121	South Gastonia	2377	Mooresville
2126	Lowell	2381	Gibsonville
2128	Smithfield	2409	Gastonia
2131	Concord	2428	Durham
2132	Mount Holly		
2138	South Gastonia	SOUTH CAROLINA	
2144	Lowell	1233	Rock Hill
2155	Durham	1661	Union
2156	Swannanoa	1664	Whitmore
2159	North Charlotte	1673	Anderson

1679	New Brookland	2060	Iva
1683	Langley	2070	Tucapau
1684	Greenville	2089	Newry
1687	Bath	2094	Belton
1705	Spartanburg	2111	Landau
1754	Graniteville	2112	Laurens
1760	Seneca	2118	Newberry
1771	Columbia	2119	Spartanburg
1780	Clifton	2135	Fairmont
1800	Winsboro	2145	Spartanburg
1804	Gaffney	2147	Liberty
1808	Pelzer	2149	Darlington
1834	Clifton	2161	Ninety-Six
1835	Drayton	2166	Great Falls
1836	Valley Falls	2171	Greenwood
1881	Spartanburg	2172	South Greenwood
1882	Spartanburg	2176	Cateechee
1883	Converse	2182	Clinton
1884	Clifton (c)	2186	Wellford
1888	Abbeville	2189	Glendale
1895	Blacksburg	2190	Greer
1896	Gaffney	2191	Lyman
1903	Bamberg	2200	Westminster
1908	Cherokee Falls	2202	Clearwater
1909	Piedmont	2210	Ware Shoals
1912	Bennettsville	2218	Greer
1913	Camden	2219	Spartanburg (c)
1914	Walhalla	2224	Laurens
1934	Cowpens	2227	Anderson
1935	Inman	2231	Gaffney (c)
1936	Spartanburg	2232	Woodruff
1946	Honea Path	2236	Enoree
1977	Union	2237	Jonesville
1994	Pacolet Mills	2238	Conestee
1995	Paris	2244	Taylors
2001	Clover	2254	Lockhart
2005	Calhoun Falls	2255	Simpsonville
2011	Slater	2266	Pacolet Mills (c)
2013	Newberry	2275	Fairmont (c)
2014	Newberry	2286	McColl
2017	Whitney	2287	Clinton
2029	Buffalo	2288	Goldville

2297	Union	1758	Knoxville
2298	Greer	1761	Knoxville
2304	Chester	1785	Chattanooga
2321	Lexington	1838	Bemis
2369	Easley	1985	Lenoir City
2406	Columbia (c)	2076	Dyersburg
2411	Camden	2207	Elizabethton
		2216	Chattanooga
TENNESSEE		2282	Trenton
1747	Chattanooga	2309	East Lake
1751	Chattanooga	2345	Chattanooga
1757	Harriman		

Key: (c) denotes "colored" locals

Source: "Report of Local Unions for Six Months from October 1, 1934 to March 1, 1935" in Locals, Status folder, Box 674, Textile Workers Union of America Papers, State Historical Society of Wisconsin.

Note: Some of the locals were much more substantial and durable than others. Fragile union locals went in and out of existence rapidly in the period from 1933 to 1936. Of the UTWA lists in existence, this list comes closest to accurately naming the locals active at the time of the general strike.

APPENDIX B

Estimates of Southern Membership in the UTWA in 1934

No existing data directly measures southern UTW membership. Below are three different types of estimates.

1. In August 1934, AFL southern representative George Googe estimated the number of union members as follows:[1]

North Carolina	80,000
South Carolina	50,000
Georgia	30,000
Alabama	20,000
Tennessee	8,000
Total	188,000

This statistic has some value, for it comes remarkably close to the number of southern workers who actually participated in the general strike. However, Googe does not explain the source of his estimates, and this number is higher than the UTW's own estimate of its membership nationwide in cotton textiles only (see below).

2. A second approach to estimating UTW southern membership starts with the UTW's stated membership in the cotton textile industry nationwide, estimated at 185,000 in July 1934. Because the overwhelming majority of southern textile workers were cotton mill workers, this is a helpful statistic. Available data indicates that, as of 1937, the South had 73 percent of the industry's cotton mill workforce. Assuming union membership to be evenly distributed throughout the cotton mill industry (and this is disputable), southern UTW membership would be 73 percent of 185,000, or 135,050 southern members.[2]

3. In August 1934, UTW President Thomas McMahon reported 270,000 members nationwide, representing six hundred new locals since July 1933. According to UTW records there were 317 UTW locals in the South in October 1934 (49 in Alabama, 60 in Georgia, 99 in North Carolina, 95 in South Carolina, and 14 in Tennessee; see appendix A). Since this number represents slightly over half the six hundred new locals, southern UTW membership could be estimated at approximately one-half of the total membership, or 135,000. This figure jibes with the estimate in method #2.

The number of southern UTW locals in UTW records seems high, however. Many of these locals must have been weak or very small. For estimates of membership it is more realistic to rely on sources counting the number of locals able to send a delegate to a state convention. Such estimates suggest the following number of locals: 70 in North Carolina; approximately 60 in South Carolina; 42 in Alabama; and 16 in Georgia. By this reckoning, UTW southern membership would be roughly proportional to the ratio of southern locals to locals nationwide. One hundred eighty-eight out of 600 equals 31.6 percent of the total membership of 270,000, or 85,320 southern UTW members. This figure seems a realistically low estimate, since one source estimated 55,000 UTW members in North Carolina alone in the spring of 1934, and another cited South Carolina membership at 20,000 at about the same time, making a total 75,000 without counting membership in Georgia or Alabama.[3]

NOTES

Introduction

1. Affidavit of F. R. Summers, Kings Mountain, North Carolina, September 13, 1934, in Box 103, J. C. B. Ehringhaus Papers, North Carolina Division of Archives and History.

2. The *New York Times* estimated that at its peak, 172,476 workers in the South had not reported to their jobs. A total of over four hundred thousand textile workers struck across the country. Nationally, only the 1922 coal miners' strike was larger. *New York Times*, September 18, 1934; Foner, *Women and the American Labor Movement*, 286.

3. Author's interview with Joseph Jacobs, Atlanta, Georgia.

4. *Walker County (Alabama) Union News*, September 6, 20, and October 18, 1934.

5. Benjamin Gossett to J. C. B. Ehringhaus, September 14, 1934, Box 104, J. C. B. Ehringhaus Papers, North Carolina Division of Archives and History.

6. See, for example, labor leader Sidney Hillman's discussion of new union members in 1933–34 as "NRA-babies." Fraser, *Labor Will Rule*, 424–25.

7. Bernstein, *The Turbulent Years*, 315.

8. A useful account is Goldfield, *The Decline of Organized Labor in the United States*. See also Moody, *An Injury to All*.

9. See Fraser, "The 'Labor Question'"; Dubofsky and Van Tine, *Labor Leaders in America*.

10. The importance of pre-1935 labor insurgency was first suggested by Lynd, "The Possibility of Radicalism in the Early 1930s." Other recent accounts of labor struggles during the early New Deal include: Nelson, *Workers on the Waterfront*, on the San Francisco General Strike; Faue, *Community of Suffering and Struggle*, on the

Minneapolis strike of 1934; and the essays in Lynd, ed., *"We Are All Leaders": The Alternative Unionism of the Early 1930s.*

11. A pioneering book in this new wave of historical literature is Hall et al., *Like a Family.* Other important accounts include Flamming, *Creating the Modern South;* Newby, *Plain Folk in the New South;* and Tullos, *Habits of Industry.* A review of the recent literature on southern textile workers is Zieger, "Textile Workers and Historians." On early southern textile labor protest see McLaurin, *Paternalism and Protest;* G. Mitchell, *Textile Unionism and the South;* and Nolan and James, "Textile Unionism in the Piedmont."

12. For an outstanding account of political activism among southern textile workers see Simon, *A Fabric of Defeat.*

13. For an in-depth account of the politicization of northern industrial workers see Cohen, *Making a New Deal.*

14. No authoritative estimate exists of voter participation of textile workers. The figure of 35 percent represents the percentage of mill workers in northwest Georgia who voted in the September 1934 gubernatorial primary. This figure, however, probably overestimates general levels of voter participation by southern textile workers, since events of that month probably elevated voter turnout to unusually high levels. See Brittain, "The Politics of Whiteness," 23. One should also be cognizant of state-by-state variations in voter participation by southern mill workers. In South Carolina, the all-white primary ensured that no poll tax stood in the way of textile worker participation in politics. The best general overview of voter participation in the South is still Key, *Southern Politics in State and Nation.*

15. An excellent discussion of the impact of the political power of southern elites on the shape of the New Deal is Brinkley, "The New Deal and Southern Politics."

16. According to the industry analyst Jack Blicksilver, the strikes "of 1929 and the early thirties temporarily slowed down the movement toward applying the concepts of scientific management to cotton textiles." Blicksilver, *Cotton Manufacturing in the Southeast,* 125.

17. This insight was first advanced in Boyette, "The General Textile Strike of 1934 in Greenwood County."

18. See, for example, Flamming, *Creating the Modern South* (Dalton, Georgia); Waldrep, "Politics of Hope and Fear" (Spartanburg, South Carolina); Frankel, "Women, Paternalism, and Protest" (Henderson, North Carolina); Wingerd, "Rethinking Paternalism" (Cooleemee, North Carolina).

19. For one published account, see Findlay, "The Great Textile Strike of 1934," 17–29. A useful unpublished account is Bennett, "Textile Workers in New England, 1920–1940."

20. The price of this silence on strike survivors and their children is explored in moving and revealing interviews with strike survivors in Stoney and Helfand's documentary film *The Uprising of '34.* See also DuPlessis, "Honea Path Confronts 60 Years of Repressed Memories."

21. An excellent account of the Gastonia strike is Salmond, *Gastonia, 1929.* Older

accounts that also provide a valuable first-hand perspective include Beal, *Proletarian Journey;* and Vorse, *Strike!.* The place of the Gastonia strike in textile labor history will be discussed in greater detail in chapter 2.

22. Minchin, *What Do We Need a Union For?;* Clark, *Like Night and Day.*

Chapter 1: Customary Rights

1. This description is based on a description of mill owners in Henderson, North Carolina, in Frankel, "'Jesus Leads Us,'" 105.

2. In later years, when electricity freed mills from falling water and mills sprung up near cities, textile villages were again politically marginalized, excluded from participation in city politics by gerrymandering. On the poll tax see Stoney, "Suffrage in the South." For a state-by-state survey of voter participation see Key, *Southern Politics in State and Nation.* For an analysis of the effect of the poll tax on labor union power see Norrell, "Labor at the Ballot Box." South Carolina workers were an exception, since no poll tax barred them from voting in the all-important "white primary." For an analysis of the political power of South Carolina textile workers see Simon, *A Fabric of Defeat.*

3. Herring, "The Industrial Worker," 347–48. See also Gaston, *The New South Creed.*

4. James Barrett, "Resolution," passed by the North Carolina Federation of Labor Convention, August 1923, Greensboro, North Carolina, reprinted in the *Charlotte Labor Herald,* August 17, 1923.

5. McHugh, *Mill Family,* especially 71–74; Hall et al., *Like a Family;* Frankel, "'Jesus Leads Us,'" 26; Freeze, "Poor Girls Who Might Otherwise Be Wretched," 105.

6. Newby, *Plain Folk in the New South,* 233.

7. Hall et al., *Like a Family,* chapter 3; Flamming, *Creating the Modern South,* 180–82; Newby, *Plain Folk in the New South,* part III; Herring, *Welfare Work in Mill Villages,* 206–10.

8. Author and Eula McGill's interview with Burns Cox, Gadsden, Alabama; Wingerd, "Rethinking Paternalism"; McLaurin, *Paternalism and Protest,* 158.

9. Letter from Ethel Durnall, Employment Manager, Wateree Mills, Camden, South Carolina, in *Survey,* August 16, 1919, 736.

10. Kohn, *The Cotton Mills of South Carolina;* Beardsley, *A History of Neglect,* 60.

11. McLaurin, *Paternalism and Protest,* 77–119.

12. W. B. Smith Whaley, President of Gramby Mills, Columbia, South Carolina, in McLaurin, *Paternalism and Protest,* 172.

13. Newby, *Plain Folk in the New South,* 549.

14. See, for example, the 1897 strike to keep out black workers at the Fulton Bag and Cotton Mills, discussed in Fink, *The Fulton Bag and Cotton Mills Strike of 1914–1915,* 40. As I. A. Newby puts it, "The shortage of white labor was a valid reason for looking into the possibilities of black labor. But that motivation would have required treating the subject as a matter of economics rather than race." Newby, *Plain Folk in*

the New South, 482. For another look at the role played by black labor in textile labor relations see McLaurin, *Paternalism and Protest*, 60–64. On black workers in southern textiles generally, see Frederickson, "Four Decades of Change."

15. See, for example, Simon, "Choosing Between the Ham and the Union," 84.

16. Flamming, *Creating the Modern South*, chapters 5 and 6, especially the chart on p. 129, which illustrates the coincidence in time between labor turnover and mill owners' efforts to improve conditions in the mill villages.

17. Wingerd, "Rethinking Paternalism," 881.

18. It was a widespread practice for supervisors to designate relatives, friends, or "loyal workers" for choice jobs. See author's interviews with Inez and Leola Allen, Shelby, North Carolina, and author and Eula McGill's interviews with Gertrude Stewart, Huntsville, Alabama. Some scholars have suggested that this practice may be a crucial factor in determining whether or not particular workers struck in 1934. See Hall et al., *Like a Family*, 346; Carlton, "Paternalism and Southern Textile Labor," 24.

19. Stoney and Helfand, *The Uprising of '34.*

20. Newby, *Plain Folk in the New South*, 329.

21. *Textile World Journal*, December 16, 1916, 41.

22. DeNatale, "Traditional Culture and Community in a Piedmont Textile Mill Village," 105; Theotis Williamson, Southern Oral History Project, quoted in Newby, *Plain Folk in the New South*, 182. Mills were also run at a relaxed pace because they were technologically primitive. Power based on falling water was notoriously unreliable, and belt-driven machines broke easily. Because machines were driven by a central motor, when one loom broke, everything stopped. Irregular work was thus common. See Hall et al., *Like a Family*, 105–9.

23. For a theoretical understanding of worker culture and employer dominance, I am indebted to Scott, *The Moral Economy of the Peasant*, and Benson, *Counter Cultures.*

24. For workers' responses to World War I generally see McCartin, *Labor's 'Great War.'*

25. Speech by James Barrett before the 1921 convention of the United Textile Workers, reprinted in *Textile Worker*, February 1922, 517–18.

26. For a general account of textile unionism during World War I, see G. Mitchell, *Textile Unionism and the South.*

27. When scattered UTW locals appeared in the South in 1913–15, they comprised only weavers and loom fixers. See *Textile Worker*, July 1915, 9. A dramatic attempt to establish a union local at the Fulton Bag and Cotton Mills failed. See Fink, *The Fulton Bag and Cotton Mills Strike of 1914–1915.*

28. *Textile Worker*, April 1918, 7; March 1919, 423; *Southern Textile Bulletin*, November 21, 1918, 4, 6, 12, 28; author's interview with Mary Woodell, Columbus, Georgia; *Textile Worker*, March 1919, 473.

29. The quote is from Douty, "The North Carolina Industrial Worker," 274. For the story of this wave of organizing see *Textile Worker*, May 1919, 64–65; *Southern*

Textile Bulletin, June 5, 1919; Hall et al., *Like a Family*, 187–90; Johnson, "The Cotton Strike." One UTW organizer reported that forty thousand textile workers had joined the UTW from January through September 1919 (*Textile Worker*, September 1919). That this membership included all types of workers in the mill may be suggested by the fact that in one mill, the Chadwick Hoskins Mill in Charlotte, North Carolina, 80 percent of the workers had joined their union local. MacDonald, *Southern Mill Hills*, 85.

30. The experience of southern textile workers during these wartime strikes supports David Montgomery's contention that World War I battles "presaged" the labor struggles of the thirties, "at least the early thirties, that is, before the founding of the Committee for Industrial Organizations and the enactment of the Wagner Act." Montgomery, *The Fall of the House of Labor*, 457.

31. Observing a walkout in North Carolina in 1921, the *New Bedford (Mass.) Morning Mercury* noted with some interest "the fact that leaders developed from the workers themselves as the strike was prolonged." *New Bedford (Mass.) Morning Mercury*, October 7, 1921, in *Textile Worker*, October 1921, 324.

32. Letter from Neal Bass to Cole Blease, February 9, 1914, in Carlton, *Mill and Town in South Carolina*, 251, n.74; Flamming, *Creating the Modern South*, 195.

33. Author and Eula McGill's interview with Burns Cox, Gadsden, Alabama.

34. G. Mitchell, "The Cotton Mills Again," 412.

35. Hearden, *Independence and Empire*.

36. *Southern Textile Bulletin*, November 6, 1919, 18.

37. *Manufacturer's Record*, November 21, 1918, 67–68, cited in *Textile Worker*, December 1918, 320.

38. Carlton, *Mill and Town in South Carolina*; Herring, *Welfare Work in Mill Villages*.

39. Resolution passed by the North Carolina Federation of Labor Convention, August, 1923, Greensboro, North Carolina, reprinted in the *Charlotte Labor Herald*, August 17, 1923.

40. It should be noted that UTW locals were formed in 1919 in Rock Hill, South Carolina, on the North Carolina border near Gastonia, and in the Horse Creek Valley, South Carolina, on the Georgia border opposite Augusta. These two union hot spots are in a sense the exceptions that prove the rule, for upon seeing successful union organization in these regions, South Carolina Governor Manning quickly intervened to ensure that these unions were not "affiliated with a national labor organization." See *Southern Textile Bulletin*, October 2 1919, and *Daily News Record*, September 30, 1919, in Miscellany file, Box 3, G. S. Mitchell Papers, Manuscripts Department, Duke University Library.

41. *Charlotte Observer*, December 2, 1919, article reprinted in the *Southern Textile Bulletin*, December 4, 1919, 18.

42. Whitley, "Fuller E. Callaway and Textile Mill Development in LaGrange," 295–306.

43. On the response of the North Carolina Federation of Labor see Douty, "The

North Carolina Industrial Worker," 284–86; Johnson, "The Cotton Strike," 646–47.

44. Statement of U.S. Commissioner of Labor Ethelbert Stewart in *Knoxville News Sentinel*, May 6, 1929.

45. Some excellent descriptions of the stretch-out can be found in Hall et al., *Like a Family*, 200–212; and Tullos, *Habits of Industry*, 172–204.

46. Author's interview with Vance and Zelleree Donnahoo, Inman, South Carolina.

47. See Rhyne, *Some Southern Cotton Mill Workers*, 18; and Hall et al., *Like a Family*, 201.

48. See description of the worklife of Lora Wright in Tullos, *Habits of Industry*, 173–204.

49. Hall et al., *Like a Family*, 212.

50. Federal Writers' Project interview, cited in Beardsley, *A History of Neglect*, 72–73.

51. Interview with Lora League in Tullos, *Habits of Industry*, 187–90.

52. By 1920 the percentage of children working in the southern mills was 5 percent of the workforce, compared to 1 percent in northern textile mills in 1930. See Wright, *Old South, New South*, and "Cheap Labor in Southern Textiles, 1880–1930," 605–29, especially the chart on p. 611, showing age-sex composition of the textile labor force from 1880 to 1920. See also pp. 608–11 on the higher productivity of adult workers. Other sources include Evans, "Southern Labor Supply and Working Conditions in Industry," 158; and Lahne, *The Cotton Mill Worker*, 290, appendix, table 6.

53. On the work of the "nannies," who were black women, see "The Uprising of '34 Video Project," transcripts, Southern Labor Archives, Georgia State University.

54. The observer was the union organizer Alfred Hoffman, quoted in Frankel, "'Jesus Leads Us,'" 108. For more on Henderson see Hoffman, "Hell in Henderson, A Walkout in Darkest America," 2–5; Herring, "12 Cents, the Troops, and the Union," 199–202; and untitled manuscript, Miscellaneous folder, Box 3, G. S. Mitchell Papers, Manuscripts Department, Duke University Library.

55. Salmond, *Gastonia, 1929*, 13.

56. McLaurin, *Paternalism and Protest*, 8, 30, 43; quote is on 30. See also Carlton, "The Revolution from Above."

57. Douty, "The North Carolina Industrial Worker," 107–9; Wright, *Old South, New South*, 151–55. Scholars are still attempting to determine why workers resisted wage cuts so passionately at the end of World War I. The economist Gavin Wright describes this phenomenon as "sticky wages," that is, workers will oppose wage cuts more than they will oppose wages that are already low. Wright also suggests that workers resisted wage cuts because high wages were more valued by experienced adult male heads of families who now comprised an increasingly large percentage of the southern cotton mill workforce (by 1930 women made up only about one-third of the workforce).

Whether only male workers valued higher wages in the 1920s is hard to determine. I will argue below that both male and female workers valued their higher wages because of their increasing integration into the consumer economy of the 1920s.

58. Blicksilver, *Cotton Manufacturing in the Southeast*, 105. An important recent analysis of the harmful consequences of mobile capital and overproduction is Greider, *One World, Ready or Not*.

59. Edmunds, *Cotton Mill Labor Conditions in the South and New England*, 6–26, quote is on 10.

60. See, for example, author and Eula McGill's interview with Jesse Ryland, Cordova, Alabama.

61. For two examples, see accounts of the 1923 organizing drive in North Charlotte (*Charlotte Labor Herald*, August 11, 17, 31, and September 14, 1923); and the 1930 organizing drive in Gadsden, Alabama (Letter to George H. Van Fleet, Commissioner of Conciliation, U.S. Department of Labor, from H. L. Kerwin, April 10, 1930, Folder 16, Box 1, Philip Taft Papers, Birmingham Public Library, Birmingham, Alabama).

62. Myers, *Representative Government in Industry*, 37.

63. Tannenbaum, "The South Buries Its Anglo-Saxons," 56.

64. Mitchell and Mitchell, *The Industrial Revolution in the South*, 33. Portions of this book, including the passage cited, were published in 1927, evidence that sentiment against mill owners on the part of reformers had begun to build even before the 1929 strikes. For other examples see Singal, *The War Within*, 74–75.

65. B. Mitchell, "The End of Child Labor," 750. A similar point was made in 1921 by *Survey* editors in their introduction to "The Cotton Strike," by Gerald Johnson. On Mitchell's change of perspective see the essay about him in Singal, *The War Within*. On townspeople's attitudes see Carlton, *Mill and Town*; and Hall et al., *Like a Family*, 132. On shifting public attitudes towards the mills in general, see Herring, "Cycles of Cotton Mill Criticism." Critical works of this era include: MacDonald, *Southern Mill Hills*; Herring, *Welfare Work in Mill Villages*; Rhyne, *Some Southern Cotton Mill Workers*; G. Mitchell, *Textile Unionism and the South*; Blanshard, *Labor in Southern Cotton Mills*.

66. Singal, *The War Within*, 303.

67. Blanshard, *Labor in Southern Cotton Mills*, 12.

68. Marshall, *Labor in the South*, 123.

69. *Atlanta Constitution*, March 28, 1927, 6; "Industry Replies to Church Appeal," *New York Times*, April 18, 1927.

70. MacDonald, *Southern Mill Hills*, 53; Hall et al., *Like a Family*, 222.

71. On workers living in town see Lahne, *The Cotton Mill Worker*, 41; and Tripplette, "One-Industry Towns," 108: "During the 1920–1930 decade the textile mills found that they did not have to build a 'village' to secure a labor supply; this era also coincided with the state's highway paving program and the increasingly widespread ownership and use of the automobile."

72. Hall et al., *Like a Family*, 252.

73. Burke, *Call Home the Heart*, 186; Herring, "The Industrial Worker," 354–55.

As the *Charlotte Observer* noted on August 13, 1919: "Fifty years ago the farmer made everything he needed on his farm. Now everything we eat or wear is bought." See also *Charlotte Observer*, July 16, 1919.

74. Observation by a staffperson for the northern-based United Textile Workers who had been visiting the South for over twenty years, cited in *Textile Worker*, May 1919, 65.

Thanks in part to major public health campaigns of the second decade of the century, diseases like hookworm were on the run. With more income, workers had better diets, decreasing the incidence of pellagra to its lowest levels since records had been kept. There was a new outbreak of pellagra in the mid-twenties but, interestingly, it was more quickly eliminated precisely because the links between pellagra, diet, and poverty were now openly discussed. Welfare work in the mill villages had also improved sanitation levels. A wave of incorporation of mill villages into towns increased the likelihood that sewage systems would be installed. The number of South Carolina mill houses with foul, open privies was cut in half from 1915 to 1925. Progress was scattered and uneven, but the change was noticeable and permanent. See Beardsley, *A History of Neglect*, 58, 195, 197; Hall et al., *Like a Family*, 119; Herring, *Welfare Work in Mill Villages*.

Finally, the new generation of textile workers was more literate. The writer and social scientist Harriet Herring reported that from 1910 to 1922 illiteracy in southern industrial states was "practically halved." A study of a group of cotton mills from 1922 to 1932 found that the number of workers who attended high school increased from 10 to 19 percent. Herring, "The Industrial Worker," 352.

75. MacDonald, *Southern Mill Hills*, 29.

76. *Charlotte Observer*, August 13, 1919. The *Observer* noted that mill workers now talked openly about an education for their children. *Charlotte Observer*, July 16, 1919. See also MacDonald, *Southern Mill Hills*, 76.

77. Letter from Mary E. Fraser, Division of Home Economic Research, Winthrop College, Rock Hill, South Carolina, to G. S. Mitchell, April 20, 1929, in Violence, Textiles folder, Box 4, G. S. Mitchell Papers, Manuscripts Department, Duke University Library.

78. Letter from Fraser to G. S. Mitchell, April 20, 1929, in Violence, Textiles folder, Box 4, G. S. Mitchell Papers, Manuscripts Department, Duke University Library.

79. Waldrep, "Politics of Hope and Fear," 70.

Chapter 2: Homegrown Unions

1. For a similar assessment, see Herring, "The Industrial Worker," 357. For a general history of the Gastonia strike see Salmond, *Gastonia, 1929*; and Vorse, *Strike!*

2. Barrett had been an advocate of North Carolina textile workers' unions since World War I. In 1921 he became president of the North Carolina Federation of Labor on a platform of justice for textile workers; in 1923, when he lost a bid for re-election, he started the *Charlotte Labor Herald*. By 1929 Barrett had become frustrated

with the AFL's sometime commitment to textile workers—to be examined in chapter 3—and had retreated out of the textile district to edit a newspaper in Brevard, in the far western region of North Carolina. In 1929 he wrote a private letter to AFL President James Green warning him that a drive to organize workers in southern textiles would fail unless "textile workers of the South form their own organization, with their membership confined to those who are actually engaged in the mills of the South, with general and subordinate offices filled by men and women who are engaged in actual work in the textile industry of the South." Industry officials acquired a copy of Barrett's letter and, delighted to see an attack on the AFL, reprinted the letter with an editorial in the *Southern Textile Bulletin*, October 17, 1929, 22; and November 28, 1929, 12, 36–37. A careful reading of the letter, however, reveals that Barrett advocated goals such as collective bargaining that were anathema to the position of southern textile manufacturers.

3. "Outlook Bright in Textile Strike," April 7, 1929, Textiles, North and South Carolina folder, Box 4, G. S. Mitchell Papers, Manuscripts Department, Duke University Library.

4. Myers, "Field Notes." For information on a similar approach used by textile workers in Passaic, New Jersey, during the war years, see Goldberg, *A Tale of Three Cities*, 46–83.

5. George Googe, "Union Progress in South Carolina," *American Federationist*, June 1929, 679.

6. Myers, "Field Notes," 11.

7. Myers, "Field Notes," 9.

8. *Knoxville News Sentinel*, May 1, 1929, 18.

9. Myers, "Field Notes," 11.

10. The labor leader was the AFL's southern representative George Googe. *American Federationist*, June 1929, 679.

11. *Spartanburg Herald* editorial reprinted in the *Gastonia Gazette*, April 6, 1929.

12. Myers, "Field Notes," 8–11. Myers noted that "other mills in this section have adjusted wages or the number of machines per operative in view of the general opposition to the 'stretch-out' system." Harriet Herring came to the same conclusion, cautioning that "we must not let the failures at the spectacular strikes at Gastonia and Marion . . . blind us to the fact that in 1929 workers in dozens of mills won their strikes against the stretch out." Herring, "The Industrial Worker," 356. An similar analysis can be found in Van Osdell, "Cotton Mills, Labor, and the Southern Mind," 124–39. A more pessimistic analysis is Simon, *A Fabric of Defeat*, 52–55.

13. For an example of a UTW-supported strike in South Carolina that produced just such a humiliating end, see Simon, *A Fabric of Defeat*, 54–55.

14. Williams, "The Cotton Manufacturing Industry in Alabama"; Cobb, *The Selling of the South*, 64. George Tindall notes that the proportion of textile mills fully owned by northern interests "rose markedly as one progressed from North Carolina to Alabama, which suggested a larger northern influence in the newer development." Tindall, *Emergence of the New South*, 76.

15. *Textile Worker,* August 1930, 274.

16. *Birmingham Labor Advocate,* May 31, 1930. See also July 19, 1930: "Thousands of textile workers have joined in Columbus"; and G. Mitchell, "Organization of Labor in the South," 186: "Columbus has been brilliantly unionized." On Anniston see the *Birmingham Labor Advocate,* May 3, 1930. Workers from four textile mills in Anniston joined the UTW. According to the *Labor Advocate* for May 31, 1930, six charters were issued in Gadsden over the previous six weeks. See also *Labor Advocate,* September 20, 1930: "A week's labor Chautaqua held in Huntsville and Columbus, attended by thousands of mill hands."

17. *Textile Worker,* June 1930, 187.

18. *Birmingham Labor Advocate,* July 26, 1930. See also report of Paul J. Smith, chairman of the AFL Southern Organizing Committee, *Textile Worker,* June 1930, 169.

19. *Birmingham Labor Advocate,* July 6, 1929, and May 31, 1930. In November 1929, UTW President Thomas McMahon came to Anniston to address the textile workers as part of a southern tour. *Labor Advocate,* November 9, 1929.

20. Hall, "Disorderly Women," 368, 380–81.

21. Speech by McMahon at UTW convention in 1930, cited in Garrison, "Paul Revere Christopher," 9. See also Prior, "From Community to National Unionism," 12, who cites unemployment for factory workers in North Carolina in 1931 to have been 19.5 percent.

22. *Textile Worker,* May 1932, 65.

23. Lawrence Hogan, a southern textile organizer in 1932, reported only four mills running out of 104 that he visited in the North Carolina piedmont. "There have been more wage-cuts, more lay-offs, short time and piece work, in the past five weeks, than ever before." Huff, "A Conference of Southern Workers," 4.

24. Author and Eula McGill's interview with Earl Richardson, Cordova, Alabama.

25. Author and Eula McGill's interviews with Burns Cox, Laura Beard, Gadsden, Alabama; Garrison, "Paul Revere Christopher," 21–22.

26. One reason for the outburst of strikes in the summer of 1932 was the sudden surge in demand for cotton textiles, which gave workers hope of some bargaining leverage. See Vittoz, *New Deal Labor Policy and the American Industrial Economy,* 32.

27. The defense was conducted by Olin Johnston, later to become governor of South Carolina. *Textile Worker,* July 1932, 126.

28. *Textile Worker,* March 1931, 742; and April, 1931, 11. 90 percent of the workers in the Augusta/Horse Creek Valley area were organized.

29. *Textile Worker,* April 1932, 9.

30. Hall et al., *Like a Family,* 217.

31. On Rockingham and High Point see Prior, "From Community to National Unionism," 19–28.

32. Huff, "A Conference of Southern Workers," 5. About one month later, the superintendent at the White Oak Mill in Greensboro committed suicide. *Textile Worker,* April 1932, 17.

33. Douty, "Labor Unrest in North Carolina"; Lawrence Hogan, "Rumblings in Southern Textiles," 8.

34. Van Osdell, "Cotton Mills, Labor, and the Southern Mind," 110.

35. *Raleigh News and Observer*, April 8, 1929, qtd. in Schultz, "Reaction of Southern Textile Communities," xxi.

36. Report in *Columbia State*, April 19, 1929, in Textiles, North and South Carolina folder, Box 4, G. S. Mitchell Papers, Manuscripts Department, Duke University Library.

37. G. Mitchell, "Organization of Labor in the South," 187. The *Raleigh Times* called the refusal of the mill at Rockingham, North Carolina, to arbitrate a "callous display of capitalistic atavism." Douty, "Labor Unrest in North Carolina," 580.

38. Marshall, *Labor in the South*, 123.

39. The statement was dated February 16, 1930, and is cited in Prior, "From Community to National Unionism," 8–10.

40. Bright, "The South Afire!" 16.

41. See the report of the Social Service Commission of the Georgia Baptist Convention affirming the right of textile workers to "employment under healthful physical and moral conditions" and "to organize in any way they desire to promote their life's interests." Wills, "Southern Baptists and Labor," 174.

42. *Cotton*, May 1934, 47.

43. Willie S. Ethridge, "Liberalism Stirs Southern Churches." The president of Bibb Mills, William Anderson, later referred to the agitation by the "local gentry" as being responsible for the unrest among his workers. Such a reference suggests that the pastor of the Mulberry Church was only one of many "socially concerned citizens" to voice support for the protests of southern millhands.

44. As many as twelve thousand strikers were involved in the 1932 strikes. Prior, "From Community to National Unionism," 12.

45. Douty, "Labor Unrest in North Carolina," 586.

46. See appendix B.

Chapter 3: Union-Management Cooperation

1. David Brody has called this "market unionism." See Brody, *In Labor's Cause*, 139–40, who calls national union agreements "as much an industry as a labor agreement."

2. Goldberg, *A Tale of Three Cities*, 38.

3. Dubofsky, *We Shall Be All*, 236.

4. Goldberg, *A Tale of Three Cities*, 17.

5. Hearden, *Independence and Empire*, 100–101. For a general discussion see McLaurin, *Paternalism and Protest*.

6. Editorial in the *New Bedford (Mass.) Morning Mercury*, October 7, 1921, reprinted in the *Textile Worker*, October 1921, 324.

7. *Textile Worker*, November 1921, 371.

8. Adamic, "Tragic Towns of New England," 755; Hearden, *Independence and*

Empire, 147; Mitchell and Mitchell, "The Plight of Cotton Mill Labor," 205. On workers sending their own machinery South see *Textile Worker*, April 1933, 107–8.

9. *Atlanta Journal of Labor*, November 1, 1929, in Van Osdell, "Cotton Mills, Labor, and the Southern Mind," 187. For the "assimilation" sentiments see Googe, "Organizing the Workers of Georgia," 1326; *Augusta Labor Review*, September 5, 1925.

10. *American Federationist*, June 1929, 658. A good overview of the AFL's southern organizing campaign is Trepp, "Union-Management Cooperation and the Southern Organizing Campaign."

11. Nolan and James, "Textile Unionism in the Piedmont," 64. These words were spoken at an AFL planning meeting that took place after the southern organizing drive was approved at the AFL convention in October 1929.

12. Hall et al., *Like a Family*, 214 (Elizabethton); Brooks, "United Textile Workers," 316 (Marion). A good overview of the 1929 strikes is Bernstein, *The Lean Years*, 1–43; and Schultz, "Reaction of Southern Textile Communities." For a more in-depth look at Elizabethton see Holly, "Elizabethton, Tennessee, A Case Study"; Hall, "Disorderly Women"; Minton, "The South Fights the Unions," 202–3. On Marion see Stolberg, "Madness in Marion"; Gorman, Tippett, and Muste, *The Marion Murder*.

13. "Union Labor's Drive in the South," *Literary Digest* 102 (August 3, 1929), 10–11.

14. "Statements of Employees," United States Commission on Industrial Relations, *Hearings*, vol. 1 (May 1915), 1016–19.

15. Testimony of Adolph Lessig, Secretary, National Industrial Union of Textile Workers, United States Commission on Industrial Relations, *Hearings*, vol. 3 (May 1915), 2453.

16. "If this scientific plan is another means of still grinding more out of the employee, . . . then organized labor will fight against it, as it has at all times fought against industrial exploitation of the wage workers." John Golden, President of the United Textile Workers of America, in a speech made at the Economic Club in Boston, March 21, 1911, reprinted in the testimony of John Golden, United States Commission on Industrial Relations, *Hearings*, vol. 1 (May 1915), 1012.

17. Dubofsky, *We Shall Be All*, 266–67; see also John Golden, President of the United Textile Workers of America, testimony, United States Commission on Industrial Relations, *Hearings*, vol. 1 (May 1915), 988–1019. In general see Nadworny, *Scientific Management and the Unions*, especially 48–57.

18. Nadworny, *Scientific Management and the Unions*, 48–57; Goldberg, *A Tale of Three Cities;* John Golden, President of the United Textile Workers of America, testimony, United States Commission on Industrial Relations, *Hearings*, vol. 1 (May 1915), 988–1019; Dubofsky, *We Shall Be All*, 266–67.

19. McMahon, quoted in Brooks, "United Textile Workers," 333. In 1928, rank and file opposition from northern workers did force McMahon to modify his endorsement. Now McMahon criticized the "multiple-loom system" because it increased the stress of one worker while it took away the job of another, bringing about

"results detrimental to both." McMahon at the UTW Convention, cited in Brooks, "United Textile Workers," 334.

20. *Textile World*, November 24, 1928, 39.

21. Nyman and Smith, *Union-Management Cooperation in the "Stretch Out,"* 135.

22. Nyman and Smith, *Union-Management Cooperation in the "Stretch Out,"* 93.

23. Nyman and Smith, *Union-Management Cooperation in the "Stretch Out,"* 127.

24. Nyman and Smith, *Union-Management Cooperation in the "Stretch Out,"* 67–84. The relationship between Brown and the AFL goes back at least to 1925. See Brown, "Scientific Management and Organized Labor"; and Brown, "Workers' Participation in Job Study."

25. *Textile Worker*, May 1932; Hodges, *New Deal Labor Policy*, 44.

26. McMahon, analyzing the 1932 Horse Creek Valley strike, *Textile Worker*, May 1932.

27. J. Mitchell, "Here Comes Gorman," 204.

28. See Gorman, Tippett, and Muste, *The Marion Murder*; J. Mitchell, "Here Comes Gorman," 204.

29. Schultz, "A Study of the Reaction of Southern Textile Communities to Strikes," 122–23. Nor did the union have the financial base to sustain four thousand workers through the winter. The UTW received no assistance from the AFL. Marshall, *Labor in the South*, 126–29.

30. *Labor Age*, October 1930, March 1931; and *Textile Worker*, March 1931.

31. Letter from Francis Gorman to Honorable W. A. Harriman, Divisional Administrator of the NRA, March 19, 1934, Box 1814, E25, RG9, National Archives.

32. Letter from Lawrence Rogin to author, June 17, 1987, in author's possession; Marcus, "Organizing the Unorganized: Paul Fuller and His Southern Campaign."

33. *Textile Worker*, March 1931, 742.

34. *Textile Worker*, February 1931, 654–56.

35. Garrison, "Paul Revere Christopher."

Chapter 4: New Rules

1. Fraser, "The 'Labor Question.'"

2. General Counsel of the National Recovery Adminstration, Release no. 536, 5, cited in a letter from presidents of eighteen UTW locals in South Carolina to Hugh Johnson, NRA Administrator, November 15, 1933, in South Carolina State Board folder, E397, RG9, National Archives.

3. Fraser, "The 'Labor Question,'" 68–69.

4. Liberal Taylorism has been the focus of much recent scholarly attention. In addition to Fraser, "The 'Labor Question,'" see Fraser, *Labor Will Rule*, 135–210; Haber, *Efficiency and Uplift*; Jacoby, *Employing Bureaucracy*; Jacoby, "Union-Management Cooperation in the United States"; Gilbert, "Defining Industrial Democracy." Gary Gerstle discusses how these ideas informed New Deal thinking in *Working-Class Americanism*, 182–87.

5. The statement was made in the spring of 1933. Himmelberg, *The Origins of the National Recovery Administration*, 208.

6. Statement of Cone Mill worker in 1930, cited in Bell, *Hard Times*, 32.

7. Simon, *A Fabric of Defeat*, 64–66, quote is on 65. For a penetrating look at South Carolina mill workers' ideas about how to respond to the Depression see chapter 3 of *A Fabric of Defeat*.

8. Levine, *Class Struggle and the New Deal*, 30.

9. Speech at meeting of the Piedmont Organizing Council, Greensboro, North Carolina, April 28, 1929, reprinted as "Women Workers in Textiles," *American Federationist* 36:6 (June 1929), 697.

10. Bernstein, *The Lean Years*, 482.

11. Hearings before House Committee on Labor, 72nd session, January 18–30, 1933, 2.

12. Testimony of Thomas McMahon, thirty-hour week bill, hearings before House Committee on Labor, 73–1, April 25–May 5, 1933, 538.

13. Schlesinger, *The Coming of the New Deal*, 90–96.

14. Burns, *Roosevelt: The Lion and the Fox*, 163–64.

15. On the significance of a "medium-size best practice firm," see Ferguson, "From Normalcy to New Deal," 41–94, esp. 69.

16. Van Osdell, "Cotton Mills, Labor, and the Southern Mind," 228.

17. Letter from Gardner to George Gordon Battle, September 7, 1932, in Prior, "From Community to National Unionism," 29.

18. Letter from Gardner to George Gordon Battle, September 7, 1932, in Prior, "From Community to National Unionism," 29.

19. Gossett, "Textile Conditions in the South," 33–36.

20. For a general history of the CTI see Galambos, *Competition and Cooperation*, 89–138.

21. Galambos, *Competition and Cooperation*, 136–99.

22. Galambos, *Competition and Cooperation*, 143–44.

23. Compliance in 1929 was 63 percent, in 1930, 73 percent, and in 1931, 83 percent. But even the 1931 figure represents compliance by only 63 percent of the southern producers. Galambos, *Competition and Cooperation*, 117–38.

24. Comer to William Anderson, June 23, 1933, in Hodges, *New Deal Labor Policy*, 50.

25. Schlesinger, *The Coming of the New Deal*, 87–89.

26. *New York Times*, June 28, 1933.

27. Hodges, *New Deal Labor Policy*, 55; *New York Times*, June 28, 1933.

28. *New York Times*, June 28, 1933.

29. For a summary of the code-formation process see Hodges, *New Deal Labor Policy*, 48–53; Galambos, *Competition and Cooperation*, 178–226; and Himmelberg, *The Origins of the National Recovery Administration*, chapter 10.

30. Bailey et al., *Biographical Dictionary of the South Carolina Senate, 1776–1985*.

31. Newspaper clipping, undated, in 1933–34 scrapbook, James F. Byrnes Papers, Robert Muldrow Cooper Library, Clemson University.

32. *Spartanburg Journal*, June 21, 1933, in 1933–34 scrapbook, James F. Byrnes Papers, Robert Muldrow Cooper Library, Clemson University.

33. The amendment was not included in the final House bill, but Taylor was able to persuade Senator Wagner and Senator James Byrnes, from South Carolina, to support it in the Senate. The Senate had passed the industrial recovery bill with the Taylor Amendment included, but the amendment was killed in a House-Senate conference. The story of the Taylor amendment can be found in the *Anderson Independent*, May 27, May 30, June 1, June 6, June 11, June 15, 1933. Text of amendment can be found in the *Columbia State*, June 8, 1933.

34. A copy of this provision and the entire Code can be found in the November 1933 issue of the *Textile Worker* and in Dearing et al., *The ABC of the NRA*, 134–35. Roosevelt later penned an amendment to the Code that approximated this wording and expressed the same point, although it differed in minor details.

35. Open letter from George Sloan, Thomas Marchant, and Ernest Hood to Hugh Johnson, printed in the *New York Times*, June 20, 1933. My thanks to Sara Judson for sharing this article with me.

36. *Textile Worker*, July 1933, 216. For an in-depth discussion of the role played by race in shaping Code wages as well as the role played by the National Consumers' League, see Storrs, "An Independent Voice for Unorganized Workers," 24–30.

37. From the beginning, Section 15 was designed as a stopgap measure, to remain in effect "until the adoption of further provisions that may prove necessary to prevent any improper speeding up of work (stretch-outs)."

38. Senator Byrnes tried but failed to get Johnson to agree to appoint a representative of the United Textile Workers. Haskett, "Ideological Radicals," 302. According to Irving Bernstein, Hugh Johnson's assistant secretary of labor Edward McGrady also objected to the appointment of Berry. Bernstein, *The Turbulent Years*, 301.

39. *Knoxville News Sentinel*, May 10–14, 1929; quote is from May 13 issue.

40. Berry, "Printing Pressman's Achievements," 1368. Michael Rogin claims that Berry had a reputation for suppressing insurgent strikes with "unsavory techniques." See Rogin, "Voluntarism," 529.

41. "Berry Says Stretch-out Exists," undated newspaper clipping, 1933–34 scrapbook, Byrnes Papers, Robert Muldrow Cooper Library, Clemson University.

42. Langston, "Greenville, Unionism, and the General Strike," 7.

43. Langston, "Greenville, Unionism, and the General Strike," 8–9.

44. Bernstein, *The Turbulent Years*, 304.

45. See chapter 3.

46. Robert Bruere, "West Lynn," 23. Before the war, Bruere was director of the New York Association for the Poor and co-author of the book, *Increasing Home Efficiency*. See Papers of the American Association for Labor Legislation, Index to Correspondence, 1905–1910, Cornell University Labor Documentation Center. During World War I, Bruere worked with the Fuel Adminstration. See Robert Bruere, "Produce or Perish." After the war, Bruere and his colleague Ordway Tead founded the Bureau of Industrial Research, whose goal was to provide the hard scientific data necessary to implement "modernized" labor relations in industry. Its

reports endorsed both collective bargaining and scientific management. See Jacoby, "Union-Management Cooperation in the United States," 20.

47. The other was Lester Frey of Washington, D.C. See "Berry Says Stretch-out Exists," undated newspaper clipping, 1933–34 scrapbook, Byrnes Papers, Robert Muldrow Cooper Library, Clemson University.

Chapter 5: Dirty Deal

1. Jacquelyn Hall, interview with Eula McGill, February 3, 1976, Southern Oral History Collection, University of North Carolina at Chapel Hill.

2. Letter from Mrs. C. R. Burton, August 22, 1933 to Franklin D. Roosevelt in Avondale Mills, Alexander City folder, E398, RG9, National Archives. For other examples see letter from Mrs. L. L. Barber, West Point Manufacturing, Georgia, August 19, 1933, Box 1815, E25, RG9, or letter from Avondale Mills worker in Alexander City, June 22, 1934, in Avondale Mills, Alexander City folder, E398, RG9, National Archives. The absence of the name of the letter's author does not necessarily mean that the letter itself was anonymous. The folders of employee complaints in the textile industry contain both original letters and carbon copies of excerpted portions of the letters. The excerpts were selected by the staff of the NRA's Cotton Textile National Industrial Relations Board (see below), to be forwarded, without name of author attached, to the Cotton Textile Code Authority for investigation. Occasionally only the excerpt of a letter was found; occasionally only the original; sometimes, both. If the source indicates that the original letter was anonymous then that information is included in the citation.

3. *New Republic*, September 19, 1934, 149.

4. *High Point Enterprise*, July 9, 1933, in Prior, "From Community to National Unionism," 54.

5. *New Republic*, September 5, 1934, 95.

6. Author's interview with Lawrence Rogin, Washington, D.C. Technical bureaucrats made the same point using more words: "With a greater labor content for industry, it will be more necessary than ever to see that the maximum amount of work is given by employees." "Speed-Up—Aim of Industry Under N.R.A.," *Textile Notes* III, No. 5 (1933), 5; cited in Ramsay, "Industrial Relations in the Southern Cotton Textile Industry," 147.

7. For example, Avondale Mills of Birmingham, Alabama, began a second shift on May 8, 1933, "in view of the re-employment program and in anticipation of the shorter work week under the textile code." Letter from Donald Comer to the NRA, May 10, 1934, in Avondale Mills, Birmingham folder, E398, RG9, National Archives. Indian Head Mills at Cordova, Alabama, went from one to three eight-hour shifts in the spring of 1933 before the Code went into effect, and hired three hundred additional people. See *Birmingham Labor Advocate*, June 3, 1933. In May 1933, labor organizers in the South Carolina piedmont reported to the UTW magazine, the *Textile Worker*, their astonishment that area mills had raised wages 10 percent. See *Textile Worker*, May 1933, 139–40.

8. Burns, *Roosevelt: The Lion and the Fox*, 182.

9. Letter from Ellis Covan, Pelzer, South Carolina, to Hugh Johnson, no date, received August 4, 1933, in Labor folder, Box 1812, E25, RG9, National Archives.

10. Letter from textile worker, July 25, 1933, Merrimack Manufacturing Company folder, E398, RG9, National Archives.

11. Anonymous letter from Samoset Cotton Mill worker to Hugh Johnson, undated, received October 13, 1933, in Talledega Cotton Mill folder, E398, RG9, National Archives.

12. Letter from A. C. Carter to Hugh Johnson, July 22, 1933, Labor folder, Box 1812, E25, RG9, National Archives ("dropped . . ."); letter from H. S. Busby, August 1, 1933, in Dwight Manufacturing Company folder, E398, RG9, National Archives ("families . . .").

13. Letter from Mrs. Margaret Pearson, August 6, 1933, in Dwight Manufacturing Company folder, E398, RG9, National Archives.

14. *Textile Worker*, May 1934, 173.

15. Letter from Monroe Jordan to Hugh Johnson, Springs Mills, Lancaster, South Carolina, July 17, 1933, in Box 1813, E25, RG9, National Archives.

16. Letter from Gastonia worker to the *Charlotte Observer*, no date, in Cleveland Cloth Mills folder, E398, RG9, National Archives.

17. Letter from textile worker in Sanford Cotton Mill, Sanford, North Carolina, August 3, 1933, Box 1813, E25, RG9, National Archives. See also author's interview with Allen sisters, Shelby, North Carolina; Allen Tullos interview with Ada Mae Wilson, February 1, 1980, Southern Oral History Collection, University of North Carolina at Chapel Hill: "I wasn't near as tired in twelve hours as I was in eight hours, because they overloaded you."

18. U.S. Department of Labor, Bureau of Labor Statistics, *Textile Report, Part I, Wage Rates and Weekly Earnings in the Cotton Goods Industry from July 1933 to August 1934*, Washington, February 4, 1935, 10, cited in Ramsay, "Industrial Relations in the Southern Cotton Textile Industry," 152.

19. "Textile Machines Increase in South," *Textile Notes* 4:11 (1935), 2, cited in Ramsay, "Industrial Relations in the Southern Cotton Textile Industry," 169.

20. *Textile Worker*, June 1934, 232.

21. Bureau of Labor Statistics, *Handbook of Labor Statistics*, 1936, cited in McLaughlin, "The Atlanta Cotton Mills and the 1934 Textile Strike," 11.

22. Letter from Mrs. Reaves, September 5, 1933, in Samoset Cotton Mill folder, E398, RG9, National Archives. For a similar anecdote see anonymous letter from worker in Samoset Cotton Mill, undated, received October 13, 1933, Samoset Cotton Mill folder, E398, RG9, National Archives.

23. Letter from Ester Steel to Franklin D. Roosevelt, August 22, 1933, in Box 1813, E25, RG9, National Archives.

24. L. J. Kines to Franklin D. Roosevelt, July 25, 1933, in Labor folder, Box 1812, E25, RG9, National Archives.

25. Letter from Pell City worker, August 4, 1933, Avondale Mills, Pell City folder, E398, RG9, National Archives.

26. Lawrence Hogan to North Carolina State Federation of Labor, *Charlotte Observer,* August 16, 1933, in Prior, "From Community to National Unionism," 59. Even the more cautious UTW conceded that violators represented a "substantial minority" of textile mills. According to Arthur Schlesinger, NRA Administrator Hugh Johnson thought that compliance was as low as 60 percent. The liberal journalist Lorena Hickock did not believe it was even that high. See Schlesinger, *The Coming of the New Deal,* 21.

27. Letter from eighteen employees to Hugh Johnson, August 2, 1933, Eagle and Phenix Mills, general folder #1, E398, RG9, National Archives.

28. Letter from Eva Brantley, November 4, 1933, in Lincoln Mills folder, E398, RG9, National Archives.

29. Letter from W. L. Hilton of Gadsden, Alabama, September 23, 1933, Dwight Manufacturing Company folder, E398, RG9, National Archives.

30. Letter from thirteen people from the Saratoga Victory Mills, Albertville, Alabama, September 25, 1933, Saratoga Victory Mills folder, E398, RG9, National Archives.

31. For statistics on the period from August 8, 1933, to August 8, 1934, see Hodges, *New Deal Labor Policy,* 92. The Code Authority apparently did not begin receiving the letters of complaint until sometime in August. Those written in July remained in the files of Hugh Johnson.

32. Griffith, *The Crisis of American Labor,* 58.

33. Author's interview with Cecil Aultman, Gadsden, Alabama. For more on Comer see Brannon, "Donald Comer, Dean of the Alabama Textile Industry"; and "The Comers and their Cotton Mills," *Fortune* 29 (May 1944), 140–45.

34. Galambos, *Competition and Cooperation,* 117.

35. Letter from S. J. Gwyn to Hugh Johnson, June 6, 1934, Cannon Mills Plant #6, Concord, North Carolina folder, E398, RG9, National Archives. On spies at Cannon see also Prior, "From Community to National Unionism," 60.

36. Letter from G. T. Duffie, no date, misfiled in Avondale Mills, Birmingham folder, E398, RG9, National Archives.

37. Anonymous letter, December 26, 1933, Avondale Mills, Childersburg folder, E398, RG9, National Archives.

38. Letter, June 22, 1934, misfiled in Avondale Mills, Stevenson folder, E398, RG9, National Archives.

39. Letter to Franklin D. Roosevelt from textile worker in Pell City, Alabama, undated, misfiled in Avondale Mills, Birmingham folder, E398, RG9, National Archives.

40. The "We will not work union labor" message was sent by Roxie Dunnaway, from Avondale Mills, Alexander City, October 31, 1933, misfiled in Avondale, Birmingham folder, E398, RG9, National Archives. On being fired at Sylacauga Mill see letters dated August 23, 1933, October 30, 1933, June 22, 1934, all misfiled in Avondale Mills, Alexander City folder, E398, RG9, National Archives.

41. For more on Greenville see Langston, "Greenville, Unionism, and the General Strike," 59.

42. Letter from John Peel to Edward McGrady, July 2, 1933, Box 1815, E25, National Archives.

43. Hodges, *New Deal Labor Policy*, 61. For more on Googe see *Richmond Times Dispatch*, August 6, 1933, and *Raleigh Union Herald*, August 3, 1933, in Labor, Georgia folder, Box 2, G. S. Mitchell Papers, Manuscripts Department, Duke University Library.

44. Cannon, "Social Deterrents to the Unionization of Southern Cotton Textile Mill Workers," 293; author's interview with Vance Donnahoo, Inman, South Carolina.

45. The Santee Mills in Bamberg, South Carolina, consisting of two hundred workers, recognized its union local; after a tense strike, employers in Augusta, Georgia, mills also recognized the unions there. *Augusta Labor Review*, December 15, 1933, and February 13, 1934.

46. *Birmingham Labor Advocate*, September 2, 1933, cited in Taft, *Organizing Dixie*, 71. See also interview with retired textile workers at Cordova, Alabama, by the author and Eula McGill.

47. *Raleigh Union Herald*, February 15, 1934, in Labor, Alabama folder, Box 1, G. S. Mitchell Papers, Manuscripts Department, Duke University Library. Irwin and Merrimack Mills also formed local unions. See *Birmingham Labor Advocate*, November 25, 1933, and December 19, 1933.

48. See chapter 2.

49. *Textile Worker*, February 1933, 42.

50. *Textile Worker*, May 1933, 139–40.

51. Prior, "From Community to National Unionism," 54.

52. Author's interview with John Howard Payne, Charlotte, North Carolina.

53. Prior, "From Community to National Unionism," 55.

54. *Birmingham Labor Advocate*, September 23, 1933; and Langston, "Greenville, Unionism, and the General Strike," 18–19.

55. Mercer Evans, "History of the Organized Labor Movement in Georgia," 97.

56. Theodore M. Forbes, retired executive Vice President of the Cotton Manufacturers Association of Georgia, interviewed by John Earl Allen, June 1976, in Allen, "The Governor and the Strike," 65. See also the report of the meeting of the Cotton Manufacturers Association of Georgia in transcript of interview by Allen Tullos and Billy Mass with Mildred Andrews, February 14, 1980, Southern Oral History Collection, University of North Carolina at Chapel Hill.

57. List of North Carolina Union Locals, box 2, uncataloged, Paul Christopher Papers, Southern Labor Archives, Georgia State University; letter from Mrs. B. M. Miller to Frances Perkins, December 13, 1933, in Chadwick Hoskins Company folder, E398, RG9, National Archives.

58. On the role of women in southern textile labor protest generally, see Frederickson, "'I Know Which Side I'm On'"; Frederickson, "Heroines and Girl Strikers"; Frankel, "Women, Paternalism, and Protest"; and Hall, "Disorderly Women." A historical overview of female textile labor is Beatty, "Gender Relations in Southern Textiles." On the marginalization of women and the shift toward ex-

clusively male imagery in textile unions after 1934 see Faue, "'The Dynamo of Change.'"

59. The other textile towns were Gaffney, Clifton, Fairmont, and Pacolet Mills, South Carolina, and Erwin and Hillsborough, North Carolina. UTW—Status, Locals, Box 674, Records of the Textile Workers Union of America, Wisconsin State Historical Society.

60. See for example, letter from "Fourteen Colored Men" to Hugh Johnson, January 5, 1934, in Mary Lelia Cotton Mill, Greensboro, Georgia folder, E398, RG9, National Archives. My thanks to Judith Helfand for sharing this letter with me.

61. Interviews with black textile workers in Stoney and Helfand, *The Uprising of '34*, and discussion of black southern textile union locals in the 1940s in Minchin, *What Do We Need a Union For?*

62. "The only way you can learn about conditions as they exist is for someone to muster up the courage to write you a statement then you have a starting point." Letter from Charles Reid, July 10, 1934, Avondale Mills, Sylacauga folder, E398, RG9, National Archives.

63. "Probably the biggest funeral they've every had over there." Author's telephone conversation with Taylor Myers, Huntsville, Alabama, July 26, 1986.

64. Letter from James Foster, November 27, 1933, in Merrimack Mill folder, E398, RG9, National Archives.

65. In addition to industry representatives, a few government officials also sat on the Code Authority, but they performed no active function. Hodges, *New Deal Labor Policy*, 54 and 213, n. 41.

66. Memo from L. R. Gilbert to Blanshard, Deputy Administrator, Textile Section, May 29, 1934, Box 1814, E25, RG9, National Archives.

67. *Textile Worker*, January 1934, 2–4.

68. Hodges, *New Deal Labor Policy*, 92.

69. *Textile Worker*, January 1934, 2–4.

70. Anonymous letter, June 22, 1934, in Avondale Mills, Stevenson folder, E398, RG9, National Archives.

71. Hodges, *New Deal Labor Policy*, 71.

72. Compare the Code Authority's record on investigating labor complaints to their record responding to complaints that mills had violated machine-hour limitations. So concerned was the Code Authority that no mill operate more than forty hours per week that two firms were taken to court on criminal charges for violating the limit. They paid fines totaling $2,250. See Galambos, *Competition and Cooperation*, 250–51.

73. Galambos, *Competition and Cooperation*, 234–35.

74. Galambos, *Competition and Cooperation*, 228–29.

75. Anonymous letter to Hugh Johnson, August 2, 1933, in Eagle and Phenix Mills, general folder #1, E398, RG9, National Archives.

76. *Raleigh Union Herald*, November 15, 1934, in Textiles, Georgia folder, Box 3, G. S. Mitchell Papers, Manuscripts Department, Duke University Library.

77. Letter from Clarence J. Swink to Hugh Johnson, November 6, 1933, in Cannon Mills #6, Concord, North Carolina folder, E398, RG9, National Archives.

78. *New York Times*, September 16, 1933, in Hodges, *New Deal Labor Policy*, 56.

79. Speech before the Committee of Code Authorities in Washington, Tuesday March 6, 1934, in Avondale Mills, Birmingham folder, E39, RG9, National Archives.

80. See Hodges, *New Deal Labor Policy*, 56, 60. An exception is Ramsay, "Industrial Relations in the Southern Cotton Textile Industry."

81. In June 1933 the UTW's *Textile Worker* reported strikes in Rock Hill, Lonsdale, and Orangeburg, South Carolina, Charlotte, North Carolina, and Prichard, Alabama. "There are many labor troubles," reported a UTW organizer in June, "too many to mention." *Textile Worker*, June 1933, 175–76. The *Birmingham News* on July 28, 1933 reported the following strikes: 4,000 hosiery workers and 400 cotton mill workers out in High Point, North Carolina; 1,000 workers out at F. W. Pee Manufacturing Company in Greenville, South Carolina; 550 out at Arial and Alice Mills in Easley, South Carolina; 850 out at Appleton Mills in Anderson, South Carolina. This is just a sampling.

82. Memo from Labor Advisory Board to Hugh Johnson, July 29, 1933, in Hodges, *New Deal Labor Policy*, 68.

83. Lorwin and Wubnig, *Labor Relations Boards*, 87–89, quote is on 87. See also "The NRA at Grips with the Labor Problem," *Literary Digest*, August 19, 1933, cited in Huthmacher, *Senator Robert F. Wagner*, 153; and "Labor: Strikes and Bombs Punctuate Planning of Codes," *Newsweek*, July 29, 1933, 8.

84. Lorwin and Wubnig, *Labor Relations Boards*, 87.

85. See chapter 4.

86. Hodges, *New Deal Labor Policy*, 67.

87. "Summary of Findings," submitted to Hugh Johnson from Robert Bruere, Benjamin Geer, and George Berry, July 21, 1933, in Box 5c/a, E25, RG9, National Archives.

88. "Analysis of Complaint Letters Alleging Violations of the Cotton Textile Code, August 8, 1933–August 8, 1934," Box 1814, E25, RG9, National Archives.

89. The new procedure received the formal approval of AFL President William Green three months later. Haskett, "Ideological Radicals," 203.

90. Minutes of the meeting of the Cotton Textile Industry Committee or CTIC, August 1, 1933, Meetings folder, Box 1799, E25, RG9, National Archives.

91. Hodges, *New Deal Labor Policy*, 68. This summary of events closely follows Hodges, although it reverses the sequence of events that led to the creation of a permanent industrial relations board. Sloan's suggestion came first; Johnson's followed a day later.

92. Dearing et al., *The ABC of the NRA*, 52. On the timing of the creation of the NLB see also Berkowitz and McQuaid, *Creating the Welfare State*, 87.

93. *New York Times*, August 5, 10, 1933. See also Tomlins, *The State and the Unions*, 109. Tomlins suggests that the NLB was conceived from the outset as a temporary board that would mediate disputes until each industry had set up its own dispute

mediation board. In fact, however, cotton textiles was the only industry for which the exemption applied. The Code Authority moved to permanently seal the authority of its own Cotton Textile Industrial Relations Board at its meeting on October 17, 1933, when it made a formal decision not to open up the Code for "labor questions." Hodges, *New Deal Labor Policy*, 76.

94. Letter from Mrs. C. A. Morgan, Bath, South Carolina, August 15, 1933, in Box 1814, E25, RG9, National Archives.

Chapter 6: A Battle of Righteousness

1. In 1901 workers elected the union organizer G. R. Webb to represent the Valley in the state legislature. *American Federationist* 8 (May 1901), 182. Unionism was so strong in the town of Aiken in the Horse Creek Valley at the turn of the century that unionists spoke of the "free air of the Valley." Carlton, *Mill and Town in South Carolina*, 200. See also Simon, *A Fabric of Defeat*, 97.

2. McLaurin, *Paternalism and Protest*; German, "The Queen City of the Savannah," 93–120.

3. *Textile Worker*, March 1931, 742.

4. This story is drawn from *Textile Worker*, March–April 1931; April 1932, esp. 6–8; May 1932, 53; August 1932, 150–51; and September–October 1932, as well as the *Augusta Labor Review* for this period. See also Hogan, "The Strikes at Langley, Bath, and Clearwater," 12.

5. Fuller was criticized by the *Labor Age* for not taking a more active role in the 1932 strike. See Hogan, "The Strikes at Langley, Bath, and Clearwater."

6. For more on Fuller's role in southern textile union organizing see Marcus, "Organizing the Unorganized: Paul Fuller and his Southern Campaign."

7. Copy of union notice, no date, in Aiken Mills, Bath, South Carolina folder, E398, RG9, National Archives. On the magnitude of discharges after the Code went into effect see telegram from Fuller to McGrady, July 18, 1933, in Labor folder, Box 1812, E25, RG9, National Archives.

8. Investigation by R. F. Howell, September 20, 1933, in Aiken Mills folder, E398, RG9, National Archives; investigation of Aiken Mills, Langley, South Carolina, by Lewis F. Sawyer, October 10, 1933, cited in Haskett, "Ideological Radicals," 304.

9. Fuller learned about the Bruere Board in a conference in Washington with members of the NRA Labor Advisory Board. *Augusta Labor Review*, September 22, 1933.

10. Transcript of December 2, 1933, hearing before Bruere Board, Aiken Mills folder, E398, RG9, National Archives.

11. *Augusta Labor Review*, October 20, 1933, and October 27, 1933.

12. *Augusta Labor Review*, November 10, 1933, and October 27, 1933.

13. *Augusta Labor Review*, October 27, 1933. The demands, according to Googe, were modest. The workers wanted grievances to be heard by the appropriate government board; they wanted no discrimination against union members; and they wanted the mills to recognize the union as the workers' collective bargaining agent.

14. *Augusta Labor Review*, October 27, 1933.

15. Hodges, *New Deal Labor Policy*, 76.

16. *Augusta Labor Review*, November 10, 1933. The visit of Bruere and Geer was also prompted when one Augusta mill, the King Mill, attempted to reopen. The attempt resulted in skirmishes between pickets and police, who used tear gas on the strikers.

17. Letter from G. A. Franklin, Manager, Aiken Mills, to L. R. Gilbert, January 4, 1934; transcript of Hearing of Horse Creek Valley workers before CTNIRB, December 2, 1933; in Aiken Mills folder, E398, RG9, National Archives.

18. *Augusta Labor Review*, November 10, 1933.

19. The managment did finally concede that it would rehire about 50 percent of the strikers, an offer rejected by the workers as a divisive tactic. *Augusta Labor Review*, November 24, 1933.

20. Berry may have been a decisive factor in getting some kind of language out of the Board validating worker rights. At the December 2 hearing he was so offended by the attitude of general manager Franklin towards his workers that he admonished him: "These people down there on strike are two-legged human beings and are entitled to treatment as such." *Augusta Labor Review*, December 8, 1933.

21. See especially the complaint investigation by A. S. Thomas, May 7, 1934, in Aiken Mills folder, E398, RG9, National Archives.

22. Untitled newspaper article, dateline Columbia, South Carolina, February 14, 1934, in Aiken Mills folder, E398, RG9, National Archives.

23. *Augusta Labor Review*, February 16, 1934.

24. *Textile Worker*, July 1934, 292.

25. Decision of CTNIRB, March 9, 1934, in Aiken Mills folder, E398, RG9, National Archives.

26. *Augusta Labor Review*, March 9, 1934.

27. The process remains an interesting illustration of the ability of real power to influence supposedly neutral, or balanced, bureaucratic bodies. Did the members of the Board know they were tailoring their understanding of justice to conform to their lack of enforcement power? The question is almost impossible to answer with certainty. Willis, who became very distraught during the controversy, likely did not. Bruere, an experienced mediator, likely did. An exchange between Willis and Bruere reveals that in his November 6 decision, Bruere had considered the possibility that Horse Creek Valley workers might not be immediately reemployed. Willis, on the other hand, had been promised by the mills that they would rehire workers eventually. Willis felt helpless when he realized that the mill was not fulfilling its promise to the State Board. "We have two different promises that the mill would carry it out," he confided to Bruere. "I don't know what the mill has been doing. I don't know what we will be able to do." Bruere never expressed such feelings of frustration. Transcript of telephone conversation between Willis and Bruere, November 23, 1933, in telephone conversations folder, E397, RG9, National Archives. See also telegram from Bruere to Willis, November 10, 1933, in folder 5c/a, E25, RG9, National Archives.

28. Transcript of telephone conversation between L. R. Gilbert and Alabama State

Board Chair Davis, October 31, 1933, in telephone conversations folder, E397, RG9, National Archives; transcript of telephone conversation between Googe and Bruere, March 20, 1934, in Adjustment, Alabama area folder, E398, RG9, National Archives.

29. Letter from V. C. Finch to P. O. Davis, December 18, 1933, in Decisions Book, folder 5c/a, E26, RG9, National Archives.

30. Letter from O. E. Petry to Robert Bruere, June 23, 1934, in George Berry folder, E397, RG9, National Archives. Bruere had hired Gilbert, past president of the Southern Textile Association, sometime in the fall of 1933. For more on Gilbert see *American Federationist*, November 1928, 1322.

31. Quote from O. E. Petry to Robert W. Bruere, June 23, 1934, George Berry folder, E397, RG9, National Archives. On Arnall Mills see telegram from Thomas A. Quigley to Robert W. Bruere, January 1, 1934, and letter from Duke Overby, Secretary to UTW Local 1880, to President Roosevelt, July 11, 1934, in Arnall Mills folder, E398, RG9, National Archives.

32. Telegram from L. E. Oates to Franklin D. Roosevelt, October 21, 1933, in Anchor Duck Mills folder, E398, RG9, National Archives.

33. Letter from Albert Cox to Senator Edward Costigan, January 11, 1934, Box 1814, E25, RG9, National Archives.

34. Meeting of Georgia-Carolina Textile Council, June 30–July 1, 1934, *Textile Worker*, July 1934, 293.

35. Affadavits to the Alabama State Textile Industrial Relations Board from millhands claiming discrimination or documenting code violations, November 1933, Dwight Manufacturing Company folder, E398, RG9, National Archives.

36. Letter from J. P. Holland to Frances Perkins, January 6, 1934, and letter from CTNIRB to Holland, January 30, 1934, in Dwight Manufacturing Company folder, E398, RG9, National Archives.

37. *Textile Worker*, December 1933, 350.

38. *Textile Worker*, November 1933, 336.

39. Wagner radio speech, October 18, 1933, cited in Tomlins, *The State and the Unions*, 109–10.

40. On the strategy of the AFL union leaders see Haskett, "Ideological Radicals," especially 59–63 and 299.

41. *Textile Worker*, September 1933, 259–61.

42. *Textile Worker*, Supplement to December 1933 issue, 10, 13.

43. Letter from Berry to Thomas McMahon, January 8, 1934, George Berry folder, E397, RG9, National Archives.

44. *Textile Worker*, December 1933, 340.

45. *Textile Worker*, January 1934, 3.

46. Hodges, *New Deal Labor Policy*, 74. Of course, McMahon was not incorrect in concluding that the problem was the Board's lack of enforcement power.

47. *American Wool and Cotton Reporter*, March 27, 1934, cited in Hodges, *New Deal Labor Policy*, 14.

48. Thomas Marchant to Hugh Johnson, March 23, 1934, cited in Hodges, *New Deal Labor Policy*, 75.

49. Author's interview with Mr. and Mrs. J. B. Cashion, Shelby, North Carolina; Van Osdell, "Cotton Mills, Labor, and the Southern Mind," 228.

50. Author's interview with Leola and Inez Allen, Shelby, North Carolina; memorandum of hearing before the CTNIRB, February 4, 1934, E397, RG9, National Archives.

51. Memorandum of hearing before the CTNIRB, February 4, 1934; telegram from L. R. Gilbert to O. M. Mull, conveying contents of telegram from Paul Christopher to Thomas McMahon, January 27, 1934; in Cleveland Cloth Mills folder, E398, RG9, National Archives.

52. *Charlotte Observer*, February 24, 1934.

53. Transcript of telephone conversations between L. R. Gilbert and O. Max Gardner, February 1, 1934, telephone conversations folder, E397, RG9, National Archives.

54. Transcript of telephone conversations between L. R. Gilbert and Gardner, and between Gilbert and Mull, both February 1, 1934, telephone conversations folder, E397, RG9, National Archives.

55. Letter from Mill Committee (Fred Senter, C. W. Bolick, and Thomas Veal), February 3, 1934, to CTNIRB State Chair Theodore Johnson, Cleveland Cloth Mills folder, E398, RG9, National Archives; *Charlotte Observer*, February 3, 1934.

56. *Charlotte Observer*, February 16, 25, 1934.

57. *Raleigh News and Observer*, February 5, 1934, Cleveland Cloth Mills folder, E398, RG9, National Archives.

58. *Raleigh News and Observer*, February 18, 1934, and *Charlotte Observer*, February 18, 1934. See also John P. Prior, "From Community to National Unionism," 69.

59. Hearing and Determination in the Case of Cleveland Cloth Mills, Washington, D.C., March 28, 1934, Cleveland Cloth Mills folder, E398, RG9, National Archives.

60. *Charlotte Observer*, February 26, 1934, and February 28, 1934, March 3, 1934.

61. Untitled press clipping, Saturday, February 24, 1934, Cleveland Cloth Mills folder, E398, RG9, National Archives; *Charlotte Observer*, February 25–27, 1934.

62. *Raleigh News and Observer*, February 27, 1934, Cleveland Cloth Mills folder, E398, RG9, National Archives.

63. Berkowitz and McQuaid, *Creating the Welfare State*, 89.

64. Transcript of telephone conversation between Robert Bruere and George Googe, March 20, 1934, in Adjustment, Alabama area folder, E398, RG9, National Archives.

65. Transcript of telephone conversation between Gilbert and Gardner, March 8, 1934, telephone conversations folder, E397, RG9, National Archives.

66. Transcript of telephone conversation between Bruere and George Sloan, May 28, 1934, telephone conversations folder, E397, RG9, National Archives.

67. Memorandum from Thomas J. Emerson, Assistant Counsel, NRA Legal Division, to Bruere, March 20, 1934, cited in Prior, "From Community to National Unionism," 62. On March 25, Roosevelt announced his support of the concept of proportional representation. This meant, in effect, that a union could not represent

a workforce unless every member of that workforce voted for or was a member of that union.

68. Letter from Bruere to Donald Comer, March 27, 1934, Avondale Mills, Birmingham folder, E398, RG9, National Archives. On the "showdown" with the NLB and its subsequent loss of power see Tomlins, *The State and the Unions*, 126–28; Berkowitz and McQuaid, *Creating the Welfare State*, 89–90.

69. Turner Battle, "Confidential Memo to the Secretary," September 18, 1934, Textile Workers Strike folder, Box 38, Papers of Secretary Frances Perkins, RG174, National Archives; transcript of telephone conversation between Googe and Bruere, April 14, 1934, Cleveland Cloth Mills folder, E398, RG9, National Archives.

70. *Charlotte Observer*, March 23, 1934.

71. Telegram from Cleveland Cloth Mill employee representatives to Robert Bruere, March 23, 1934; Hearing and Determination in the Case of Cleveland Cloth Mill, Washington D.C., March 28, 1934; in Cleveland Cloth Mills folder, E398, RG9, National Archives. See also *Charlotte Observer*, March 24, 1934.

72. Transcript of telephone conversation between O. Max Gardner and L. R. Gilbert, April 7, 1934, telephone conversations folder, E397, RG9, National Archives.

73. Hearing and Determination in the Case of the Cleveland Cloth Mill, Washington, D.C., March 28, 1934; telegram from Robert Bruere to Theodore Johnson, April 10, 1934; letter from Bruere to the Cleveland Cloth Mills workers' committee, April 20, 1934; all in Cleveland Cloth Mills folder, E398, RG9, National Archives. See also *Charlotte Observer*, April 1, 3, and 12, 1934.

74. Transcript of telephone conversation between George Googe and Robert Bruere, April 14, 1934, telephone conversations folder, E397, RG9, National Archives.

75. See in particular the case at the Stonecutter Mills at Spindale, reported in Prior, "From Community to National Unionism," 69–71.

76. North Carolina State Federation of Labor, minutes of Executive Meeting, April 14, 1934, in Prior, "From Community to National Unionism," 75.

77. The workers' anger was also partly directed against Googe, who had counseled cooperation and had been proven wrong. "The textile workers are up in arms," Googe complained to Bruere after the decision had been announced. "I am about to be lynched down here; I am afraid to go out of the hotel." Transcript of telephone conversation between George Googe and Robert Bruere, April 14, 1934, Cleveland Cloth Mills folder, E398, RG9, National Archives.

78. The original petitions are in North Carolina State Board folder, E397, RG9, National Archives. On the State Federation of Labor resolution see *Hosiery Worker*, April 20, 1934, Labor, North and South Carolina folder, Box 2, G. S. Mitchell Papers, Manuscripts Department, Duke University Library.

79. Letter from the presidents of seventeen union locals in South Carolina to Hugh Johnson, November 15, 1933, South Carolina State Board folder, E397, RG9, National Archives. Peel claimed that Willis had been handpicked by Geer to be the South Carolina State Board Chair. *Textile Worker*, May 1934, 175.

80. Letter from John Peel to H. H. Willis, chairman of South Carolina State Board, April 11, 1934, South Carolina State Board folder, E397, RG9, National Archives.

81. The group elected J. A. Frye, of Columbia, South Carolina, president and E. W. McAbee, of Inman, South Carolina, vice president. McAbee sat on the UTW Executive Committee in 1935. *Charlotte Observer*, April 22, 1934; *Textile Worker*, May 1934, 166.

82. *Columbia State*, May 19, 1934.

83. *Textile Worker*, May 1934, 175.

84. *Textile Worker*, May 1934, 175–76; *Columbia State*, May 20, 1934.

85. Telegram from George Googe to Robert Bruere, May 15, 1934, Eagle and Phenix Mills folder, E398, RG9, National Archives. For Georgia, see *Augusta Labor Review*, May 4, 1934.

86. Paul Christopher to James Starr, May 20, 1934, in letters folder, Box 2, Paul Christopher Papers, Southern Labor Archives, Georgia State University.

Chapter 7: We Must Get Together in Our Organization

1. Letter from Thomas McMahon to L. R. Gilbert, March 22, 1934, Alabama State Board folder, E397, RG9, National Archives.

2. Hodges, *New Deal Labor Policy*, 76.

3. *Augusta Labor Review*, March 16, 1934; Hodges, *New Deal Labor Policy*, 78. See also UTW letter to Sidney Hillman, Labor Advisor to the Textile Administration, reprinted in the *Textile Worker*, March 1934, 90–94.

4. *Textile Worker*, March 1934, 89.

5. *Textile Worker*, March 1934, 94–96; *Charlotte Observer*, March 7, 1934.

6. *Textile Worker*, March 1934, 87. See also letter from Francis Gorman to all organizers, May 9, 1934, in folder 3, Box 2, Paul Christopher Papers, Southern Labor Archives, Georgia State University.

7. *Augusta Labor Review*, February 16, 1934; *Textile Worker*, April 1934.

8. Author and Eula McGill, interviews with Alabama veteran UTW organizers and cotton mill workers Burns Cox and Clyde Ware, Gadsden, Alabama; author's conversations with Eula McGill, Birmingham, Alabama.

9. Lou Lipsitz, interview with Eula McGill, Fall 1975, Southern Oral History Collection, University of North Carolina at Chapel Hill.

10. On Alice Berry see letter from Carl Gill to Samuel R. McClurd, Executive Assistant, Textile Labor Relations Board, March 4, 1935, McClurd folder, E403, RG9, National Archives. On Welch see Callaway Mills folder, E398, RG9, National Archives. The *Textile Worker* for July 1934 suggests that Welch had been hired as a UTW organizer by July. On Welch's legendary status see author and Eula McGill, interviews with retired Cordova textile workers, Cordova, Alabama, and author's interview with Lloyd Davis, Birmingham, Alabama.

11. Author and Eula McGill's interview with Clyde Ware, Gadsden, Alabama.

12. *Augusta Labor Review*, April 27 and May 18, 1934.

13. Gaylord, "Alabama Textile Labor Turned the Other Cheek," 482. This num-

ber is a low estimate. Forty-two Alabama locals were said to have voted on whether to hold a general strike when the Alabama Textile Council gathered in Birmingham in July 1934. For Georgia, see below.

14. Author's interview with John Howard Payne, Charlotte, North Carolina.

15. Letter from James Starr to Mr. G. H. Kanupp, Hickory, North Carolina, May 9, 1934, folder 3, Box 2, Paul Christopher Papers, Southern Labor Archives, Georgia State University.

16. Author and Eula McGill's interview with Clyde Ware, Gadsden, Alabama; author's conversations with Eula McGill.

17. Author and Eula McGill's interviews with Burns Cox and Laura Beard, Gadsden, Alabama; author's interviews with James Cortez, Edgefield, South Carolina, formerly of Graniteville, South Carolina; and Ruby Page, Columbus, Georgia.

18. *Rock Hill Evening News*, September 28, 30, 1929, in Textiles, North and South Carolina folder, Box 4, G. S. Mitchell Papers, Manuscripts Department, Duke University Library.

19. Telegram from E. B. Newberry to C. W. Bolick, May 2, 1934, folder 3, Box 2, Paul Christopher Papers, Southern Labor Archives, Georgia State University.

20. Gretchen McLaughlin, "The Atlanta Cotton Mills and the 1934 Textile Strike," 14; and testimony of George Googe, hearings, April 1–2, 1935, Calloway Mills folder, E402, RG9, National Archives.

21. *Textile Worker*, July 1934, 294.

22. *Textile Worker*, July 1934, 293.

23. Author's interview with Joe Jacobs, Atlanta, Georgia.

24. Martin, "Southern Labor Relations in Transition"; Tripplette, "One-Industry Towns."

25. Report by an organizer for the Boot and Shoe Workers in Alabama who had attempted to organize workers in Gadsden in 1930, described in letter from H. L. Kerwin to George H. Van Fleet, Commissioner of Conciliation, April 10, 1930, File 16, Box 1, Philip Taft Papers, Birmingham Public Library, Birmingham, Alabama.

26. Author and Eula McGill's interview with Laura Beard, Gadsden, Alabama.

27. There is little doubt that Pearson is the author of these words. They were accidentally included in the final incorporation papers of the Dixie Federation of Labor filed at the County Courthouse in Gadsden, Alabama, July 27, 1933. On Pearson's authorship see author and Eula McGill's interviews with Laura Beard and Burns Cox and author's interview with Roscoe Pearson, all from Gadsden, Alabama.

28. Author and Eula McGill's interview with Burns Cox, Gadsden, Alabama.

29. Author and Eula McGill's interview with Burns Cox, Gadsden, Alabama.

30. Letter from Francis Gorman to W. A. Harriman, Divisional Administrator of the NRA, March 19, 1934, Box 1814, E25, RG9, National Archives.

31. *Charlotte Observer*, April 24, 1934. See also *Textile Worker*, April 1934, 150. On Wagner generally see Huthmacher, *Senator Robert F. Wagner*.

32. For examples of workers' responses see *Textile Worker*, April 1934, 150; May 1934, 170.

33. Report on UTW Emergency Committee meeting, April 24–26, 1934, *Textile Worker*, May 1934, 165.

34. *Charlotte Observer*, April 21, 1934, 3.

35. *Textile Worker*, May 1934, 170–71.

36. *Textile Worker*, May 1934, 178.

37. *Charlotte Observer*, April 24, 1934.

38. Letter from Robert Bruere to James Byrnes, May 7, 1934, in Box 1814, E25, RG9, National Archives.

39. *Textile Worker*, May 1934, 166.

40. Letter from James Starr to Paul Christopher, June 14, 1934, folder 3, Box 2, Paul Christopher Papers, Southern Labor Archives, Georgia State University.

41. *Textile Worker*, May 1934, 171.

42. Statement by UTW Research Department submitted to General Johnson, May 29, 1934, in *Textile Worker*, June 1934, 233. A summary by McMahon of the June negotiations can be found in *Textile Worker*, June 1934, 223–26.

43. Statement by John Peel to the Greenville press, quoted in letter from F. S. Blanchard, Deputy NRA Administrator, to Hugh Johnson, May 28, 1934, Box 1798, E25, RG9, National Archives. It is hard to gauge exactly how upset southern workers were over the curtailment, as they were accustomed to slowdowns of work in the summer.

44. Hodges, *New Deal Labor Policy*, 87; Galambos, *Competition and Cooperation*, 257–60.

45. Transcript of telephone conversations between L. R. Gilbert and Theodore Johnson and between L. R. Gilbert and George Googe, both June 4, 1934, in telephone conversations folder, E397, RG9, National Archives.

46. Transcript of telephone conversation between Robert Bruere and Benjamin Geer, May 31, 1934, in telephone conversations folder, E397, RG9, National Archives.

Chapter 8: No Turning Back

1. Transcript of telephone conversation between Googe and Bruere, June 6, 1934, telephone conversations folder, E397, RG9, National Archives.

2. Anonymous letter to Hugh Johnson, June 9, 1934, Labor folder, Box 1812, E25, RG9, National Archives.

3. Telegram from George Googe to George Berry, June 23, 1934, George Berry folder, E397, RG9, National Archives.

4. Telephone conversation between Theodore Johnson and Robert Bruere, May 26, 1934, and between L. R. Gilbert and the vice president and general manager of Waverly Mills, A. M. Fairley, May 28, 1934, telephone conversations folder, E397, RG9, National Archives.

5. Transcript of telephone conversation between Robert Bruere and George Googe, July 11, 1934, telephone conversations folder, E397, RG9, National Archives.

6. Confidential memo from L. R. Gilbert to Robert Bruere, May 12, 1934, in Labor folder, Box 1814, E25, RG9, National Archives.

7. Meeting of UTW Executive Council, June 14–16, 1934, *Textile Worker*, June 1934, 229; Southern Conference of Organizers, June 23, in Greenville, South Carolina, *Textile Worker*, July 1934, 290.

8. Letter from Gorman to Christopher, August 8, 1934, discussing meeting with southern organizers on June 23, 1934, in Greenville, South Carolina, folder 3, Box 2, Paul Christopher Papers, Southern Labor Archives, Georgia State University.

9. Letter from Paul Christopher to Mr. C. E. Lorrance, Recording Secretary, Shelby Local 1901, letters folder, Box 2, Paul Christopher Papers, Southern Labor Archives, Georgia State University.

10. Telegram from J. C. Penny, Laurinburg, North Carolina, to R. Lee Guard, May 29, 1934, claiming that strikers had been subject to gunfire for two nights in a row; letter from Paul Christopher to James Starr, June, 13, 1934, on strikers being armed; in letters folder, Box 2, Paul Christopher Papers, Southern Labor Archives, Georgia State University.

11. Transcript of telephone conversation between Robert Bruere and George Googe, July 11, 1934, telephone conversations folder, E397, RG9, National Archives.

12. Letter from Paul Christopher to Robert Bruere, August 6, 1934, North Carolina State Board folder, E397, RG9, National Archives.

13. The background to the Piedmont strike is described in a letter from John Peel to Robert Bruere, February 13, 1934, and from Peel to George Berry, March 4, 1934, both in Piedmont Manufacturing Company folder, E398, RG9, National Archives.

14. *Columbia State*, May 29, June 21, 1934.

15. The ten mills included mills at Belton, Hamrick, Lonsdale, Monaghan, Gastonia, Waverly, Queen City, Pequot, Selma, and Mobile. Transcript of telephone conversation between Robert Bruere and Benjamin Geer, July 10, 1934, telephone conversations folder, E397; transcript of telephone conversation between Willis and Robert Bruere, July 13, 1934, Piedmont Manufacturing Company folder, E398; both in RG9, National Archives.

16. Night letter from Neal Bass, Piedmont Textile Union President, to Frances Perkins, July 11, 1934, Adjustment, Piedmont Manufacturing Company folder, E398, RG9, National Archives. This was the same day that McMahon threatened Bruere with a statewide strike in North Carolina due to the Laurinburg situation.

17. Letter from Benjamin Geer to Robert Bruere, July 14, 1934, Piedmont Manufacturing Company folder, E398, RG9, National Archives.

18. Letter from Benjamin Geer to Robert Bruere, July 14, 1934, Piedmont Manufacturing Company folder, E398, RG9, National Archives.

19. Transcript of telephone conversation between Robert Bruere and Willis, July 13, 1934, Piedmont Manufacturing Company folder, E398, RG9, National Archives. Langston, "Greenville, Unionism, and the General Strike," 25–26, writes that the local press reported that Geer aided in producing a "settlement" at Piedmont.

20. Telegram from Robert Bruere to Benjamin Geer, July 14, 1934, Piedmont Manufacturing Company folder, E398, RG9, National Archives.

21. *Greenville News,* July 15 and 16, 1934, cited in Langston, "Greenville, Unionism, and the General Strike," 25.

22. Telegram from C. W. Bolick to Frances Perkins, July 14, 1934, Conciliation, Strikes, Georgia folder, Box 38, RG174, National Archives.

23. Letter from John Peel to Frances Perkins, July 30, 1934, Adjustment, Alabama area folder, E398, RG9, National Archives; Langston, "Greenville, Unionism, and the General Strike," 25.

24. Letter from Textile Workers' Committee, Greenwood, South Carolina, to Ibra C. Blackwood, Governor of South Carolina, July 15, 1934, Conciliation and Arbitration Board folder, Box 40, Ibra C. Blackwood Papers, South Carolina State Archives.

25. *Daily News Record,* July 9, 1934, Adjustment, Alabama area folder, E398, RG9, National Archives.

26. This story is drawn from *Daily News Record,* July 12, 1934, and telegram from Robert Bruere to Thomas McMahon, July 14, 1934, both in Dwight Manufacturing Company folder, E398, RG9, National Archives; *Birmingham Age-Herald,* July 13, 1934; Dwight Manufacturing Company, summary argument, employees brief, no date, Dwight Manufacturing Company folder, E402, RG9, National Archives.

27. AP report, untitled, July 16, 1934, Adjustment, Alabama area folder, E398, RG9, National Archives.

28. *Birmingham Age-Herald,* July 13, 16, 1934.

29. *Birmingham Age-Herald,* July 17, 19, 1934. The meetings were not entirely unexpected. On June 23, Gorman had already announced a series of meetings of textile workers in each state to poll the membership on issues such as the stretch-out, discrimination, wages, and hours. Georgia's meeting was to take place June 30–July 1; it did. Alabama's was to be held at an undetermined date; events forced a meeting on July 15 to respond to the walkouts at Dwight and Saratoga Victory mills. South Carolina's was to be in Spartanburg on July 7, but in view of the pace of events in that state it was pushed back to July 20. North Carolina's was to be held in Gastonia at an undetermined date; it turned out to be Salisbury on July 21. Alabama textile leaders agreed to travel to Salisbury to meet with Gorman on July 21. On the June 23 Conference of Southern Organizers see *Columbia State,* June 24, 1934. On subsequent state textile workers' meetings see *Textile Worker,* July 1934, 307–8, Langston, "Greenville, Unionism, and the General Strike, " 25–26.

30. Transcript of telephone conversation between George Googe and Robert Bruere, July 23, 1934, telephone conversations folder, E397, RG9, National Archives.

31. *Birmingham Age-Herald,* July 16, 1934. The meeting was marred by continual bickering between AFL representative George Googe and UTW organizer John Dean. Transcript of telephone conversation between Googe and Robert Bruere, July 23, 1934, Adjustment, Alabama area folder, E398, RG9, National Archives.

32. *Greenville News,* July 22, 1934, cited in Langston, "Greenville, Unionism, and the General Strike," 25–26.

33. Letter from Albert Cox to Hugh Johnson, June 17, 1934, Box 1814, E25; see also telegram from Commissioners of Conciliation C. W. Richardson and J. R.

Steelman to H. L. Kerwin, Director of Conciliation, U.S. Department of Labor, August 30, 1934, Adjustment, Eagle and Phenix Strike Case folder, E398; both in RG9, National Archives.

34. Letter from J. R. Steelman and C. L. Richardson to H. L. Kerwin, Director of Conciliation, U.S. Department of Labor, August 15, 1934, Adjustment, Eagle and Phenix Mill folder, E398, RG9, National Archives.

35. Telegram from E. B. Newberry, President UTW Local 1605, to Franklin Roosevelt, June 25, 1934, Eagle and Phenix Mill folder #3, E398, RG9, National Archives.

36. Letter from G. A. Bland, Lee Carroll, and Robert Stewart to L. R. Gilbert, August 8, 1934, Eagle and Phenix Mill Strike Case folder, E398, RG9, National Archives.

37. Disputes in other Columbus mills in July included the Columbus Manufacturing Company, Muscogee Mills, and Georgia Webbing and Tape Company. A strike of one thousand workers at Muscogee Mills in Columbus was settled peacefully. *Birmingham Age-Herald*, July 31, 1934, Textile and Hosiery Clippings folder, Box 4, G. S. Mitchell Papers, Manuscripts Department, Duke University Library.

38. *Columbia State*, August 14, 1934; Allen, "The Governor and the Strike," 104.

39. *Birmingham News*, August 12, 1934, in Textiles, Georgia folder, Box 3, G. S. Mitchell Papers, Manuscripts Department, Duke University Library; telegram from C. L. Richardson to Hugh Kerwin, August 12, 1934, Adjustment, Eagle and Phenix Strike Case folder, E398, RG9, National Archives.

40. Telegram from C. L. Richardson and J. R. Steelman, Commissioners of Conciliation, to H. L. Kerwin, Director of Conciliation, U.S. Department of Labor, August 13, 1934, Adjustment, Eagle and Phenix Strike Case folder, E398, RG9, National Archives. The owner of Georgia Webbing and Tape resisted this advice and instead remained closed on Monday, August 13. A week later, upon the advice of its lawyer, Georgia Webbing and Tape signed a contract with the union and everyone was back at work. Workers were apparently so satisfied with their victory that they insisted that they would not, even in sympathy, join a general strike. Transcript of telephone conversation between C. L. Richardson and L. R. Gilbert, August 17, 1934, Adjustment, Eagle and Phenix Strike Case folder, E398, RG9, National Archives.

41. Telegram from E. B. Newberry to Frances Perkins, August 13, 1934, Eagle and Phenix Mill folder #3, E398, RG9, National Archives.

42. Letter from "A Committee of half-starved human beings looking to you for help" to Franklin Roosevelt, August 11, 1934, Eagle and Phenix Mill, general folder, E398, RG9, National Archives.

43. Letter from Robert Bruere to Thomas McMahon, August 15, 1934, Eagle and Phenix Mill folder #3, E398, RG9, National Archives.

44. Letter from Richardson and Steelman to H. L. Kerwin, U. S. Department of Labor, August 15, 1934, Adjustment, Eagle and Phenix Mill Strike Case folder, E398, RG9, National Archives. See also transcript of telephone conversation between Richardson and L. R. Gilbert, August 17, 1934, Adjustment, Eagle and Phenix Strike Case folder, E398, RG9, National Archives. Appalled at Bradley's lack of coopera-

tion, Richardson asked L. R. Gilbert to authorize him to act. But Gilbert demurred, indicating that the Cotton Textile Board intended to send Geer down to handle the situation.

45. Transcript of telephone conversation between Bradley and L. R. Gilbert, August 22, 1934, telephone conversations folder, E397, RG9, National Archives.

46. Telegram from E. B. Newberry to Hugh Kerwin, August 16, 1934, Adjustment, Eagle and Phenix Strike Case folder, E398, RG9, National Archives.

47. Telegram from Richardson and Steelman to H. L. Kerwin, Director of Conciliation, U.S. Department of Labor, August 13, 1934, Adjustment, Eagle and Phenix Strike Case folder, E398, RG9, National Archives.

48. *Salisbury (North Carolina) Sunday Post*, August 26, 1934, Textiles, Georgia folder, Box 3, G. S. Mitchell Papers, Manuscripts Department, Duke University Library.

49. Northern textile manufacturers were not unalterably opposed to collective bargaining. Northern silk workers actually achieved, briefly, a nationally binding agreement with silk manufacturers as a result of a protracted strike in the fall of 1933. See Gorka, "It Raised More Questions Than It Provided Answers"; and Bennett, "Textile Workers in New England, 1920–1940."

50. Reeve, "A Million Workers Say Strike," 212.

51. Statement by Sol Stetin, videotaped interview for "The Uprising of '34," Southern Labor Archives, Georgia State University. Stetin later became the president of the Amalgamated Clothing and Textile Workers Union, now part of UNITE.

52. *New York Times*, August 17, 1934 (McMahon quote); *Columbia State*, August 17, 1934 (delegate quote).

53. Whether non-cotton textile workers should also join the strike was the subject of a separate vote. But this vote passed unanimously. From Paterson, New Jersey, a center of the silk industry, workers argued that conditions in silk and rayon were as bad as conditions in cotton. The strike vote in non-cotton textiles passed in spite of the concern expressed by Hosiery Federation President Emil Rieve that the union was biting off "more than it can chew." *New York Herald Tribune*, August 18, 1934.

54. *Columbia State* (AP reports), August 20, 1934. For another report of workers' grievances see *Columbia State* (AP reports), August 21, 1934, where Gorman listed three outstanding grievances: the stretch-out, code violations, and hostility to labor organization. For another example, see *Washington Star*, August 27, 1934, Textile Workers' Strikes folder, Box 38, RG174, National Archives. Workers' grievances were listed as: "1. stretch-out; 2. volume of employment has declined; 3. average weekly earnings have declined; and 4. sweeping and intolerable practice of discharging workers for union affiliation."

55. *New York Times*, September 6, 1934.

56. *Textile Worker*, July 1934, 290.

Chapter 9: Anatomy of a Strike

1. Author's interview with Joe Jacobs, Atlanta, Georgia.

2. *Salisbury (North Carolina) Sunday Post*, August 26, 1934, in Textiles, Georgia

folder, Box 3, G. S. Mitchell Papers, Manuscripts Department, Duke University Library. The UTW's three-week assessment can be found an interview with Francis Gorman in Haskett, "Ideological Radicals," 331, n.74. UTW southern organizer John Peel predicted that the strike could be won in ten days. Langston, "Greenville, Unionism, and the General Strike," 31. See also author's interview with John Howard Payne, Charlotte, North Carolina.

3. In June 1933, the federal government had adopted a policy of granting relief to the destitute whether or not they were on strike. When union officials announced that the textile strikers would be entitled to relief, southern employers counterattacked with arguments that such a practice was "indefensible." Bernstein, *The Turbulent Years*, 307–8. See also "Government Will Pay For Strike, Officials Think," *Salisbury (North Carolina) Sunday Post*, August 26, 1934, Textiles, Georgia folder, Box 3, G. S. Mitchell Papers, Manuscripts Department, Duke University Library. For an example of southern elites' responses to federal relief efforts see Badger, *North Carolina and the New Deal*, chapter 3. The reference to "unworthy" people is on 47.

4. Hodges, *New Deal Labor Policy*, 112. Research still needs to be done on the practical effect of federal relief policy on the textile strike. I have found little evidence that southern textile strikers actually received federal relief.

5. *New York Times*, September 3, 1934.

6. *New York Herald Tribune*, August 18, 1934. Dubinsky eventually contributed $10,000 from the International Ladies Garment Workers Union to the strike fund. Bernstein, *The Turbulent Years*, 313.

7. Strikers quoted in letter from Jack P. Lang, Chief Inspector, North Carolina Department of Labor, to A. L. Fletcher, Commissioner, Sept. 7, 1934, Strikes, 1933–1937, Box 103, J. C. B. Ehringhaus Papers, North Carolina Division of Archives and History. For a similar example of rank and file unionists striking to implement their notion of a just government see Winn, *Weavers of Revolution*.

8. *New York Times*, September 3, 1934.

9. *New York Times*, September 3, 1934.

10. Gaylord, "Alabama Textile Labor Turned the Other Cheek," 482. On the religious basis of southern textile organizing see Marcus, "Organizing the Unorganized: Paul Fuller and His Southern Campaign"; and Simon, "'I Believed in the Strongest Kind of Religion.'"

11. The total number of textile workers in the South, 272,000, includes 20,000 workers in Virginia, most of whom did not strike. Sources for estimates on the strike include the following: Independent AP reports, September 5, 1934; United Press estimates, September 5, 1934; *Columbia Record*, September 7, 13, 18, 1934, courtesy of Tom Terrill; *New York Times*, September 8, 18, 19, 1934; *Newsweek*, September 22, 1934. Estimates on the number of textile workers in the southern industry can be found in the *Greensboro Daily News*, August 25, September 1, 1934, cited in Schultz, "Reaction of Southern Textile Communities," 133. Surprisingly, these numbers did not diverge significantly from those predicted by AFL southern representative George Googe, who, a week before the strike date, claimed that 196,000 out of

272,000 southern workers would strike. His state-by-state breakdowns only slightly overestimated the UTW's strength in the Carolinas, and underestimated the union's strength in Georgia. *Salisbury (North Carolina) Sunday Post*, August 26, 1934, in Textiles, Georgia folder, Box 3, G. S. Mitchell Papers, Manuscripts Department, Duke University Library.

12. On John Dean's kidnapping see Kendrick, "Alabama Goes on Strike"; and Gaylord, "Alabama Textile Labor Turned the Other Cheek," 482.

13. *Daily News Record*, July 24, 1934, Adjustment, Alabama area folder; anonymous letter to FDR, August 29, 1934, Pell City, Alabama, misfiled in Avondale Mills, Birmingham folder; both in E398, RG9, National Archives.

14. *Huntsville Times*, September 7, 1934. The doctor was asked by the millhands at Alexander City to speak on their behalf. See Avondale Mills Alexander City folder, E398, RG9, National Archives.

15. Pendleton, "The 1934 Textile Strike in Alabama," 13.

16. Testimony of Esther Lee Grover, proprietor of a dry cleaning plant in Lanett, Alabama, testifying before a Senate committee in 1939, cited in Wyche, "Southern Industrialists View Organized Labor," 163.

17. Pendleton, "The 1934 Textile Strike in Alabama," 13.

18. Letter from C. W. Lineburger Jr. et al. to J. C. B. Ehringhaus, September 5, 1934, in Strikes, 1933–37 folder, Box 103, J. C. B. Ehringhaus Papers, North Carolina Division of Archives and History.

19. Flamming, *Creating the Modern South*, 199.

20. *Charlotte Observer*, September 4, 1934.

21. Schultz, "Reaction of Southern Textile Communities," 158–60.

22. Schultz, "Reaction of Southern Textile Communities," 157.

23. Fellowship of Reconciliation, "Can Guns Settle Strikes?" 9.

24. Schultz, "Reaction of Southern Textile Communities," 148.

25. Author and Eula McGill's interview with Burns Cox, Gadsden, Alabama.

26. Telegram from Huntsville Retail Clerks International Protective Association to Hugh Kerwin, July 26, 1934, Adjustment, Alabama area folder, E398, RG9, National Archives.

27. *Charlotte Observer*, September 12, 1934.

28. Flamming, *Creating the Modern South*, 200.

29. Howard E. Coffin, chair, Southeastern Cottons, Inc., to J. C. B. Ehringhaus, September 7, 1934; telegram from Groves Thread Co. to J. C. B. Ehringhaus, September 5, 1934, both in Strikes 1933–37 folder, Box 103, J. C. B. Ehringhaus Papers, North Carolina Division of Archives and History; Editorial, *Textile World*, September 1934, Textile Strike folder, Official File 407B, Franklin D. Roosevelt Papers, Hyde Park, New York.

30. Letter from Benjamin Gossett to J. C. B. Ehringhaus, September 14, 1934, Strike Situation folder, Box 104, J. C. B. Ehringhaus Papers, North Carolina Division of Archives and History.

31. Letter from John Howard Payne to J. C. B. Ehringhaus, September 9, 1934,

in Strikes 1933–37 folder, Box 103, J. C. B. Ehringhaus Papers, North Carolina Division of Archives and History.

32. Letter from J. L. Hamme and fifty other people to J. C. B. Ehringhaus, Strikes 1933–37 folder, Box 103, J. C. B. Ehringhaus Papers, North Carolina Division of Archives and History.

33. "Textile Outtakes," newsreel footage, Instructional Services Center, University of South Carolina.

34. Affadavit of F. R. Summers, King's Mountain, September 13, 1934, Strike Situation folder, Box 104, J. C. B. Ehringhaus Papers, North Carolina Division of Archives and History.

35. Letter from Earl Yelton to J. C. B. Ehringhaus, September 10, 1934, in Strikes 1933–37 folder, Box 103, J. C. B. Ehringhaus Papers, North Carolina Division of Archives and History.

36. *Charlotte Observer*, September 5, 1934.

37. The words were those of UTW organizer George Kendall. *Gastonia Gazette*, September 5, 1934.

38. Schultz, "Reaction of Southern Textile Communities," 135.

39. Letter from William F. Gaffney, Inspector, to Major A. L. Fletcher, Commissioner, North Carolina Department of Labor, September 6, 1934, Strikes 1933–37 folder, Box 103, J. C. B. Ehringhaus Papers, North Carolina Division of Archives and History.

40. *Gastonia Gazette*, September 3, 4, 1934; *Raleigh News and Observer*, September 5, 1934.

41. Fellowship of Reconciliation, "Can Guns Settle Strikes?" 8.

42. Author's interview with Joe Jacobs, Atlanta, Georgia. The *LaGrange Daily News* described a "human chain" around the mills, September 3, 1934.

43. For an in-depth account of the '34 strike in Rhode Island see Gerstle, *Working-Class Americanism*, chapter 4, and Findlay, "The Great Textile Strike of 1934." On the AP independent survey see the *New York Times*, September 19, 1934. The survey counted four hundred thousand idle the previous week.

44. *New York Times*, September 15, 1934.

45. Schultz, "Reaction of Southern Textile Communities," 163–64.

46. There is no definitive study of the differences between workers who struck and workers who crossed the picket line within the same mill. For an analysis that supports the idea that workers who were favorites of supervisors were less likely to strike see Hall et al., *Like a Family*, 346–47; and Carlton, "Paternalism and Southern Textile Labor," 24.

47. *Charlotte Observer*, September 7, 1934; letter from William F. Gaffney to A. L. Fletcher, Commissioner, North Carolina Department of Labor, Sept 11, 1934, Strikes 1933–37 folder, Box 103, J. C. B. Ehringhaus Papers, North Carolina Division of Archives and History.

48. Telegram from Robert L. Thompson, president of Local 2084, Waverly Mills, Laurinburg, to Paul Christopher, September 4, 1934, Box 2, uncataloged, Paul Christopher Papers, Southern Labor Archives, Georgia State University.

49. *Birmingham Post,* September 5, 1934, Textiles, Georgia folder, Box 3, G. S. Mitchell Papers, Manuscripts Department, Duke University Library; *Augusta Labor Review,* September 28, 1934.

50. Brittain, "The Politics of Whiteness," 92.

51. Langston, "Greenville, Unionism, and the General Strike," 32.

52. Langston, "Greenville, Unionism, and the General Strike," 32; *Charlotte Observer,* September 6, 1934.

53. "Textile 'Strike,'" *Textile World,* September 1934, Official File 407B, Franklin D. Roosevelt Papers; Langston, "Greenville, Unionism, and the General Strike," 33–37.

54. Hopkins, "Adventures in Carolina Textile Mills," 59.

55. *New York Times,* September 18, 1934.

56. The opening of the Loray Mill provided a wedge with which mill owners pressed their advantage, and by September 12 four mills in Gastonia had reopened. But those mills reopened only after their owners had loaded workers into automobiles and driven them to the mills in between two lanes of troops to prevent crowds from blocking their paths. Schultz, "Reaction of Southern Textile Communities," 155.

57. *New York Times,* September 18, 1934.

58. *Charlotte Observer,* September 4, 5, 1934.

59. Brittain, "The Politics of Whiteness," 92; Hodges, *New Deal Labor Policy,* 110.

60. Jack P. Lang, Chief Inspector, North Carolina Department of Labor, to Major A. L. Fletcher, Commissioner of Labor, September 22, 1934, Strikes 1933–37 folder, Box 103, J. C. B. Ehringhaus Papers, North Carolina Division of Archives and History.

61. *Gastonia Gazette,* September 5, 1934.

62. At Henderson the mills closed for Labor Day but then opened as usual. One hundred and fifty men were sworn in as deputies and sixty-four National Guardsmen were held in readiness. All workers worked all week. *Raleigh News and Observer,* Septmber 5, 8, 12, 1934.

63. Letter from Paul Christopher to UTW Secretary-Treasurer James Starr, September 9, 1934, in Box 2 (uncataloged), Paul Christopher Papers, Southern Labor Archives, Georgia State University.

64. Report of Van B. Metts, Adjutant General, North Carolina, Exhibit B: "Resume of Situation by Areas, United Textile Workers' Strike, 1934," Adjutant General's Department Papers, North Carolina Division of Archives and History (courtesy Jacquelyn Hall).

65. Telegram from John Peel to Ibra C. Blackwood, August 29, 1934; reply from Blackwood to Peel, August 29, 1934; telegram from E. A. McKern to Ibra Blackwood, August 29, 1934; all in 1934 Conciliation and Arbitration Board folder, Box 40, Ibra C. Blackwood Papers, South Carolina State Archives.

66. *Gastonia Gazette,* September 5, 1934, 11. Guardsmen used tear gas to disperse about two hundred strikers who were attempting to close the Woodside Mill. *Charlotte Observer,* September 8, 1934; "Textile 'Strike,'" *Textile World,* September 1934, Official File 407B, Franklin D. Roosevelt Papers.

67. Allen, "The Governor and the Strike," 111–12, quote is on 116. On Talmadge generally see Anderson, *The Wild Man from Sugar Creek*. For a fascinating analysis of Talmadge's campaign speeches to textile workers in September 1934, see Brittain, "The Politics of Whiteness."

68. Author's inteview with Lloyd Davis, Birmingham, Alabama.

69. The number four thousand is cited in the *New York Times*, September 15, 1934. Quotation is from Allen, "The Governor and the Strike," 125.

70. This was the case of workers at the Anchor Duck Mills in Rome, Georgia. See Brittain, "The Politics of Whiteness," 101.

71. *New York Times*, September 21, 1934.

72. *New York Times*, September 20, 1934.

73. *New York Times*, September 21, 1934.

74. *Columbia Record*, September 19, 1934.

75. *New York Times*, September 3, 1934.

76. *New Republic*, September 26, 1934, 172.

77. The *Birmingham Post* suggested that southern manufacturers feared that they would lose "important orders" to their New England competitors as a result of the strike. See *Birmingham Post*, September 5, 1934, in Textiles, Georgia folder, Box 3, G. S. Mitchell Papers, Manuscripts Department, Duke University Library.

78. Turner Battle, "Confidential Memo to the Secretary," September 18, 1934, Textile Workers' Strike folder, Box 38, RG174, National Archives.

79. Letter from J. L. Hamme to J. C. B. Ehringhaus, September 6, 1934, Strikes 1933–37 folder, Box 103, J. C. B. Ehringhaus Papers, North Carolina Division of Archives and History.

80. Letter from O. Max Gardner to O. M. Mull, September 6, 1934, in Box 4, O. Max Gardner Papers, Southern Historical Collection, Wilson Library, University of North Carolina at Chapel Hill.

Chapter 10: Which Side Are You On?

1. Letter from Mrs. L. H. Anderson, Statesville, to J. C. B. Ehringhaus, September 15, 1934, in Box 103, J. C. B. Ehringhaus Papers, North Carolina Division of Archives and History.

2. Letter from Mrs. Vernon L. Ward, President-elect, American Legion Auxiliary, Martin County, to J. C. B. Ehringhaus, September 9, 1934, Box 104, J. C. B. Ehringhaus Papers, North Carolina Division of Archives and History.

3. J. L. Hamme, attorney from Gastonia, to J. C. B. Ehringhaus, September 5, 1934, in Box 103, J. C. B. Ehringhaus Papers, North Carolina Division of Archives and History.

4. Letter from Mr. and Mrs. J. Q. Thornton, sellers of grain and feedstuffs for animals, to Franklin D. Roosevelt, September 20, 1934, in folder 407B, Franklin D. Roosevelt Papers, Hyde Park, New York. The Thorntons made a point of emphasizing that they were not connected with mill owners or strikers.

5. *New York Times*, August 31, 1934.

6. Letter from G. W. McCommon, president, Atlantic Cotton Mills, to L. R. Gilbert, September 17, 1934, Atlantic Cotton Mills folder, E398, RG9, National Archives.

7. "The Meaning of the Textile Strike," *New Republic*, September 26, 1934, 173.

8. *Birmingham Labor Advocate*, September 15, 1934. Georgia labor leaders also provided at best lukewarm support of the strike. See McLaughlin, "The Atlanta Cotton Mills and the 1934 Textile Strike."

9. Turner Battle, "Confidential Memo to the Secretary," September 18, 1934, in Textile Workers' Strike folder, Box 38, RG174, National Archives. Battle was heir to the Cool Springs Plantation in Edgecomb County, North Carolina, and some family-owned industry in nearby Rocky Mount, North Carolina. His uncle, George Gordon Battle, was active in Democratic party politics and a New York lawyer.

10. *New York Times*, September 4, 1934.

11. Haskett, "Ideological Radicals," 331; Freidel, *FDR and the South*, 64.

12. On Roosevelt believing that Socialists were behind the strike see Haskett, "Ideological Radicals," 316. There is some evidence that Roosevelt involved himself in maneuvers to marginalize the left wing of the UTW. *New York Herald Tribune*, August 17, 1934; *Columbia State*, August 18, 1934. See also Reeve, "A Million Workers Say Strike," 211–13. My thanks to Jacquelyn Hall for providing me with a copy of this article.

13. Letter from Josiah Bailey to Franklin Roosevelt, September 13, 1934, in Cotton Textile folder, Box 8, OF407b Labor folder, Franklin D. Roosevelt Library. Roosevelt also failed to send troops to Gorman's home state of Rhode Island, where full-scale rioting had broken out, despite requests from the Rhode Island governor. Findlay, "The Great Textile Strike of 1934."

14. *Columbia State* (AP reports), August 19, 1934. The statement that the union was striking against the government was "attributed to George Sloan," chairman of the Cotton Textile Code Authority. Later the Code Authority made this charge explicit. See *New York Times*, August 30, 1934.

15. *New York Times*, August 28, 1934, 3.

16. *New York Times*, August 19, 1934.

17. *New York Times*, August 31, 1934. Gorman did suggest that mill owners were being allowed to "hide their exploitation behind a cloak of governmental protection." But this was not the centerpiece of his speech, and he did not explain what he meant.

18. *New York Times*, August 25, 1934.

19. *Columbia State* (AP reports), August 26, 1934.

20. *New York Times*, August 26, 1934.

21. *New York Times*, August 30, 1934.

22. *New York Times*, August 17, 1934.

23. *New York Herald Tribune*, August 17, 1934.

24. *New York Times*, August 16, 1934. Hosiery workers were covered by the NLB and not the Bruere Board, and Rieve was a member of the regional National Labor Board in Philadelphia.

25. Bruere said to Geer: "It is Mr. Hillman's idea also that this talk about stretch-out is nonsense. He does feel, however, that the experience of the year shows that we should make some modification in the matter of hours." Transcript of telephone conversation between Robert Bruere and Benjamin Geer, August 20, 1934, in telephone conversations folder, E397, RG9, National Archives. That Hillman privately suggested the need for shorter hours in the textile industry was quite plausible, since Hillman had won shorter hours for workers in his own union, the clothing industry, only weeks before the textile strike began.

26. Kennedy, "The General Strike in the Textile Industry," 37.

27. *New York Times*, August 27, 1934.

28. The full story of the killings at the Chiquola Mill has only recently been told. The account in this book is based primarily on interviews conducted in the late 1970s by students of Dr. James Gettys at Erskine College, South Carolina. Those interviewed were residents of Honea Path who recounted the strike and the shootings on the condition that their identities never be revealed. Copies of the cassette recordings of the interviews are on file at the Erskine College Library. I am grateful to Dr. Gettys and to Dr. Lowry Ware for helping me to understand the words on these tapes. In the late 1980s, the journalist James DuPlessis began an intensive study of the Honea Path tragedy. Finally, in the early 1990s, the producers of the documentary film, *The Uprising of '34*, aided by DuPlessis, also interviewed dozens of residents, both participants and descendents of participants in the 1934 events. A group of Honea Path citizens subsequently began to reevaluate this tragic episode and, in 1996, commemorated it with the erection of a memorial in Honea Path to the seven men who were killed on September 6, 1934. DuPlessis, "Honea Path Confronts 60 years of Repressed Memories, History."

29. Telegram from G. E. Henderson, chairman Local 1881 Strike Committee, to Secretary of Labor Frances Perkins, September 7, 1934, in Textile Workers' Strike folder, Box 38, RG174, National Archives.

30. *Greenville News*, September 7, 1934.

31. *Greenville News*, September 8, 1934.

32. *Greenville News*, September 8, 1934. See also *New York Times*, September 8, 1934, for an even more ambiguous statement by Perkins.

33. Telegram from Francis Gorman to Franklin Roosevelt, September 8, 1934, in Textiles, 1933–34 folder, Box 1, OF355, Franklin D. Roosevelt Library; *New York Times*, September 9, 1934.

34. Statement of J. A. Frier, President, South Carolina Textile Workers Federation: "With human lives hanging in the balance the mills should close for a week in order to allow the people to regain their composure and secure or delay adjustment of the existing disagreement," in *Greenville News*, Greenville, South Carolina, September 10, 1934, courtesy of Tom Terrill, University of South Carolina.

35. For South Carolina Governor Ibra Blackwood's response see Simon, *A Fabric of Defeat*, 119.

36. *New York Times*, September 12, 1934.

37. Langston, "Greenville, Unionism, and the General Strike," 38.

38. *New York Times*, September 11, 1934.

39. *New York Times*, September 8, 1934. After an investigation of the violence which took place during the '34 strike, the Federation of Churches concluded that workers often claimed "intimidation" by flying squadrons as an excuse to stay home. Because they wanted to get their jobs back when the strike was over, they would publicly claim that they stayed home because they were "afraid." Privately, however, they would tell the union they were with them. Report of investigation by the Federal Council of Churches of Christ in America, reprinted in *Textile Worker*, October 1934, 447–48.

40. *New York Times*, September 13, 1934.

41. *New York Times*, September 18, 1934.

42. Letter from Mollie Dowd to her friend "Elizabeth," October 8, 1934, in UTW Organizers folder, E397, RG9, National Archives.

43. Haskett, "Ideological Radicals," 331.

44. *New York Times*, September 22, 1934; *Newsweek*, September 29, 1934, 10–11.

45. Haskett, "Ideological Radicals," 331.

46. *Newsweek*, September 29, 1934, 10–11.

47. *Textile Worker*, September 1934, 432.

Chapter 11: Aftermath

1. *Daily News Record*, quoted in *New Republic*, October 17, 1934, 272.

2. Testimony of John Brown, undated, Box 2, uncataloged, Paul Christopher Papers, Southern Labor Archives, Georgia State University.

3. Letter from Mollie Dowd to "Elizabeth," October 8, 1934, in UTW Organizers folder, E397, RG9, National Archives.

4. On Griffin see the report of AFL organizer S. A. Hollihan in *Birmingham Post*, September 25, 1934, Textiles, Georgia folder, Box 3, G. S. Mitchell Papers, Manuscripts Department, Duke University Library.

5. Letter from Christopher to Peel, October 1, 1934, Box 2, uncataloged, Paul Christopher Papers, Southern Labor Archives, Georgia State University.

6. *Southern Labor Review*, December 12, 1934, Discrimination, Textiles folder, Box 3, G. S. Mitchell Papers, Manuscripts Department, Duke University Library. Workers at the Saratoga Victory Mills at Albertville and Guntersville, Alabama, also reported widespread discrimination. *Walker County Union News*, October 18, 1934.

7. Bernstein, *The Turbulent Years*, 315.

8. *New York Times*, September 25, 1934. This was inevitably a crude estimate, based only on the number of mills that did not immediately open. In fact, some of the mills that remained temporarily closed rehired their original workforce once they reopened; others that reopened immediately refused to hire strikers or strike leaders from the beginning. The *New York Times* broke down its estimate as follows: 10,000 idle in Alabama, 17 mills closed; 32,000 idle in North Carolina, 84 mills closed;

29,000 idle in South Carolina, 62 plants closed; nearly all mills open in Georgia. *New York Times*, September 25, 1934. Education Director Lawrence Rogin estimated that, in the end, approximately twenty-five thousand workers were permanently blacklisted. Author's interview with Lawrence Rogin, Washington, D.C.

9. Letter from Paul Christopher to James Starr, September 29, 1934; letter from Christopher to Francis Gorman, September 27, 1934, Box 2, uncataloged, Paul Christopher Papers, Southern Labor Archives, Georgia State University. Gorman quickly requested that the local delay voting on a new strike pending arrival of UTW organizers to confer with them. *New York Times*, September 27, 1934.

10. *New York Times*, September 29, 1934.

11. *New Republic*, November 7, 1934, 351.

12. Fellowship of Reconciliation, "Can Guns Settle Strikes?" 18.

13. Letter from Mrs. H. M. Huskaup to Franklin Roosevelt, September 1934, Lonsdale Mill folder, E402, RG9, National Archives.

14. Letters from Mollie Dowd to "Elizabeth," October 10 and October 8, 1934, in UTW Organizers folder, E397, RG9, National Archives.

15. Gaylord, "Alabama Textile Labor Turned the Other Cheek," 484.

16. Public statement by B. M. Squires, chair, TLRB, November 6, 1934, J. L. Connor folder, E403, RG9, National Archives.

17. Letter from B. M. Squires to C. E. L. Gill, November 3, 1934, C. E. L. Gill folder, E403, RG9, National Archives.

18. Galambos, *Competition and Cooperation*, 265.

19. Editorial in *Textile Bulletin*, October 11, 1934, Bibb Manufacturing Company folder, E398, RG9, National Archives.

20. UTW testimony at 1936 congressional hearings cited in Lahne, *The Cotton Mill Worker*, 232.

21. *Raleigh Union Herald*, November 15, 1934, Textiles, Georgia folder, Box 3, G. S. Mitchell Papers, Manuscripts Department, Duke University Library.

22. The report was issued in February 1935. Hodges, *New Deal Labor Policy*, 125.

23. Statement by a group of Greenville mills at a meeting of the American Cotton Manufacturers' Association in Greenville, South Carolina, October 17, 1934, in Langston, "Greenville, Unionism, and the General Strike," 41.

24. *New York Times*, December 17, 1934.

25. Galambos, *Competition and Cooperation*, 271.

26. *New Republic*, November 7, 1934, 351.

27. Galambos, *Competition and Cooperation*, 265.

28. *Knoxville Labor News*, December 13, 1934, Discrimination, Textiles folder, Box 3, G. S. Mitchell Papers, Manuscripts Department, Duke University Library.

29. Testimony before the House Labor Committee, reported in *Huntsville Times*, February 25, 1935.

30. "List of Cotton Mills Charged With Complaints Relative to Work Assignments and Work Loads," January 17, 1935, G. Brown folder, E403, RG9, National Archives.

31. See chapter 3.

32. *Textile Worker*, March 1935, 91 (Gorman); *Augusta Labor Review*, March 1, 1935 (Hollihan).

33. Telegram from H. L. Welch to President Roosevelt, April 25, 1935, and letter from TLRB Chair Henry Wiley to H. L. Welch, April 27, 1935, both in Textile Workers' Strike folder, Box 38, RG174, National Archives.

34. *Augusta Labor Review*, May 24, 1935. The workers were also striking because the mill had effectively reduced wages by raising the house rents. But the TLRB could not find the mill guilty of wage reductions, since raising the house rent was not technically illegal.

35. *Augusta Labor Review*, May 24, 1935.

36. Gorman apparently made this statement in an issue of the *Textile Labor Banner*. It is referred to in a letter from UTW member Jack Rubenstein to Gorman, May 30, 1935, Jack Rubenstein Papers, Center for Labor Research and Studies, Florida International University.

37. Hodges, *New Deal Labor Policy*, 132. Galambos, *Competition and Cooperation*, 266, calls the report "very favorable" to management.

38. Letter from John Peel to William A. Mitchell, chairman, Textile Work Assignment Board, May 23, 1935, W. A. Mitchell folder, E403, RG9, National Archives.

39. Letter from Jack Rubenstein to Gorman, May 30, 1935, Jack Rubenstein Papers, Center for Labor Research and Studies, Florida International University.

40. "Workers Cry as They Learn of Supreme Court's NRA Decision," *Textile Labor Banner*, June 15, 1935.

41. See for example, letters from Robert L. Thompson, E. Laurinburg Local 2084, to Paul Christopher, November 12, 1935; and Jack Hinson, King's Mountain, North Carolina, to Thomas McMahon, October 14, 1935, in folder 2, Box 2, Paul Christopher Papers, Southern Labor Archives, Georgia State University.

42. Letter from Mr. P. J. Shehan, Caroleen, North Carolina, to Paul Christopher, October 24, 1935, folder 2, Box 2, Paul Christopher Papers, Southern Labor Archives, Georgia State University.

43. UTWA Status—Locals, 1934–36 folder, Box 674, Papers of the Textile Workers Union of America, State Historical Society of Wisconsin; letter from Paul Christopher to John Peel, March 3, 1936, in Box 2, uncataloged, Paul Christopher Papers, Southern Labor Archives, Georgia State University.

44. Letter from Paul Christopher to John Peel, April 22, 1936, in Hodges, *New Deal Labor Policy*, 129.

45. UTWA Status—Locals, 1934–36 folder, Box 674, Papers of the Textile Workers Union of America, State Historical Society of Wisconsin.

46. Letter from Ernest Ross, secretary, Columbus Textile Council, to Paul Christopher, October 7, 1935, folder 3, Box 2, Paul Christopher Papers, Southern Labor Archives, Georgia State University. Author's interview with Lloyd Davis, Birmingham, Alabama.

47. UTWA Status—Locals, 1934–36 folder, Box 674, Papers of the Textile Workers Union of America, State Historical Society of Wisconsin.

48. The figure 5,472 is cited in Hodges, *New Deal Labor Policy*, 130. Including Tennessee, Virginia, West Virginia, and Mississippi, the total southern membership was 8,313. Richards, "The History of the Textile Workers Union of America," 39, n.6. Nationally, UTW membership had declined from a peak of 350,000 in the summer of 1934 to 79,000 in the summer of 1935. Frankel, "Women, Paternalism, and Protest," 38.

49. Report of F. J. Gorman to 1936 UTW convention, September 14, 1936, 22 and 23, in Convention Reports 1936, General files, President's Office, Paul Christopher Papers, Southern Labor Archives, Georgia State University. See also Hodges, *New Deal Labor Policy*, 149.

50. Letter from Paul Christopher to John Peel, May 21, 1935, in letters folder, Box 2, Paul Christopher Papers, Southern Labor Archives, Georgia State University.

51. UTW Executive Committee Minutes, Friday, Dec 6, 1935, Box 674, Papers of the Textile Workers Union of America, State Historical Society of Wisconsin.

52. Author and Eula McGill's interview with Louis Holloway, Gadsden, Alabama. For a compelling example of what it meant for a southern textile worker to be "union" after the '34 strike when no organization existed, see the account of Annie Mae West in Waldrep, "Politics of Hope and Fear," chapter 5.

53. Hodges, *New Deal Labor Policy*, 146.

54. Schultz, "Reaction of Southern Textile Communities," 177.

55. The other figures were: Georgia, 13 locals with 445 members; North Carolina, 19 locals with 557 members; South Carolina, 21 locals with 726 members. See Richards, "The History of the Textile Workers Union of America," 39, n.6.

56. For more on Alabama textile unions see Pendleton, "New Deal Labor Policy and Alabama Textile Unionism." A similar sort of independent initiative in the North took place among workers in Woonsocket, Rhode Island, where the Independent Textile Union (ITU) kept the mills shut a week after the national strike had been called off. "Virtually alone among textile unions in the country," writes Gary Gerstle, "it emerged from the strike of 1934 with a solid organization and enhanced visibility in the community." As a result of this organizational strength, a former ITU lawyer told Gerstle, Woonsocket workers were "way ahead of anyone else" in the region in their ability to limit machine loads. Unlike most of the unions in New England, the Woonsocket workers managed to hold out against the "terrific drive to increase the workload" that occurred after the 1934 strike. Gerstle, *Working-Class Americanism*, 138, 141.

57. Gorman speech, draft #4, 8, in President's Office, 1936, Paul Christopher Papers, Southern Labor Archives, Georgia State University.

58. Gorman speech, draft #4, 9–10, in President's Office, 1936, Paul Christopher Papers, Southern Labor Archives, Georgia State University.

59. Gorman speech, draft #4, 9–10, in President's Office, 1936, Paul Christopher Papers, Southern Labor Archives, Georgia State University.

60. Gorman speech, draft #1, 2, in President's Office, 1936, Paul Christopher

Papers, Southern Labor Archives, Georgia State University. The disillusionment was shared by Jack Rubenstein, member of the Dyers and Finishers' Federation inside the UTW. "We were all too trustful of what the NRA would do for us," he wrote to Gorman. Letter from Jack Rubenstein to Frank Gorman, May 30, 1935, Jack Rubenstein Papers, Center for Labor Research and Studies, Florida International University.

61. Gorman speech, draft #2, 11, in President's Office, 1936, Paul Christopher Papers, Southern Labor Archives, Georgia State University.

62. Davin, "The Very Last Hurrah?," 117–71.

63. Gorman speech, draft #1, 10, in President's Office, 1936, Paul Christopher Papers, Southern Labor Archives, Georgia State University.

64. Gorman speech, draft #3, 19, in President's Office, 1936, Paul Christopher Papers, Southern Labor Archives, Georgia State University. Gorman was responding in part to circumstances in the northeast, where subdepartments of the textile union had frequently chafed at the centralized control exercised by the UTW leadership. But Gorman's advice also applied to the southern situation, and was clearly a product of his experiences during the 1934 strike.

65. Gorman speech, draft #3, 11, in President's Office, 1936, Paul Christopher Papers, Southern Labor Archives, Georgia State University.

66. Gorman speech, draft #3, 19, in President's Office, 1936, Paul Christopher Papers, Southern Labor Archives, Georgia State University.

67. Gorman speech, draft #3, 19, in President's Office, 1936, Paul Christopher Papers, Southern Labor Archives, Georgia State University.

68. Author's interview with Lloyd Davis, Birmingham, Alabama. See also author's interview with J. H. Payne, Charlotte, North Carolina.

69. Letter from Jack Rubenstein to Frank Gorman, May 30, 1935, Jack Rubenstein Papers, Center for Labor Research and Studies, Florida International University.

70. Letter from Christopher to Francis Gorman, September 7, 1934, letters folder, box 2, Paul Christopher Papers, Southern Labor Archives, Georgia State University.

71. Letter from Francis Gorman to Paul Christopher, September 10, 1934, Box 2, uncataloged, Paul Christopher Papers, Southern Labor Archives, Georgia State University.

72. Letter from Thomas McMahon to Paul Christopher, February 8, 1935, Box 2, uncataloged, Paul Christopher Papers, Southern Labor Archives, Georgia State University.

73. Paul Christopher, "Biennial Report to the UTWA," 35th Annual Convention, September 14, 1936, in UTW Minutes, Executive Council Report, 1936–37, Paul Christopher Papers, Southern Labor Archives, Georgia State University.

74. *Textile Labor Banner*, May 25, 1935.

75. Author and Eula McGill's interviews with Cordova, Alabama, workers.

76. The third candidate was Sandy Graham, who represented the state's banking interests and was vehemently opposed to the New Deal.

77. Garrison, "Paul Revere Christopher," 57–62; Badger, *North Carolina and the New Deal*, 63–67; Morrison, *Governor O. Max Gardner*, 164–68.

78. Simon, *A Fabric of Defeat*, chapter 7.

79. This can be seen in the distribution of votes. In Greenville, an area heavily populated by textile workers but without a strong union presence, Johnston lost. In the textile districts where the union was strong, however, Johnston won overwhelmingly. See Simon, *A Fabric of Defeat*, 134; and Key, *Southern Politics in State and Nation*, 139.

80. Badger, *North Carolina and the New Deal*, 37–38.

81. This analysis supports the conclusion of Alan Brinkley that the weakness of southern liberalism was a key factor in the failure of the New Deal to transform southern politics. Brinkley, "The New Deal and Southern Politics."

82. *New York Times*, October 2, 1934.

83. *Huntsville Times*, March 25, 1935.

84. Wolf, "Cotton and the Unions," 149.

85. Author's interview with Lloyd Davis, Birmingham, Alabama; Jonathan Daniels, cited in Langston, "Greenville, Unionism, and the General Strike," 64.

86. Hawes, "Organizing a Textile District," 15; Hodges, *New Deal Labor Policy*, 160.

87. TWOC "Report on Activities," cited in Richards, "The History of the Textile Workers Union of America," 40.

88. Richards, "The History of the Textile Workers Union of America," 135.

89. Hodges, *New Deal Labor Policy*, 152.

90. As Paul Richards writes, the TWOC was "a northern organization which constantly looked southward for its salvation." Richards, "The History of the Textile Workers Union of America," 81.

91. Richards, "The History of the Textile Workers Union of America," 135.

92. Letter from Christopher to Franz Daniel, cited in Hodges, *New Deal Labor Policy*, 152.

93. Richards, "The History of the Textile Workers Union of America," 140–42. In response to accusations that the TWOC was a northern union invading Dixie, TWOC leaders were careful to ensure that the union had a southern face in the South. In particular, it brought on staff many veteran southern UTW leaders, although these organizers were reassigned to parts of the South where their connection to the '34 strike would not be known. Gorman left the TWOC in 1939 because he felt his locals in Rhode Island should be permitted the autonomy to agree to independent wage concessions during a sharp economic recession in 1938. The national union balked at this demand for a local agreement; Gorman was fired. Disgusted, Gorman helped re-form the old AFL UTW, bringing a handful of disenchanted southern workers with him as he did so.

94. Richards, "The History of the Textile Workers Union of America," 142.

95. Author and Eula McGill's interviews with Margaret Drake, daughter of William Adcock, and Mrs. Harry H. Owen, both of Huntsville, Alabama.

96. Richards, "The History of the Textile Workers Union of America," 144.

97. Richards, "The History of the Textile Workers Union of America," 145.

98. Author's interview with Ruby Page, Columbus, Georgia.

99. Author's interview with James Cortez, Edgefield, South Carolina.

100. Minchin, *What Do We Need A Union For?* For an account of the failure of the CIO's Operation Dixie to "crack" the textile South see Griffith, *The Crisis of American Labor.*

Conclusion

1. Garrison, "Paul Revere Christopher," 68.

2. Waldrep, "Politics of Hope and Fear."

3. See, for one example, Green, "Democracy Comes to 'Little Siberia.'"

4. Wyche, "Southern Industrialists View Organized Labor," 170–71.

5. Historians of the Southern Tenant Farmers' Union (STFU) document a similar reluctance on the part of Roosevelt to abandon his loyalty to the South's political elites. See Grubbs, *Cry from the Cotton*; Dante, *The Great Depression* (documentary film); Naison, "The Southern Tenant Farmers' Union."

6. Haber, *Efficiency and Uplift.* It is important to acknowledge that such reformers did attempt to distance themselves from the worst abuses of the stretch-out. When workers in Gastonia had walked off their jobs in 1929, for example, the Taylor Society cancelled its annual meeting there and denounced labor practices in the Loray Mills as a misuse of the principles of scientific management. But as the role played by Geoff Brown in the UTW indicates, reformers were blind to the destructive effects of even those scientific management practices considered "legitimate."

7. Schlesinger, *The Coming of the New Deal,* 118. See also 159, where Schlesinger suggests that the NIRA had "bitten off more than it could chew."

8. Ferguson, "From Normalcy to New Deal."

9. Lippman quoted in Lash, *Dealers and Dreamers,* 259.

10. Galambos, *Competition and Cooperation,* 273–75.

11. Galambos, *Competition and Cooperation,* 268, 272–73, and 276.

12. Michl, *The Textile Industries: An Economic Analysis,* 276–77.

13. For an account of the ways that workplace issues were sacrificed in the 1930s in the coal mining industry, see B. E. Smith, *Digging Our Own Graves.*

14. Record of statement by John Peel, *Textile Worker,* July 1934, 308.

15. Christopher, "The General Strike of 1934," 28.

16. W. R. Gaylord, "Alabama Textile Labor Turned the Other Cheek," 482–84.

Appendix B

1. Googe also included eight thousand textile workers from Mississippi, making a total of 196,000. See "Government Will Pay For Strike, Officials Think," *Salisbury (North Carolina) Sunday Post,* August 26, 1934, in Textiles, Georgia folder, Box 3, G. S. Mitchell Papers, Manuscripts Department, Duke University Library.

2. For UTW cotton textile membership see Hodges, *New Deal Labor Policy*, 61, 91; and Haskett, "Ideological Radicals," 305; on percentage of cotton textile workers in the South see Hodges, 9.

3. On membership nationwide see Brooks, "United Textile Workers," 350; and Garrison, "Paul Revere Christopher," 27. On the number of locals in each southern state see Prior, "From Community to National Unionism," 75; *Textile Worker*, July 1934, 291; and *Birmingham Age-Herald*, July 13, 16, 1934. On estimates of membership in North and South Carolina see Prior, 55; *Augusta Labor Review*, May 18, 1934.

SELECTED BIBLIOGRAPHY

Archives, Manuscript Collections, and Special Library Collections

National Archives and Records Administration, Washington, D.C.
>   Records of the National Recovery Administration (RG9)
>   Records of the Department of Labor (RG174)

Southern Labor Archives, Special Collections Department, Pullen Library, Georgia State University, Atlanta
>   Records of AFL-CIO, Region 8, United Textile Workers of America, 1934–36: Papers of Paul Revere Christopher
>   Transcripts of Interviews, "The Uprising of '34 Video Project"

State Historical Society of Wisconsin, Madison
>   TWOC Historical Records
>   United Textile Workers of America

Manuscripts Department, Duke University Library, Durham, N.C.
>   George S. Mitchell Papers

Huntsville Public Library, Huntsville, Ala.
>   Vertical files

Birmingham Public Library, Birmingham, Ala.
>   Philip Taft Papers

Erskine College Library, Due West, S.C.
>   Cassette recordings of personal interviews with Honea Path Strike Survivors

South Carolina State Archives, Columbia
>   Ibra Blackwood Papers
>   Olin Johnston Papers

University of South Carolina, Columbia
>   "Textile Outtakes"—film footage located at the Instructional Services Center

North Carolina Division of Archives and History, Raleigh
     J. C. B. Ehringhaus Papers
     Adjutant General's Department Papers
Southern Historical Collection, Wilson Library, University of North Carolina,
Chapel Hill
     O. Max Gardner Papers
     Southern Oral History Collection
Robert Muldrow Cooper Library, Clemson University, Clemson, S.C.
     James F. Byrnes Papers
Franklin D. Roosevelt Library, Hyde Park, N.Y.

Interviews

By the Author
Allen, Inez, Leola, and Goldie. Personal interview, Shelby, North Carolina, June 1986
Aultman, Cecil. Personal interview, Gadsden, Alabama, July 1986
Bland, Wilene. Personal interview, Columbus, Georgia, July 1986.
Cashion, Mr. and Mrs. J. B. Personal interview, Shelby, North Carolina, June 1986
Cortez, James. Personal interview, Edgefield, South Carolina, June 1986
Davis, Lloyd. Personal interview, Birmingham, Alabama, July 1986
Donnahoo, Vance and Zelleree. Personal interview, Inman, South Carolina, June
     1986
Jacobs, Joseph. Personal interview, Atlanta, Georgia, September 1987
Knox, Robert. Personal interview, Phenix City, Alabama, July 1986
Myers, Taylor. Telephone interview, Huntsville, Alabama, July 1986
Page, Ruby. Personal interview, Columbus, Georgia, July 1986
Payne, John H. Personal interview, Charlotte, North Carolina, June 1986
Pearson, Roscoe. Personal interview, Gadsden, Alabama, July 1986
Reeves, Alice. Personal interview, Graniteville, South Carolina, June 1986
Smith, G. W. Personal interview, Easley, South Carolina, June 1986
Trammell, Dee. Personal interview, Shelby, North Carolina, June 1986
Woodell, Mary. Personal interview, Columbus, Georgia, July 1986

By the Author and Eula McGill
Beard, Laura. Personal interview, Gadsden, Alabama, July 1986
Boyanton, Arthur. Personal interview, Huntsville, Alabama, July 1986
Cox, Burns. Personal interview, Gadsden, Alabama, July 1986
Drake, Margaret. Personal interview, Huntsville, Alabama, July 1986
Holloway, Louis. Personal interview. Gadsden, Alabama, July 1986
Owen, Mrs. Harry. Personal interview, Huntsville, Alabama, July 1986
Richardson, Earl, and Dick Smith, Clifford McFarear, Lorene Ryland, Jesse Ryland,
     Donald Harbison, and George Kilby. Group interview at Cordova Town Hall,
     Cordova, Alabama, July 1986
Ryland, Jesse and Lorene. Personal interview, Cordova, Alabama, July 1986
Smith, Irving "Tynes." Personal interview, Gadsden, Alabama, July 1986

Stewart, Gertrude. Personal interview, Huntsville, Alabama, July 1986
Ware, Clyde. Personal interview, Gadsden, Alabama, July 1986

Books, Articles, and Theses

Adamic, Louis. "Tragic Towns of New England." *Harper's* 162 (May 1931): 748–60.

Akin, Edward. "'Mr. Donald's Help': Donald Comer, Avondale's Birmingham Operatives, and the United Textile Workers, 1933–34." Paper presented at the meeting of the Southern Historical Association, November 1980.

Allen, John Earl. "The Governor and the Strike: Eugene Talmadge and the General Textile Strike of 1934." Master's thesis, Georgia State University, 1977.

Anderson, William. *The Wild Man from Sugar Creek: The Political Career of Eugene Talmadge.* Baton Rouge: Louisiana State University Press, 1975.

Badger, Anthony J. *North Carolina and the New Deal.* Raleigh: North Carolina Department of Cultural Resources, 1981.

Bailey, N. Louise et al. *Biographical Dictionary of the South Carolina Senate, 1776–1985.* Columbia: University of South Carolina Press, 1986.

Beal, Fred. *Proletarian Journey.* New York: Hillman, Inc., 1937.

Beardsley, Edward H. *A History of Neglect: Health Care for Blacks and Mill Workers in the Twentieth-Century South.* Knoxville: University of Tennessee Press, 1987.

Beatty, Bess. "Gender Relations in Southern Textiles: A Historiographical Overview." In Gary M. Fink and Merl E. Reed, eds., *Race, Class, and Community in Southern Labor History* (Tuscaloosa: University of Alabama Press, 1994): 9–16.

———. "Textile Labor in the North Carolina Piedmont: Mill Owner Images and Mill Worker Response." *Labor History* 25 (Fall 1984): 485–503.

Bell, John L. *Hard Times: Beginnings of the Great Depression in North Carolina, 1929–1933.* Raleigh: North Carolina Department of Cultural Resources, 1982.

Bennett, John. "Textile Workers in New England, 1920–1940." Seminar paper, University of Pittsburgh, 1973.

Benson, Susan Porter. *Counter Cultures: Saleswomen, Managers, and Customers in American Department Stores, 1890–1940.* Urbana: University of Illinois Press, 1986.

Berkowitz, Edward, and Kim McQuaid. *Creating the Welfare State: The Political Economy of Twentieth-Century Reform.* New York: Praeger, 1980.

Bernstein, Irving. *The Lean Years: A History of the American Worker, 1933–1941.* Boston: Houghton Mifflin Co., 1960.

———. *The Turbulent Years: A History of the American Worker, 1933–1941.* Boston: Houghton Mifflin Co., 1970.

Berry, George L. "Printing Pressman's Achievements." *American Federationist* 35:11 (November 1928): 1368–72.

Blanshard, Paul. *Labor in Southern Cotton Mills.* New York: New Republic, 1927.

Blicksilver, Jack. *Cotton Manufacturing in the Southeast: An Historical Analysis.* Atlanta: Georgia State College of Business Administration, 1959.

Boyette, Lawrence. "The General Textile Strike of 1934 in Greenwood County: In

Search of Sadie Harris." Seminar paper, University of North Carolina at Chapel Hill, 1987.

Boyte, Harry. "The Textile Industry: Keel of Southern Industrialization." *Radical America* 6 (March–April 1972): 4–49.

Brannon, Peter A. "Donald Comer, Dean of the Alabama Textile Industry." *Textile History Review* 1:3 (July 1960): 118–21.

Bright, Leonard. "The South Afire!" *Labor Age* 18 (May 1929): 15–17.

Brinkley, Alan. *Liberalism and Its Discontents*. Cambridge, Mass: Harvard University Press, 1998.

———. "The New Deal and Southern Politics." In James C. Cobb and Michael Namorato, eds., *The New Deal and the South* (Jackson: University Press of Mississippi, 1984): 97–117.

Brittain, Michele. "The Politics of Whiteness: Race, Workers and Culture in the Modern South." Ph.D. dissertation, Rutgers University, 1995.

Brody, David. *In Labor's Cause*. New York: Oxford University Press, 1996.

———. *Workers in Industrial America: Essays on the Twentieth-Century Struggle*. New York: Oxford University Press, 1980.

Brooks, Robert R. "The United Textile Workers of America." Ph.D. dissertation, Yale University, 1935.

Brown, Geoff. "Scientific Management and Organized Labor." *Bulletin of the Taylor Society* 10 (June 1925): 139–45.

———. "Workers' Participation in Job Study." *Bulletin of the Taylor Society* 12 (June 1927): 416–20.

Bruere, Robert. "Produce or Perish." *The World Tomorrow* 5:12 (December 1922): 355–57.

———. "West Lynn." *The Survey* 56 (April 1, 1926): 23–27.

Burke, Fielding [Olive Tilford Dargen]. *Call Home the Heart*. New York: Longmans, Green, and Co., 1932.

Burns, James MacGregor. *Roosevelt: The Lion and the Fox*. New York: Harcourt, Brace, Jovanovich, 1956.

Cannon, Bernard. "Social Deterrents to the Unionization of Southern Cotton Textile Mill Workers." Ph.D. dissertation, Harvard University, 1951.

Carlton, David L. "How American Is the American South?" In Larry J. Griffin and Don H. Doyle, eds., *The South as An American Problem* (Athens: University of Georgia Press, 1995): 33–56.

———. *Mill and Town in South Carolina, 1880–1920*. Baton Rouge: Louisiana State University Press, 1982.

———. "Paternalism and Southern Textile Labor: A Historiographical Review." In Gary M. Fink and Merl E. Reed, eds., *Race, Class and Community in Southern Labor History* (Tuscaloosa: University of Alabama Press, 1994): 17–26.

———. "The Revolution from Above: The National Market and the Beginnings of Industrialization in North Carolina." *Journal of American History* 77:3 (September 1990): 445–75.

Christopher, Paul. "The General Strike of 1934." *Let Southern Labor Speak.* Monteagle, Tenn.: Highlander Folk School, 1938. 28–30.

Clark, Daniel J. *Like Night and Day: Unionization in a Southern Mill Town.* Chapel Hill: University of North Carolina Press, 1997.

Cobb, James C. *The Selling of the South: The Southern Crusade for Industrial Development, 1936–1980.* Baton Rouge: Louisiana State University Press, 1982.

Cohen, Lizabeth. *Making a New Deal: Industrial Workers in Chicago, 1919–1939.* New York: Cambridge University Press, 1990.

Cooke, Morris, Samuel Gompers, and Fred Miller, eds. "Labor, Management and Production." *Annals of the American Academy of Political and Social Science* 91 (September 1920).

Davin, Eric Leaf. "The Very Last Hurrah? The Defeat of the Labor Party Idea, 1934–1936." In Staughton Lynd, ed., *"We Are All Leaders": The Alternative Unionism of the Early 1930s* (Urbana: University of Illinois Press, 1996): 117–71.

Dearing, Charles L. et al., *The ABC of the NRA.* Washington, D.C.: Brookings Institute, 1934.

DeNatale, Douglas. "Traditional Culture and Community in a Piedmont Textile Mill Village." Master's thesis, University of North Carolina at Chapel Hill, 1980.

DeVyver, Frank. "Status of Labor Unions in the South." *Southern Economic Journal* 5:4 (April 1939): 485–98.

Douty, Harry M. "The North Carolina Industrial Worker, 1880–1930." Ph.D. dissertation, University of North Carolina at Chapel Hill, 1936.

———. "Labor Unrest in North Carolina." *Social Forces* 11 (May 1933): 579–88.

Dubofsky, Melvyn. *We Shall Be All: A History of the Industrial Workers of the World.* Chicago: Quadrangle Books, 1969.

Dubofsky, Melvyn, and Warren Van Tine. *Labor Leaders in America.* Urbana: University of Illinois Press, 1987.

DuPlessis, James. "Honea Path Confronts 60 Years of Repressed Memories, History." *The Greenville News* (May 28, 1995): G1, 4–5.

Edmunds, Richard. *Cotton Mill Labor Conditions in the South and New England.* Baltimore: Manufacturers' Record Publishing Company, 1925.

Etheridge, Willie S. "Liberalism Stirs Southern Churches." *Christian Century* (March 9, 1932): 317–19.

Evans, Mercer G. "History of the Organized Labor Movement in Georgia." Ph.D. dissertation, University of Chicago, 1929.

———. "Southern Labor Supply and Working Conditions in Industry." *Annals of the American Academy of Political and Social Science* 153 (January 1931): 156–62.

Faue, Elizabeth. *Community of Suffering and Struggle: Women, Men and the Labor Movement in Minneapolis, 1915–1945.* Chapel Hill: University of North Carolina Press, 1991.

———. "'The Dynamo of Change': Gender and Solidarity in the American Labour Movement of the 1930s." *Gender and History* 1:2 (Summer 1989): 138–58.

Fellowship of Reconciliation. "Can Guns Settle Strikes? A Study of the Violent Aspects of the 1934 Textile Strike in Three Southern States." New York: n.p., 1935. Copy located in Rare Book and Manuscripts Collection, Duke University Libraries, Durham, North Carolina.

Ferguson, Thomas. "From Normalcy to New Deal: Industrial Structure, Party Competition, and American Public Policy in the Great Depression." *International Organization* 38 (Winter 1984): 41–94.

Findlay, James F. "The Great Textile Strike of 1934: Illuminating Rhode Island History in the Thirties." *Rhode Island History* 42:1 (February 1983): 17–29.

Fink, Gary M. *The Fulton Bag and Cotton Mills Strike of 1914–1915: Espionage, Labor Conflict, and New South Industrial Relations.* Ithaca, N.Y.: Cornell University Press, 1993.

Flamming, Douglas. *Creating the Modern South: Millhands and Managers in Dalton, Georgia, 1884–1984.* Chapel Hill: University of North Carolina Press, 1992.

Foner, Philip. *Women and the American Labor Movement, From World War I to the Present.* New York: Free Press, 1980.

Frankel, Linda. "'Jesus Leads Us, Cooper Needs Us, The Union Feeds Us': The 1958 Harriet-Henderson Textile Strike." In Jeffrey Leiter, Michael D. Schulman, and Rhonda Zingraff, eds., *Hanging By a Thread: Social Change in Southern Textiles* (Ithaca, N.Y.: ILR Press, 1991): 101–20.

———. "Women, Paternalism, and Protest in a Southern Textile Community: Henderson, North Carolina, 1900–1960." Ph.D. dissertation, Harvard University, 1986.

Fraser, Steve. "Dress Rehearsal for the New Deal: Shop Floor Insurgents, Political Elites, and Industrial Democracy in the Amalgamated Clothing Workers." In Michael Frisch and Daniel Walkowitz, eds., *Working-Class America: Essays on Labor, Community, and American Society* (Urbana: University of Illinois Press, 1983): 212–255.

———. "From the 'New Unionism' to the New Deal." *Labor History* 25:3 (Summer 1984): 405–43.

———. "The 'Labor Question.'" In Steve Fraser and Gary Gerstle, eds., *The Rise and Fall of the New Deal Order, 1930–1980* (Princeton, N.J.: Princeton University Press, 1989): 55–84.

———. *Labor Will Rule: Sidney Hillman and the Rise of American Labor.* New York: Free Press, 1991.

Frederickson, Mary. "Four Decades of Change: Black Workers in Southern Textiles, 1941–1981." In James Green, ed., *Workers' Struggles, Past and Present: A "Radical America" Reader* (Philadelphia: Temple University Press, 1983): 62–82.

———. "Heroines and Girl Strikers: Gender Issues and Organized Labor in the Twentieth-Century American South." In Robert H. Zieger, ed., *Organized Labor in the Twentieth-Century South* (Knoxville: University of Tennessee Press, 1991): 84–112.

———. "'I Know Which Side I'm On': Southern Women in the Labor Movement in the Twentieth Century." In Ruth Milkman, ed., *Women, Work and Protest: A Century of Women's Labor History* (Boston: Routledge and Kegan Paul, 1985): 156–80.

Freeze, Gary R. "Poor Girls Who Might Otherwise Be Wretched: The Origins of Paternalism in North Carolina's Mills, 1836–1880." In Jeffrey Leiter, Michael D. Schulman, and Rhonda Zingraff, eds., *Hanging By a Thread: Social Change in Southern Textiles* (Ithaca, N.Y.: ILR Press, 1991): 21–32.

Freidel, Frank. *FDR and the South*. Baton Rouge: Louisiana State University Press, 1965.

Galambos, Louis. *Competition and Cooperation: The Emergence of a National Trade Association*. Baltimore: Johns Hopkins University Press, 1966.

Garrison, Joseph Yates. "Paul Revere Christopher, Southern Labor Leader, 1910–1974." Ph.D. dissertation, Georgia State University, 1976.

Gaston, Paul. *The New South Creed: A Study in Southern Mythmaking*. New York: Alfred A. Knopf, 1970.

Gaylord, W. R. "Alabama Textile Labor Turned the Other Cheek." *Textile Worker* (November 1934): 482–85.

German, Richard Henry Lee. "The Queen City of the Savannah: Augusta, Georgia, during the Urban Progressive Era, 1890–1917." Ph.D. dissertation, University of Florida, 1971.

Gerstle, Gary. *Working-Class Americanism: The Politics of Labor in a Textile City, 1914–1960*. New York: Cambridge University Press, 1989.

Gilbert, James. "Defining Industrial Democracy: Work Relations in Twentieth-Century America." *International Labor and Working Class History* 35 (Spring 1989): 81.

Goldberg, David J. *A Tale of Three Cities: Labor Organization and Protest in Paterson, Passaic, and Lawrence, 1916–1921*. New Brunswick: Rutgers University Press, 1989.

Goldfield, Michael. *The Decline of Organized Labor in the United States*. Chicago: University of Chicago Press, 1987.

Googe, George. "Organizing the Workers of Georgia." *American Federationist* 35:11 (November 1928): 1326–29.

———. "Union Progress in South Carolina." *American Federationist* 36 (June 1929): 678–80.

Gorka, Ted. "It Raised More Questions Than It Provided Answers: The NIRA, Section 7(a), and the Silk Strike of 1933." Unpublished paper provided to the author by Kier Jorgensen, director, Research Department, Amalgamated Clothing and Textile Workers' Union, 1988.

Gorman, Francis, Tom Tippett, and A. J. Muste. *The Marion Murder*. New York: Conference for Progressive Labor Action, Pamphlet #2, 1929.

Gossett, B. B. "Textile Conditions in the South." *Southern Textile Bulletin* (December 19, 1929): 33–36.

Green, James R. "Democracy Comes to 'Little Siberia': Steel Workers Organize in Aliquippa, Pennsylvania, 1933–1937." *Labor's Heritage* 5:2 (Summer 1993): 5–27.

Greider, William. *One World, Ready or Not: The Manic Logic of Global Capitalism.* New York: Simon and Schuster, 1997.

Griffith, Barbara. *The Crisis of American Labor: Operation Dixie and the Defeat of the CIO.* Philadelphia: Temple University Press, 1988.

Gross, James A. *The Making of the National Labor Relations Board.* Albany: State University of New York Press, 1981.

Grubbs, Donald R. *Cry from the Cotton: The Southern Tenant Farmers' Union and the New Deal.* Chapel Hill: University of North Carolina Press, 1971.

Haber, Samuel. *Efficiency and Uplift: Scientific Management in the Progressive Era, 1890–1920.* Chicago: University of Chicago Press, 1964.

Hall, Jacquelyn Dowd, James Leloudis, Robert Korstad, Mary Murphy, LuAnn Jones, and Christopher B. Daly. *Like a Family: The Making of a Southern Cotton Mill World.* Chapel Hill: University of North Carolina Press, 1987.

Hall, Jacquelyn Dowd. "Disorderly Women: Gender and Labor Militancy in the Appalachian South." *Journal of American History* 73 (September 1986): 354–82.

Haskett, William. "Ideological Radicals: The American Federation of Labor and Federal Labor Policy in the Strikes of 1934." Ph.D. dissertation, University of California at Los Angeles, 1958.

Hawes, Elizabeth. "Organizing a Textile District." *Let Southern Labor Speak.* Monteagle, Tenn: Highlander Folk School, 1938. 15–17.

Hayes, Jack Irby. "South Carolina and the New Deal, 1932–1938." Ph.D. dissertation, University of South Carolina, 1972.

Hearden, Patrick J. *Independence and Empire: The New South's Cotton Mill Campaign, 1865–1901.* DeKalb: Northern Illinois University Press, 1982.

Heiss, M. W. "The Southern Cotton Mill Village: A Viewpoint." *Journal of Social Forces* 2 (March 1924): 345–50.

Herring, Harriet. "Cycles of Cotton Mill Criticism." *South Atlantic Quarterly* 28 (April 1929): 113–25.

———. "The Industrial Worker." In W. T. Couch, ed., *Culture in the South* (Chapel Hill: University of North Carolina Press, 1934), 344–60.

———. "12 Cents, the Troops, and the Union." *The Survey* 59 (November 15, 1927): 199–202.

———. "Welfare Work." *Social Forces* 6 (June 1928): 595–97.

———. *Welfare Work in Mill Villages: The Story of Extra-Mill Activities in North Carolina.* Chapel Hill: University of North Carolina Press, 1929.

Hill, Patrick Henry. "The Ethical Emphases of the Baptist Editors in the Southeast Region of the U.S., 1915–1940." Ph.D. dissertation, Southern Baptist Theological Seminary, 1949.

Himmelberg, Robert F. *The Origins of the National Recovery Administration.* New York: Fordham University Press, 1976.

Hodges, James A. *New Deal Labor Policy and the Southern Cotton Textile Industry, 1933–1941.* Knoxville: University of Tennessee Press, 1986.

Hoffman, Alfred. "Hell in Henderson, A Walkout in Darkest America." *Labor Age* 16 (November 1927): 2–5.

Hogan, Lawrence. "Rumblings in Southern Textiles." *Labor Age* 21 (March 1932): 8, 17.

———. "The Strikes at Langley, Bath, and Clearwater." *Labor Age* 21 (May 1932): 12.

Holly, John F. "Elizabethton, Tennessee: A Case of Southern Industrialization." Ph.D. dissertation, Clark University, 1949.

Honey, Michael K. *Southern Labor and Black Civil Rights: Organizing Memphis Workers.* Urbana: University of Illinois Press, 1993.

Hood, Robin. "The Loray Mill Strike." Master's thesis, University of North Carolina at Chapel Hill, 1932.

Hopkins, Ollie. "Adventures in Carolina Textile Mills." *Let Southern Labor Speak.* Monteagle, Tenn: Highlander Folk School, 1938. 58–60.

Huff, Tess. "A Conference of Southern Workers." *Labor Age* 21 (August 1932): 4–5.

Huthmacher, J. Joseph. *Senator Robert F. Wagner and the Rise of Urban Liberalism.* New York: Atheneum, 1968.

Jacoby, Sanford. *Employing Bureaucracy: Managers, Unions, and the Transformation of Work in American Industry, 1900–1945.* New York: Columbia University Press, 1985.

———. "Union-Management Cooperation in the United States: Lessons from the 1920s." *Industrial Labor Relations Review* 37:1 (October 1983): 18–33.

Johnson, Gerald. "The Cotton Strike." *The Survey* 46 (September 1921): 646–47.

Jolley, H. E. "The Labor Movement in North Carolina: 1880–1922." *North Carolina Historical Review* 30 (July 1953): 354–75.

Kendrick, Alexander. "Alabama Goes on Strike." *The Nation* (August 29, 1934): 233–34.

Kennedy, John W. "The General Strike in the Textile Industry, September 1934." Master's thesis, Duke University, 1947.

Key, V. O. *Southern Politics in State and Nation.* New York: Alfred A. Knopf, 1949.

Kohn, August. *The Cotton Mills of South Carolina.* Columbia: South Carolina Department of Agriculture, Commerce and Immigration, 1907.

Lahne, Herbert J. *The Cotton Mill Worker.* New York: Farrar and Rinehart, 1944.

Langston, Stan. "Greenville, Unionism, and the General Strike in the Textile Industry." Unpublished paper, February 27, 1984, Greenville Public Library. Paper provided to the author by James Dunlap, University of South Carolina, Columbia.

Lash, Joseph P. *Dealers and Dreamers: A New Look at the New Deal.* Garden City: Doubleday, 1988.

Levine, Rhonda. *Class Struggle and the New Deal.* Lawrence: University Press of Kansas, 1988.

Lichtenstein, Nelson, and Howell John Harris, eds., *Industrial Democracy in America: The Ambiguous Promise.* New York: Cambridge University Press, 1993.

Lorwin, Lewis, and Arthur Wubnig. *Labor Relations Boards.* Washington, D.C.: Brookings Institute, 1935.

Lynd, Staughton, ed. "The Possibility of Radicalism in the Early 1930s: The Case of Steel." In James Green, ed., *Workers' Struggles, Past and Present: A "Radical America" Reader* (Philadelphia: Temple Univeristy Press, 1983): 190–208.

————. *"We Are All Leaders": The Alternative Unionism of the Early 1930s.* Urbana: University of Illinois Press, 1996.

Lyon, Ralph M. *The Basis for Constructing Curricular Materials in Adult Education for Carolina Cotton Mill Workers.* New York: Columbia University Contributions to Education, Teachers' College, series no. 678, 1937.

MacDonald, Lois. *Southern Mill Hills: A Study of Social and Economic Forces in Certain Textile Mill Villages.* New York: Alex L. Hillman, 1928.

Marcus, Irwin. "Organizing the Unorganized: Paul Fuller and His Southern Campaign." Unpublished paper in author's possession, September 1997.

Marshall, F. Ray. *Labor in the South.* Cambridge, Mass.: Harvard University Press, 1967.

Martin, Charles H. "Southern Labor Relations in Transition: Gadsden, Alabama, 1930–1943." *Journal of Southern History* 47 (November 1981): 545–68.

McCartin, Joseph A. *Labor's 'Great War': American Workers, Unions, and the State, 1916–1920.* Chapel Hill: University of North Carolina Press, 1997.

McHugh, Cathy. *Mill Family: The Labor System in the Southern Cotton Textile Industry, 1880–1915.* New York: Oxford University Press, 1988.

McLaughlin, Gretchen. "The Atlanta Cotton Mills and the 1934 Textile Strike." Seminar paper, Emory University, 1984.

McLaurin, Melton. *Paternalism and Protest: Southern Cotton Mill Workers and Organized Labor, 1875–1905.* Westport, Conn.: Greenwood Press, 1971.

Michl, Edward Herman. *The Textile Industries: An Economic Analysis.* Washington, D.C.: The Textile Foundation, 1938.

Minchin, Timothy J. *What Do We Need a Union For? The TWUA in the South, 1945–1955.* Chapel Hill: University of North Carolina Press, 1997.

Minton, George Fort. "The South Fights the Unions." *New Republic* (July 10, 1929): 202–3.

Mitchell, Broadus. "The End of Child Labor, or How Mill Workers Are Finishing What Social Workers Began." *The Survey* 42 (August 23, 1919): 747–50.

Mitchell, Broadus, and George S. Mitchell. *The Industrial Revolution in the South.* Baltimore: Johns Hopkins University Press, 1930.

Mitchell, George S. "The Cotton Mills Again." *The Survey* 58 (July 15, 1927): 411–13.

————. "Organization of Labor in the South." *Annals of American Academy of Political and Social Science* 153 (January 1931): 182–87.

————. *Textile Unionism and the South.* Chapel Hill: University of North Carolina Press, 1931.

Mitchell, George S., and Broadus Mitchell. "The Plight of Cotton Mill Labor." In J. B. S. Hardman, ed. *American Labor Dynamics in Light of Postwar Developments* (New York: Harcourt, Brace, and Co., 1928): 211–15.

Mitchell, Jonathan. "Here Comes Gorman!" *New Republic* (October 3, 1934): 203–5.

Montgomery, David. *The Fall of the House of Labor: The Workplace, the State, and American Labor Activism, 1865–1925.* Cambridge: Cambridge University Press, 1987.

————. *Workers' Control in America: Studies in the History of Work, Technology, and Labor Struggles*. New York: Cambridge University Press, 1980.

Moody, Kim. *An Injury to All: The Decline of American Unionism*. New York: Verso, 1988.

Morrison, Joseph L. *Governor O. Max Gardner: A Power in North Carolina and New Deal Washington*. Chapel Hill: University of North Carolina Press, 1971.

Murchison, Claudius. *King Cotton Is Sick*. Chapel Hill: University of North Carolina Press, 1930.

Muste, A. J. "A.F. of L.'s Biggest Task. Will Toronto Back Organization of the South?" *Labor Age* 18 (October 1929): 3–6.

————. "The Call of the South: Labor's Next Task." *Labor Age* 17 (August 1928): 5–6.

Myers, James. "Field Notes: Textile Strikes in the South," Typescript, 1929. Copies in Gastonia Public Library and in the North Carolina Collection at the University of North Carolina at Chapel Hill.

————. *Representative Government in Industry*. New York: George H. Doran and Co., 1924.

Nadworny, Milton. *Scientific Management and the Unions, 1900–1932*. Cambridge, Mass.: Harvard University Press, 1955.

Naison, Mark. "The Southern Tenant Farmers' Union." In Staughton Lynd, ed., *"We Are All Leaders": The Alternative Unionism of the Early 1930s* (Urbana: University of Illinois Press, 1996), 102–16.

Nelson, Bruce. *Workers on the Waterfront: Seamen, Longshoremen, and Unionism in the 1930s*. Urbana: University of Illinois Press, 1988.

Newby, I. A. *Plain Folk in the New South: Social Change and Cultural Persistence, 1880–1915*. Baton Rouge: Louisiana State University Press, 1989.

Newman, Dale. "Work and Community Life in a Southern Textile Town." *Labor History* 19 (Spring 1978): 204–25.

Nichols, Jeanette Paddock. "Does the Mill Village Foster Any Social Types?" *Social Forces* 2 (March 1924): 350–57.

Nolan, Dennis R., and Donald E. James. "Textile Unionism in the Piedmont, 1901–1932." In Gary M. Fink and Merle E. Reed, eds., *Essays in Southern Labor History: Selected Papers, Southern Labor History Conference, 1976* (Westport, Conn.: Greenwood Press, 1977): 48–79.

Norrell, Robert J. "Labor at the Ballot Box: Alabama Politics from the New Deal to the Dixiecrat Movement." *Journal of Southern History* 62:2 (May 1991): 201–34.

Nyman, Richard C., and Elliot Dunlap Smith. *Union-Management Cooperation in the "Stretch Out": Labor Extension at the Pequot Mills*. New Haven: Yale University Press, 1934.

Ohl, John Kennedy. *Hugh S. Johnson and the New Deal*. DeKalb: Northern Illinois University Press, 1985.

Page, Myra. *Southern Cotton Mills and Labor*. New York: Workers' Library Publishers, 1929.

Pendleton, Deborah. "New Deal Labor Policy and Alabama Textile Unionism." Master's thesis, Auburn University, 1988.

———. "The 1934 Textile Strike in Alabama." Seminar paper, Auburn University, 1985.

Prior, John P. "From Community to National Unionism: North Carolina Textile Labor Organizations, July 1932–September 1934." Master's thesis, University of North Carolina at Chapel Hill, 1972.

Pope, Liston. *Millhands and Preachers: A Study of Gastonia.* New Haven: Yale University Press, 1942.

Ramsay, Anne Marshall. "Industrial Relations in the Southern Cotton Textile Industry, 1933–1935." *Vassar Journal of Undergraduate Studies* 9 (May 1935): 135–74.

Reeve, Carl. "A Million Workers Say Strike!" *New Masses* (August 28, 1934): 211–13.

Rhyne, J. Jennings. *Some Southern Cotton Mill Workers and Their Villages.* Chapel Hill: University of North Carolina Press, 1930.

Richards, Paul David. "The History of the Textile Workers Union of America, CIO, in the South, 1937–1945." Ph.D. dissertation, University of Wisconsin, 1978.

Robertson, David. *Sly and Able: A Political Biography of James F. Byrnes.* New York: W. W. Norton and Co., 1994.

Rogin, Michael. "Voluntarism: The Political Functions of an Antipolitical Doctrine." *Industrial and Labor Relations Review* 15:4 (July 1962): 521–35.

Salmond, John A. *Gastonia, 1929: The Story of the Loray Mill Strike.* Chapel Hill: University of North Carolina Press, 1995.

Schlesinger, Arthur, Jr. *The Age of Roosevelt: The Coming of the New Deal.* Boston: Houghton Mifflin, Co., 1959.

Schultz, Robert Grissom. "A Study of the Reaction of Southern Textile Communities to Strikes." Master's thesis, University of North Carolina at Chapel Hill, 1949.

Scott, James. *The Moral Economy of the Peasant: Rebellion and Subsistence in Southeast Asia.* New Haven: Yale University Press, 1976.

Selby, John. "Industrial Growth and Worker Protest in a New South City: High Point, North Carolina, 1859–1959." Ph.D. dissertation, Duke University, 1984.

Simon, Bryant. "Choosing Between the Ham and the Union: Paternalism in the Cone Mills of Greensboro, 1925–1930," In Jeffrey Leiter, Michael D. Schulman, and Rhonda Zingraff, eds., *Hanging by a Thread: Social Change in Southern Textiles* (Ithaca, N.Y.: ILR Press, 1991): 81–100.

———. *A Fabric of Defeat: The Politics of South Carolina Millhands, 1910–1948.* Chapel Hill: University of North Carolina Press, 1998.

———. "'I Believed in the Strongest Kind of Religion': James Evans and Working Class Protest in the New South." *Labor's Heritage* 4 (Fall 1992): 60–77.

Singal, Danel Joseph. *The War Within: From Victorian to Modernist Thought in the South: 1919–1945.* Chapel Hill: University of North Carolina Press, 1982.

Smith, Barbara Ellen. *Digging Our Own Graves: Coal Miners and the Struggle over Black Lung Disease.* Philadelphia: Temple University Press, 1987.

Smith, B. H. "The Social Significance of the Southern Cotton Mill Community." Master's thesis, Emory University, 1925.

Smith, Fenelon DeVere. "The Economic Development of the Textile Industry in the Columbia, South Carolina Area from 1790 through 1916." Ph.D. dissertation, University of Kentucky, 1952.

Smith, Sarah Margaret. "A Social Study of High Point." Master's thesis, University of North Carolina at Chapel Hill, 1933.

Spier, William. "We Was All Poor Then: The Sub-Economy of a Farming Community, 1900–1925." *Southern Exposure* 2:3 (Fall 1974): 80–91.

Stewart, Ethelbert. "The Present Situation in Textiles." *American Federationist* 36 (June 1929): 683–91.

Stolberg, Benjamin. "Madness in Marion." *The Nation* 129 (October 23, 1929): 462–63.

Stoney, George C. "Suffrage in the South, Part I: The Poll Tax," *Survey Graphic* 29:1 (January 1940): 5–43.

Storrs, Landon R. Y. "An Independent Voice for Unorganized Workers: The National Consumers' League Speaks to the Blue Eagle." *Labor's Heritage* 6:3 (Winter 1995): 24–30.

Taft, Philip. *Organizing Dixie: Alabama Workers in the Industrial Era.* Westport, Conn.: Greenwood Press, 1981.

Tannenbaum, Frank. "The South Buries Its Anglo-Saxons." *Darker Phases of the South* (New York: G. P. Putnam's Sons, 1924): 39–73.

Terrill, Tom E., and Jerrold Hirsch. *Such As Us: Southern Voices of the Thirties.* New York: W. W. Norton and Co., 1979.

Thompson, Holland. *From the Cotton Field to the Cotton Mill.* New York: Macmillan Co., 1906.

Tindall, George B. *Emergence of the New South: 1913–1945.* Baton Rouge: Louisiana State University Press, 1967.

Tippett, Tom. *When Southern Labor Stirs.* New York: Jonathan Cape and Harrison Smith, 1931.

Tomlins, Christopher. *The State and the Unions: Labor Relations, Law, and the Organized Labor Movement in America, 1880–1960.* Cambridge: Cambridge University Press, 1985.

Trepp, Jean Carol. "Union-Management Cooperation and the Southern Organizing Campaign." *Journal of Political Economy* 41 (1933): 602–24.

Triffin, Susan. *In Whose Best Interest? Child Welfare Reform in the Progressive Era.* Westport, Conn.: Greenwood Press, 1982.

Tripplette, Ralph R. "One-Industry Towns: Their Location, Development, and Economic Character." Ph.D. dissertation, Univeristy of North Carolina at Chapel Hill, 1974.

Tullos, Allen. *Habits of Industry: White Culture and the Transformation of the Carolina Piedmont*. Chapel Hill: University of North Carolina Press, 1989.

United Textile Workers of America. 6th Biennial and 33rd Annual Convention, *Proceedings*, New York, August 1934.

———. 7th Biennial and 35th Annual Convention, *Proceedings*, New York, September 1936.

Vance, Rupert B. "Rebels and Agrarians All." *The Southern Review* 4 (1938–39): 34.

Van Osdell, John Garrett. "Cotton Mills, Labor, and the Southern Mind." Ph.D. dissertation, Tulane University, 1966.

Vittoz, Stanley. *New Deal Labor Policy and the American Industrial Economy*. Chapel Hill: University of North Carolina Press, 1987.

Vorse, Mary Heaton. (1930). *Strike!* Urbana: University of Illinois Press, 1991.

Waldrep, George C. III. "Politics of Hope and Fear: The Struggle for Community in the Industrial South." Ph.D. dissertation, Duke University, 1996.

Werner, Randolph D. "Hegemony and Conflict: The Political Economy of a Southern Region, Augusta, Georgia, 1865–1895." Ph.D. dissertation, University of Virginia, 1977.

Whitley, Donna Jean. "Fuller E. Calloway and Textile Mill Development in LaGrange, 1895–1920." Ph.D. dissertation, Emory University, 1984.

Williams, Clinton E. "The Cotton Manufacturing Industry in Alabama." Master's thesis, University of Alabama, 1927.

Williamson, Gustavas G. "South Carolina Cotton Mills and the Tillman Movement." *Proceedings of the South Carolina Historical Association*, Columbia, 1949: 36–49.

Wills, Keith C. "Southern Baptists and Labor, 1927–1956." Ph.D. dissertation, Southwestern Baptist Theological Seminary, 1958.

Wingerd, Mary Lethert. "Rethinking Paternalism: Power and Parochialism in a Southern Mill Village." *Journal of American History* 83:3 (December 1996): 872–902.

Winn, Peter. *Weavers of Revolution: The Yarur Workers and Chile's Road to Socialism*. New York: Oxford University Press, 1986.

Wolf, Herman. "Cotton and the Unions." *Survey Graphic* 27 (March 1938): 146–50; 189–90.

Wright, Gavin. *Old South, New South, Revolutions in the Southern Economy Since the Civil War*. New York: Basic Books, 1986.

———. "Cheap Labor and Southern Textiles, 1880–1930." *Quarterly Journal of Economics* 96 (November 1981): 605–29.

Wyche, Billy H. "Southern Industrialists View Organized Labor in the New Deal Years." *Southern Studies* 19 (Summer 1980): 157–71.

Zieger, Robert H. "Textile Workers and Historians." In Robert H. Zieger, ed., *Organized Labor in the Twentieth-Century South* (Knoxville: University of Tennessee Press, 1991): 35–59.

Zieger, Robert H. ed. *Southern Labor in Transition, 1940–1995*. Knoxville: University of Tennessee Press, 1997.

Documentary Films

Dante, James, producer. *The Great Depression: Mean Things Happening.* PBS Film
    Documentary, Henry Hampton, Executive Producer, 1993.
Stoney, George, and Judith Helfand, producers. *The Uprising of '34.* 1934 Strike
    Consortium, Vera Rony, Executive Producer, 1995.

INDEX

Adamic, Louis, 40
Adcock, William, 118, 172–73
AFL. *See* American Federation of Labor
Alabama State Federation of Labor, 143, 151
Alabama State Textile Council, 95
Alabama textile industry, 32
Alabama textile workers: and union organizing (1929–30), 32–33; experience with Bruere Board, 84–85; and general textile strike, 114, 123–24; and union organizing (1935–38), 162–63
Alamance County, N.C., 16
Albertville, Ala., 67
American Cotton Manufacturers' Association, 65, 88
American Federation of Labor (AFL): and migration of textile industry, 40; and Southern Organizing Campaign, 41–42; 1932 convention of, 52; reaction to general textile strike, 142. *See also* Green, William
American Spinning Company, 31
Anderson, Mary, 52
Anderson, William, 35
Anderson, S.C., 21, 171
Anniston, Ala., 32, 33, 123
Apalache Mill, 130 (photo)
Appleton Mill, 95
Arcadia Mills, 34

Arnall Mill, 85, 125
Augusta, Ga., 17, 47, 111, 125. *See also* Horse Creek Valley
automobiles: purchased by southern textile workers, 26–27; used in flying squadrons, 129, 130 (photo)
Avondale Mills: workers' letters to FDR, 63, 68; and general strike, 123–24; after strike settlement, 154

Bailey, Josiah, 143
Barrett, James, 19, 30
Bass, Neal, 20, 112–13
Battle, Turner, 138, 143
Beacham, Dan, 147
Beard, Laura, 33
Beattie, S. M., 113
Bedaux system, 159–60. *See also* scientific management
Beddow, Noel, 169
Belmont, N.C., 125, 126 (photo), 134
Bernstein, Irving, 5
Berry, Alice, 100
Berry, George, 61, 76, 82, 88
Bessemer City, N.C., 106
Bibb Mill, 35, 136
Birmingham, Ala., 123, 154
Black Bill, 52–53
black southern textile workers: prevented from working by strikes, 17;

join UTW, 71; "colored" locals in 1934, 183–87. *See also* white supremacy
Blackwood, Ibra, 135
Bland, G. A., 117
Blease, Cole, 168
Bolick, C. W., 70, 102
boll weevil, 25
"boomlet" of 1933, 64, 74
Borah, William E., 63
Bradley, Frank J., 116
Brandeis, Louis, 43
Brinkley, Alan, 175
Brookwood Labor College, 46, 47
Brown, Geoff, 45, 61, 159
Bruere, Robert W.: biography, 61–62; as chair of stretch-out committee, 76; speech before American Cotton Manufacturers' Association, 105; response to Sen. Byrnes, 106; complaint about North Carolina strikers, 111; comment on Eagle and Phenix strike case, 117; offer to mediate textile labor dispute, 145. *See also* Bruere Board
Bruere Board (aka Cotton Textile National Industrial Relations Board): origins of, 75–78; procedures of, 79–80; impact on textile union organizing, 80; in Horse Creek Valley dispute, 81–83; supported by UTW, 87–88; in Cleveland Cloth Mills dispute, 89–93; opposed by southern unionists, 93–96, 105, 107, 111; expansion of, 108–9; and Eagle and Phenix Mills dispute, 116–17; not well understood by public, 145
Burke, Fielding (aka Olive Tilford Dargen), 27
Byrnes, James F., 58–59, 106

Calloway, Cason, 143
Calloway Mills, 100, 159. *See also* LaGrange, Ga.
Calvert, Rob, 148
Cannon Mills: workers' letters to FDR, 67–68: layoffs not reflected in payrolls, 74; and general strike, 131–32, 132 (photo), 135
Cedartown, Ga., 133, 136
Chadwick Hoskins Mill, 54, 70, 100, 126
Charlotte, N.C., 70; during WWI, 20,

21; and 1921 strike, 22; and general strike, 122, 125, 126
Chattahoochee Valley, 70, 124
Chickamauga, Ga., 102
Chiquola Mill, 134, 147–50. *See also* Honea Path, S.C.
Christopher, Paul: biography, 33, 47–48; as president of North Carolina Federation of Textile Workers, 90; hired by UTW, 100; and general strike, 135; after strike settlement, 154–55; frustrated with UTW, 110, 162, 165–66; frustrated with TWOC, 171–72; assesses general strike, 175, 180
CIO. *See* Congress of Industrial Organizations
Clark, David, 91
Cleveland Cloth Mill, 47, 89–93
Columbia, S.C., 17, 122, 125, 126–27
Columbus, Ga.: and National Union of Textile Workers, 17; during WWI, 20, 21; and UTW, 32, 102; and August 1934 strike, 115–18; and general strike, 125; after strike settlement, 161. *See also* Eagle and Phenix Mills
Comer, Donald, 56, 67–68, 91, 143. *See also* Avondale Mills
communism, 11, 29, 41 (photo)
Cone Mills, 23, 135. *See also* Greensboro, N.C.
Congress of Industrial Organizations (CIO), 6, 170–73
Cooleemee, N.C., 16
Cordova, Ala., 167. *See also* Walker County, Ala.
Cortez, James, 173
Cotton Textile Code: origins of, 56–57; sec. 15 of, 59; response of southern textile workers to, 64; impact on workloads, 64–65; impact on wages, 66; sec. 17 of, 75–76, 89; assessed, 95, 140–41, 159. *See also* National Industrial Recovery Act
Cotton Textile Code Authority: and investigations of Code violations, 72–73, 156–57; and data collection, 73–74; public relations, 74, 157–58; creates Bruere Board, 76–77; declares industry exempt from NLB oversight, 77; curtails production hours, 97–98, 107. *See also* Sloan, George
Cotton Textile Institute: attempts self-

regulation, 55–56; and creation of NIRA, 49, 56–57, 59. *See also* Sloan, George

Cotton Textile National Industrial Relations Board. *See* Bruere Board

Covan, Ellis, 65

Cox, Albert, 85, 100, 115

Cox, Burns, 15, 103–4

Crawford, Lee, 148

Crow, Tom, 20

CTNIRB. *See* Cotton Textile National Industrial Relations Board

Dalton, Ga., 20, 122, 125, 127

Daniels, Josephus, 35

Danville, Va., 46

Dargen, Olive Tilford. *See* Burke, Fielding

Davis, Ira, 149

Davis, Lloyd, 100, 161, 162, 165

Dean, John, 20, 100, 114, 123

Democratic party, 6, 9, 168–69, 176. *See also* New Deal; Roosevelt, Franklin D.

direct action: by southern textile workers, 8, 9, 15, 121, 129–30; endorsed by UTW, 111–12

Donnahoo, Vance, 23, 69

Donnahoo, Zelleree, 23, 69

Dowd, Mollie, 100, 151, 154, 155, 169

Dubofsky, Melvyn, 40

Dunean Mills, 128, 132–33

Durham, N.C., 125–26, 161

Dwight Manufacturing Company (Dwight Mills): and sexual harassment, 15–16; workers' letters to FDR, 65, 67; experience with Bruere Board, 85–86; union organizing, 103–4; and general strike, 114; after strike settlement, 162. *See also* Gadsden, Ala.

Eagle and Phenix Mills, 67, 73, 115–18. *See also* Columbus, Ga.

East Tallassee, Ala., 106–7

Elizabethton, Tenn., 29, 33, 42, 61

Ellenbogen Bill (National Textile Bill), 179

Exposition Mill, 127 (photo)

Federation of Churches, 30–31

fences: used around textile mills, 24, 171

Finch, V. C., 85

Florence, Ala., 123

flying squadrons: described, 3, 128–31, 130 (photo), 133–34, 135; response of mill owners to, 128–29; called off in South Carolina, 150

Foster, J. R., 71–72

Fox, Council M., 100, 114, 150

Fuller, Paul, 34, 47, 81–84

Gadsden, Ala., 20, 29, 33, 123, 127, 162. *See also* Dwight Manufacturing Company

Gaffney, S.C., 161

Galambos, Louis, 156, 158, 178

Gardner, O. Max: and Rockingham strike, 34; philosophy of labor, 54; and creation of Cotton Textile Institute, 55–56; and Cleveland Cloth Mills dispute, 89–93; and general strike, 139; and 1936 North Carolina gubernatorial campaign, 167

Gaston County, N.C., 130. *See also* Gastonia, N.C.

Gastonia, N.C., 11, 29–30, 35, 65, 125 (photo), 143 (photo), 167. *See also* Gaston County, N.C.; Loray Mill

Gay, J. Ralph, 84, 100, 133, 137

Gaylord, W. R., 122, 180

Geer, Benjamin: attitude toward unions, 61; as member of stretch-out committee, 76; and Bruere Board controversies, 82, 92–93; attacked by John Peel, 94; and June agreement with UTW, 109; and Piedmont strike settlement, 113

general textile strike: dimensions of, 3, 4, 122–23, 150–51; described, 3–4, 123–38; mill owners' reaction to, 4, 123–24; violence in, 4, 133–34, 148–49; distortions of accounts of, 4–5, 146–50; legacy of, 11–12, 173; begins in Alabama, 114; demands formulated, 114–15; federal relief during, 120–21; meaning of, 121–22, 139, 141–42; public support for, 126–27, 140–41; in the North, 131; use of National Guard in, 135–38

Georgia Federation of Labor, 101–2

Georgia textile manufacturers: response to Cotton Textile Code, 70; and Eugene Talmadge's campaign, 137; and TLRB, 157

Georgia textile workers: and union orga-

nizing (1929–33), 70; experience with
Bruere Board, 85; and UTW, 101–2;
and general strike, 125, 131, 137; and
violence, 133–34; after general strike,
161
Georgia Webbing and Tape Company,
117–18
Gilbert, L. R., 89–92, 108–9, 111
Gluck and Equinox Mills, 21
Golden, John, 39, 43
Googe, George, 42, 69, 92–93, 102, 146
Gorman, Francis: and southern organizing (1930–31), 32, 46; biography, 45–
46; at conference of Cotton Textile
Code Authority, 98; and southern organizing (1933–34), 99, 101–2, 114;
opposes stretch-out, 107; and general
strike, 119, 120–21, 144–45; refuses
Bruere's offer to mediate, 145; pro-
poses arbitration, 150; regrets settle-
ment, 158; denounces TLRB, 159–60;
on loss of UTW membership, 161–
62; assesses failure of strike, 163–65,
164 (photo)
Gossett, B. B., 54, 55–56, 128
Graham, Frank Porter, 35
Graniteville, S.C., 83. See also Horse
Creek Valley, S.C.
Great Depression, 7, 33, 49. See also un-
employment
Green, William, 42, 52, 142, 146, 160.
See also American Federation of Labor
Greensboro, N.C., 131. See also Cone
Mills
Greenville, S.C., 31–32, 69, 135, 157.
See also Dunean Mills
Greer, S.C., 130 (photo)
Griffin, Ga., 154
Grover, N.C., 165
Gwyn, S. J., 68

Hamme, J. L., 128, 138–39, 140–41
Hare, W. O., 142. See also Alabama State
Federation of Labor
Harriet and Henderson Mill, 24. See also
Henderson, N.C.
Hauskaup, Mrs. H. M., 155
Henderson, N.C., 135. See also Harriet
and Henderson Mill
Herring, Harriet, 14
High Point, N.C., 33, 36, 54, 70, 90
Hillman, Sidney, 146, 171

Hilton, W. L., 67
Hodges, James, 73
Hoey, Clyde, 167
Hoffman, Alfred, 64
Hogan, Lawrence, 67
Hogansville Mills, 73–74
Holland, J. P., 64, 85–86
Hollihan, S. A., 159
Holloway, Louis, 162
Honea Path, S.C., 4, 134, 147–50
Hood, Ernest, 44, 59
Hopkins, Ollie, 133
Horse Creek Valley, S.C.: and 1932
strike, 34, 47, 81; early history of, 80;
and Bruere Board, 81–84; and general
strike, 132
Huntsville, Ala.: and union organizing,
32, 33, 69; and general strike, 122,
123, 127; after general strike, 162

industrial democracy, 19, 29
Industrial Workers of the World
(IWW), 39, 43
Inman, S.C., 23, 69, 161
IWW. See Industrial Workers of the
World

Jacobs, Joseph, 102–3, 120, 131
Johnson, Hugh: on NIRA, 57, 63; and
origins of Bruere Board, 59–61, 77;
and Cotton Textile Code Authority,
73; negotiates with UTW and George
Sloan, 108–9
Johnson, Theodore, 91–92, 102, 146
Johnson and Johnson Company, 57
Johnston, Olin, 167–68
Jordan, Monroe, 65

Kendall, George, 70, 100
Keynsian economics, 51, 178–79
King's Mountain, N.C., 154
Knights of Labor, 16, 40
Knoxville, Tenn., 70

LaCons, H. F., 137–38
LaGrange, Ga., 21, 85. See also Calloway
Mills
Laurinburg, N.C., 111, 112, 167
Lawrence, Roy, 121
Lawrence, Mass., 39, 43
Liberty League, 168
Lincoln Mills, 67

Lindale, Ga., 132
Lisk, H. D., 121–22
Long Shoals Cotton Mills, 3
Lonsdale Mill, 95, 135
Loray Mill, 24, 29–30, 130, 133. *See also* Gastonia, N.C.
Lumberton, N.C., 112

Macon, Ga., 35, 133
Marchant, Thomas, 59, 88, 105
Marion, N.C.: in 1929–30, 29, 34, 35, 42, 46; and general strike, 135
market unionism, 50
McCandler, Robert, 138
McDonald, Ralph, 167
McGill, Eula, 70, 100
McMahon, Thomas: during WWI era, 40, 41 (photo); favors national wage standards, 40, 45, 115, 166; opposes militancy, 41 (photo), 86, 88, 90, 97; views on stretch-out, 43–44, 52–53, 105–6, 119; transfers Paul Fuller, 84; favors cooperation with Bruere Board, 87–88; favors labor representation on Cotton Textile Code Authority, 90, 97–98, 107–9; makes final appeals to Bruere Board, 112, 117; at August 1934 UTW convention, 118
Merrimack Mills, 65, 71
Miller, Mrs. B. M., 70
Minette Mill, 165–66
Mitchell, George, 20, 35, 40
Morgan, C. A., 77
Mulberry Methodist Church, 35
Mull, O. M., 89–93, 139
Myers, James, 30, 31

National Civic Federation, 39
National Guard: in South Carolina in 1916, 21; in North Carolina in 1922, 22; in Gastonia in 1929, 29; in Danville in 1930, 46; and general strike, 134 (photo), 135–38; at Calloway Mills in 1935, 159
National Industrial Recovery Act (NIRA): origins of, 7, 56–57; southern textile workers' response to, 7, 63–64, 71–72, 77–78; sec. 7(a) of, 69–71, 179–80; declared unconstitutional, 160; assessed, 177–78
National Labor Board (NLB): origins of, 75–77; confused with Bruere Board, 87, 145; and Cleveland Cloth Mills dispute, 91
National Labor Relations Act. *See* Wagner Act
National Textile Bill. *See* Ellenbogen Bill
National Textile Workers' Union (NTWU), 29
National Union of Textile Workers (NUTW), 16–17
Newberry, E. B., 117, 119
Newberry, S.C., 95
Newby, I. A., 15
New Deal: as response to Great Depression, 7, 49–50; impact on the South, 7, 176; as inspiration for southern textile labor protests, 8, 36–37, 140–41; shaped by liberal reformers, 50–51; shaped by industry, 51, 53, 141; shaped by working people, 51–53, 140; impact on ordinary Americans, 63, 140; as political coalition, 143–44, 168, 178. *See also* National Industrial Recovery Act
Newnan, Ga., 73, 85, 136 (photo), 137
NIRA. *See* National Industrial Recovery Act
NLB. *See* National Labor Board
North Carolina Federation of Labor, 93
North Carolina Federation of Textile Workers, 36, 90
North Carolina textile workers: during WWI era, 19, 22; viewed by middle classes, 21; characteristics of unions of, 36, 70; boycott of Bruere Board, 93, 111–12; and general strike, 123, 128–30, 135
northern textile industry, decline of, 40
northern textile manufacturers: and unionization of the South, 39–40; response to general strike, 138
northern textile workers, 10, 39–40, 41–43, 118; and general strike, 131
NTWU. *See* National Textile Workers' Union
NUTW. *See* National Union of Textile Workers

Opelika, Ala., 124
overproduction, 25, 55–56, 107

Palmetto Organizing Council, 36
Parkdale Mill, 129

Passaic, N.J., 43
Paterson, N.J., 39
Payne, John Howard, 100, 101, 126, 128, 130
Pearson, Margaret, 65, 103–4
Pearson, Walter, 103–4
Peel, John, 100; biography, 47; on NIRA, 86, 180; opposes Bruere Board, 94–95, 105, 107; and general strike, 150; denounces Textile Work Assignment Board, 160
Pelzer, S.C., 32, 65, 95
Pequot Mills, 44
Perkins, Frances, 53, 73, 86, 143; views on Honea Path murders, 149–50. *See also* U.S. Department of Labor
Petry, O. E., 85
Piedmont, S.C., 20
Piedmont Mill, 112–13
Piedmont Textile Council, 36, 48, 70
Pittsboro, N.C., 161
poll tax, 6, 30
Porterdale, Ga., 133
public attitudes toward southern textile workers, 13–14, 17, 21–22, 26, 147; impact of WWI era strikes on, 25–26; impact of 1929 strikes on, 31–36; during general strike, 126–27, 140–41

Quigley, Thomas, 85

radio, 26, 140–41
Reconstruction, 4, 7
religion. *See under* southern textile unions
Rhode Island, 41 (photo), 131
Richards, Paul, 172
Richardson, C. L., 117
Rieve, Emil, 90, 146, 173
Riley, Ernest, 134
Roanoke Rapids, N.C., 155
Robinton, Ike, 100
Rock Hill, S.C., 161
Rockingham, N.C., 33, 34
Rogin, Lawrence, 64
Rome, Ga., 85
Roosevelt, Franklin D., 49; as inspiration to ordinary Americans, 9, 63, 140, 180; and administration of New Deal, 53, 60, 91; reaction to general strike, 143–44; accepts Winant report, 152
Rubenstein, Jack, 165

Samoset Cotton Mill, 65
Sanders, W. N. "Reuben," 116–17
Sanford Cotton Mill, 65–66
Saratoga Victory Mills, 114
Sargeant Mill, 136 (photo)
scientific management, 7, 22, 43–45, 51, 177–79. *See also* Bedaux system
Selma Manufacturing Company, 100
Seneca, S.C., 135
sexual harassment in southern mills, 15–16, 19, 33, 48, 71
Shelby, N.C., 33, 47, 89–91. *See also* Cleveland Cloth Mill
Sibley Textile Mill, 100
Sloan, George, 57, 72; opposes sec. 15 of Cotton Textile Code, 59; and data collection, 74, 158; negotiates with Thomas McMahon, 108; and general strike, 144
Smith, "Cotton Ed," 168
South Carolina Federation of Labor, 60
South Carolina Federation of Textile Workers, 105–6, 115
South Carolina legislature, report on textile industry by, 35
South Carolina textile workers: during WWI, 21; and 1929 strikes, 30; characteristics of unions of, 36, 94–95; political power of, 52, 58, 167–69; and 1934 strike, 131
Southern Council on Women and Children in Industry, 35
southern textile labor force: gender as factor in recruitment of, 13, 14–15; as family labor system, 15, 23–24; and child labor, 15, 23, 57; and absenteeism, 16; and shortage of labor, 16, 24, 25; divisions within, 18, 33
southern textile manufacturers: public image challenged, 8, 31; political power of, 13, 137; hostility toward unions, 17, 21–22, 42, 111, 113–14; welfare practices of, 18; profits of, 24; tolerance for unions, 32, 138, 165–66; favors higher wages, 56; and general strike, 131–34, 138–39; and blacklisting, 154–57; responds to TLRB investigations, 157
southern textile unions: purpose of, in 1934, 8, 121–22; early organization of, 16–17; during WWI, 19–20; size of, 20, 36–37, 100, 173, 188–89; opposed

to affiliation with national union, 30, 33–34, 103–4; courting public support, 30–31, 34; religious dimension of, 82, 90, 121–22, 180; opposed to end of general strike, 153, 155
southern textile workers: political power of, 6, 13, 30, 50, 58, 136–37, 166–69, 176, 179; letters to FDR from, 6, 63–67; informal resistance to mill authority by, 8, 15, 18–19; rural ties of, 15, 127; impact of urbanization on, 26–27. *See also* southern textile unions; strikes; *names of cities and mills*
Spartanburg, S.C., 31, 122, 125, 161
Spindale, N.C., 129, 135
Spofford Mills, 112
Squires, B. M., 156
Stetin, Sol, 118
stretch-out: causes of, 7, 24–25, 64; impact of, on textile workers, 23–24, 43–44, 65–66; strikes against, 29–32, 43–44, 45; opposed by UTW, 106–7; as issue in general strike, 115, 119; legacy of failure of, in general strike, 173
Stretch-out Committee, 75–76
strikes, 17, 21–22, 29–30, 35–36, 44, 46, 89–93, 111–13, 115–18, 120–53 passim, 162, 173. *See also* general textile strike
Swift Spinning Mill, 20

Talmadge, Eugene, 135–36, 159
Taylor, John Clarence, 58–59
Taylor Society, 44, 51, 61. *See also* scientific management
Textile Labor Relations Board (TLRB), 156–57, 159–60
textile strikes. *See* general textile strike; strikes
Textile Work Assignment Board (WAB), 158–59, 160
Textile Workers Organizing Committee–CIO (TWOC), 170–71
Textile Workers' Union of America, 173
Thomas, Norman, 143
Thompson, Robert L., 167
Thornburgh, Lucille, 70
Thornton, Mr. and Mrs. J. Q., 141
TLRB. *See* Textile Labor Relations Board
Trenton Mill, 134

Trion, Ga., 102, 133–34
TWOC. *See* Textile Workers Organizing Committee–CIO

unemployment, 8, 43, 49, 51–53, 64–66, 74, 140–41. *See also* stretch-out
Union, S.C., 161
United Textile Workers (UTW): responds to industry migration, 9–10, 40; favors efficiency, 10, 42–45; size of, 20, 37, 161–63, 188–89; structure and composition of, 20, 38–39, 44; during WWI, 20–22, 40; and 1929–30 organizing drive, 32, 42; negotiating strategy of, 38–40; in the North, 38–40, 42–44, 131; opposes militancy, 39–42, 86, 97; at Cotton Textile Code hearings, 59–60; and organizing (1933–34), 69–71, 98–104; cooperates with NIRA, 87–88; opposes Cotton Textile Code Authority, 97–98; opposes wage cuts, 104–5; opposes stretch-out, 106; negotiates with Hugh Johnson, 108; favors direct action, 110–12; August 1934 convention of, 118–19; and general strike, 120–22, 144–47, 150–51, 153; collapse of, 161–63; assessment of, 177
U.S. Department of Labor, 111. *See also* Battle, Turner; Perkins, Frances
UTW. *See* United Textile Workers

Victor Monaghan Mills, 111
violence (in southern textile labor disputes), 4, 112–13, 116–17, 124, 131, 133–34, 148–49

WAB. *See* Textile Work Assignment Board
wages (of southern textile workers): increases in, 24, 32; increases proposed by mill owners, 32–33, 54, 56; cuts in, 34, 160; impact of Cotton Textile Code on, 66, 104–5; studied by Bureau of Labor Statistics, 158
Wagner, Robert, 51, 75, 87
Wagner Act (National Labor Relations Act), 6, 170 (photo)
Walker County, Ala., 69, 123, 162
Ware Shoals, S.C., 31, 42, 148
Waverly Mills, 111–12, 132. *See also* Laurinburg, N.C.

Welch, Homer, 100
West Point Manufacturing Company, 124
white supremacy, 14, 17, 168–69
Wilkie, Wendell, 168
Williams, John F., 84
Willis, H. H., 82, 94–95
Wilson, Rodney, 90
Winant, John, 144

Winant Board: creation of, 144; report of, 152–53
Wingerd, Mary, 18
Women's Trade Union League, 100, 151. *See also* Dowd, Mollie
workloads, customary, 7, 15, 16, 19, 24, 30
World War I, 19–22, 40
Wright, Chester, 164 (photo)

JANET IRONS received her Ph.D. degree from Duke University. She teaches American history and social studies education at Lock Haven University of Pennsylvania.

THE WORKING CLASS IN AMERICAN HISTORY

Worker City, Company Town: Iron and Cotton-Worker Protest in
Troy and Cohoes, New York, 1855–84   *Daniel J. Walkowitz*

Life, Work, and Rebellion in the Coal Fields: The Southern West
Virginia Miners, 1880–1922   *David Alan Corbin*

Women and American Socialism, 1870–1920   *Mari Jo Buhle*

Lives of Their Own: Blacks, Italians, and Poles in Pittsburgh,
1900–1960   *John Bodnar, Roger Simon, and Michael P. Weber*

Working-Class America: Essays on Labor, Community, and American Society   *Edited by Michael H. Frisch and Daniel J. Walkowitz*

Eugene V. Debs: Citizen and Socialist   *Nick Salvatore*

American Labor and Immigration History, 1877–1920s: Recent
European Research   *Edited by Dirk Hoerder*

Workingmen's Democracy: The Knights of Labor and American
Politics   *Leon Fink*

The Electrical Workers: A History of Labor at General Electric and
Westinghouse, 1923–60   *Ronald W. Schatz*

The Mechanics of Baltimore: Workers and Politics in the Age of
Revolution, 1763–1812   *Charles G. Steffen*

The Practice of Solidarity: American Hat Finishers in the Nine-
teenth Century   *David Bensman*

The Labor History Reader   *Edited by Daniel J. Leab*

Solidarity and Fragmentation: Working People and Class Consciousness in Detroit, 1875–1900   *Richard Oestreicher*

Counter Cultures: Saleswomen, Managers, and Customers in American Department Stores, 1890–1940   *Susan Porter Benson*

The New England Working Class and the New Labor
History   *Edited by Herbert G. Gutman and Donald H. Bell*

Labor Leaders in America   *Edited by Melvyn Dubofsky and
Warren Van Tine*

Barons of Labor: The San Francisco Building Trades and Union
Power in the Progressive Era   *Michael Kazin*

Gender at Work: The Dynamics of Job Segregation by Sex during
World War II   *Ruth Milkman*

Once a Cigar Maker: Men, Women, and Work Culture in American
Cigar Factories, 1900–1919   *Patricia A. Cooper*

A Generation of Boomers: The Pattern of Railroad Labor Conflict in
Nineteenth-Century America   *Shelton Stromquist*

Work and Community in the Jungle: Chicago's Packinghouse Workers, 1894–1922   *James R. Barrett*

Workers, Managers, and Welfare Capitalism: The Shoeworkers and
Tanners of Endicott Johnson, 1890–1950   *Gerald Zahavi*

Men, Women, and Work: Class, Gender, and Protest in the New England Shoe Industry, 1780–1910 *Mary Blewett*

Workers on the Waterfront: Seamen, Longshoremen, and Unionism in the 1930s *Bruce Nelson*

German Workers in Chicago: A Documentary History of Working-Class Culture from 1850 to World War I *Edited by Hartmut Keil and John B. Jentz*

On the Line: Essays in the History of Auto Work *Edited by Nelson Lichtenstein and Stephen Meyer III*

Upheaval in the Quiet Zone: A History of Hospital Workers' Union, Local 1199 *Leon Fink and Brian Greenberg*

Labor's Flaming Youth: Telephone Operators and Worker Militancy, 1878–1923 *Stephen H. Norwood*

Another Civil War: Labor, Capital, and the State in the Anthracite Regions of Pennsylvania, 1840–68 *Grace Palladino*

Coal, Class, and Color: Blacks in Southern West Virginia, 1915–32 *Joe William Trotter, Jr.*

For Democracy, Workers, and God: Labor Song-Poems and Labor Protest, 1865–95 *Clark D. Halker*

Dishing It Out: Waitresses and Their Unions in the Twentieth Century *Dorothy Sue Cobble*

The Spirit of 1848: German Immigrants, Labor Conflict, and the Coming of the Civil War *Bruce Levine*

Working Women of Collar City: Gender, Class, and Community in Troy, New York, 1864–86 *Carole Turbin*

Southern Labor and Black Civil Rights: Organizing Memphis Workers *Michael K. Honey*

Radicals of the Worst Sort: Laboring Women in Lawrence, Massachusetts, 1860–1912 *Ardis Cameron*

Producers, Proletarians, and Politicians: Workers and Party Politics in Evansville and New Albany, Indiana, 1850–87 *Lawrence M. Lipin*

The New Left and Labor in the 1960s *Peter B. Levy*

The Making of Western Labor Radicalism: Denver's Organized Workers, 1878–1905 *David Brundage*

In Search of the Working Class: Essays in American Labor History and Political Culture *Leon Fink*

Lawyers against Labor: From Individual Rights to Corporate Liberalism *Daniel R. Ernst*

"We Are All Leaders": The Alternative Unionism of the Early 1930s *Edited by Staughton Lynd*

The Female Economy: The Millinery and Dressmaking Trades, 1860–1930 *Wendy Gamber*

"Negro and White, Unite and Fight!": A Social History of Industrial
    Unionism in Meatpacking, 1930–90   *Roger Horowitz*
Power at Odds: The 1922 National Railroad Shopmen's
    Strike   *Colin J. Davis*
The Common Ground of Womanhood: Class, Gender, and Working
    Girls' Clubs, 1884–1928   *Priscilla Murolo*
Marching Together: Women of the Brotherhood of Sleeping
    Car Porters   *Melinda Chateauvert*
Down on the Killing Floor: Black and White Workers in Chicago's
    Packinghouses, 1904–54   *Rick Halpern*
Labor and Urban Politics: Class Conflict and the Origins of Modern
    Liberalism in Chicago, 1864–97   *Richard Schneirov*
All That Glitters: Class, Conflict, and Community in Cripple
    Creek   *Elizabeth Jameson*
Waterfront Workers: New Perspectives on Race and Class   *Edited by
    Calvin Winslow*
Labor Histories: Class, Politics, and the Working-Class
    Experience   *Edited by Eric Arnesen, Julie Greene, and Bruce Laurie*
The Pullman Strike and the Crisis of the 1890s: Essays on Labor and
    Politics   *Edited by Richard Schneirov, Shelton Stromquist, and
    Nick Salvatore*
AlabamaNorth: African-American Migrants, Community, and Work-
    ing-Class Activism in Cleveland, 1914–45   *Kimberley L. Phillips*
Imagining Internationalism in American and British Labor,
    1939–49   *Victor Silverman*
William Z. Foster and the Tragedy of American Radicalism
    James R. Barrett
Colliers across the Sea: A Comparative Study of Class Formation in
    Scotland and the American Midwest, 1830–1924
    John H. M. Laslett
"Rights, Not Roses": Unions and the Rise of Working-Class Femi-
    nism, 1945–80   *Dennis Deslippe*
Testing the New Deal: The General Textile Strike of 1934 in the
    American South   *Janet Irons*

Typeset in 10/13 Janson Text
with Officina Sans display
Designed by Paula Newcomb
Composed by Jim Proefrock
at the University of Illinois Press
Manufactured by Cushing-Malloy, Inc.

University of Illinois Press
1325 South Oak Street
Champaign, IL 61820-6903
www.press.uillinois.edu